4.95

THE TAIPING REBELLION
History

TRANSLATIONS BY

Margery Anneberg

Y. S. Chao

C. L. Chang

Shelley Cheng

Boyd Compton

Robert Crawford

C. T. Hu

Michael Ivy

William Johnson

Harry Lamley

K. H. Lu

Albert Mann

Frederick Mote

William Schultz

Keaton Shih

Leslie Tsou

Rose Tsou

Urban Whitaker

I. Wu

EDITOR: Gladys Greenwood

THIS book is a product of the Modern Chinese History Project carried on by the Far Eastern and Russian Institute of the University of Washington. Members of the group represent various disciplines in the social sciences and humanities. The work of the project is of a cooperative nature with each member assisting the others through critical discussion and the contribution of ideas and material. The responsibility for each study rests with the author.

The

TAIPING
REBELLION

History

By Franz Michael
In collaboration with Chung-li Chang

UNIVERSITY OF WASHINGTON PRESS
Seattle and London

The Taiping Rebellion: History is Volume I of the three-volume set, *The Taiping Rebellion: History and Documents,* Number 14 of the Publications on Asia of the Institute for Comparative and Foreign Area Studies, formerly Far Eastern and Russian Institute Publications on Asia.

Copyright © 1966 by the University of Washington Press
First paperback edition, 1972
Library of Congress Catalog Card Number 66-13538
ISBN 0-295-73958-4 (cloth)
ISBN 0-295-95244-X (paper)
Printed in the United States of America

Preface

WHEN this work was started ten years ago, it seemed to be a useful enterprise to collect and translate the existing Taiping documentary material and derive from it a periodization of Taiping history that would make possible a new understanding of this crucial period in the beginning of modern Chinese history. The concepts used for the period-ization soon began to develop into a new analysis of this extraordinary story. No reader of the Taiping documents can escape the startling sensation of becoming witness to events in human history that break so much out of the pattern of existing institutions that they touch on basic issues of any kind of social order. The Taiping Rebellion repre-sented as violent and complete a social revolution against an existing order as was ever attempted; indeed it can serve as a case study of revolution. The extraordinary fascination of this revolutionary attempt was accentuated by a combination of human frailties rarely found. Fantasy, madness, social experimentation, cruelty, vulgarity, vices mingle with concepts that touch on utopian dreams found in all human history. To bring order into the pressing events of this wild story became a task that was as complicated as it was intriguing. In the comments written about the documents there emerged what became the beginnings of an analytical history. It remained to put the story together and to derive from the documents and their explanation the analytical history of the Taiping Rebellion presented in the introductory volume to this work. What we then present is a history in two parts. The rich historical material that has come to us is given in Volumes II and III of this work with comments and footnotes that explain the value of the material and its importance in the story. From this was derived Volume I, the history, that deals with the Taiping Rebellion as a historical event, crucial for the course of modern China and full of interest for any student of social problems and institutions.

It has been a most rewarding study for all those who participated. The team that worked on the translations was formed by Chinese and American graduate students, many of whom have since made their way in the academic world and may, we hope, remember with pleasure the hours spent in toil on this material and welcome with us its appearance. Chang Chung-li, who for many years participated in the work on this project, is responsible for a very large part of the source material that was brought in to give substance to our plan of research and analysis. His thorough scholarship and careful evaluation of much of the material, his reworking and footnoting of much of the documentary translation, have made an invaluable contribution to these volumes. Gladys Greenwood has as research editor of this work, critically discussing all the ideas and evaluating the treatment, helped to give this study its form and content.

The work has been in the fullest degree a product of the Modern Chinese History Project. Its documentary material and its analytical text have been many times discussed in our colloquium, and all its members have taken an active share in judging and evaluating the problems with which we have dealt. George E. Taylor, the Director of the Institute, has himself written what still stands as one of the most perceptive studies of the Taiping Rebellion. Some of the other present and former members of the Modern Chinese History Project have themselves worked on the Rebellion. Vincent Shih, who in his study on the Taiping Ideology has analyzed the composition and history of the ideas held by the Taipings, has provided stirring discussions that led to new insight. Lo Jung-pang has closely followed the arguments in Communist China on the role of Taiping leaders and shared his knowledge. Hellmut Wilhelm, who has worked on the Taipings' main antagonist and defender of the traditional social order, Tseng Kuo-fan, has dealt with the ideas that the Taipings could not overcome. The senior member of our group, Professor Hsiao Kung-chuan, has given generously of his wisdom and his profound knowledge of the intellectual climate in which all Chinese history unfolded. He has enriched his always focused comments with the sparkle of a wit that comes from great learning and human understanding. As guest member of our Project, A. F. P. Hulsewé has read the first chapters of the history and made valuable suggestions. And all other present and former members of the colloquium, C. K. Yang, Marinus Meijer, Mah Feng-hua, Hsu Dau-lin, Wolfgang Bauer, Rhoads Murphey, Hsia Tsi-an, Philip Bilancia, Dan Henderson, and Jack Dull have shared the excitement of the struggle with the ideas and institutions of the Taiping world. Of special help with the bibliography, which was first worked out by Chang Chung-li, has been Shelley Cheng, whose contributions to our colloquium have been marked by extensive knowledge of Chinese source material. Stanley Spector, William Schultz and C. T. Hu have as participants in the early stages of our Project helped to organize and supervise the translation program of the documentary material. I owe special thanks to my research assistant, Teng Ju-wen, for his careful help on much of the source material.

Special recognition should be given to the famous scholar of Taiping history, Professor Jen Yu-wen, whose many books and articles have been a treasure of information. Professor Kuo T'ing-i's outstanding work on the chronology of events has been of invaluable help. Many other works of colleagues which I have used have been listed in the footnotes and the bibliography. The help and previous work of all these friends and scholars have made this study possible. To all of them I am most grateful. The responsibility for the story and for the argument, and for whatever mistakes may appear, is entirely mine.

I hope that my analysis will bring to life a story that in sheer drama cannot be surpassed. In trying to do it justice and to relate it to the problems of Chinese history as we see them today, I have attempted to bring out what seemed to me to be the true issues of that time as well as ours.

FRANZ MICHAEL
Chairman, Modern Chinese
History Project
University of Washington

June, 1964
Seattle

Contents

Maps

THE TAIPING REBELLION

History and Documents

VOLUME I: HISTORY

The Setting of the Rebellion

ONE may well say that modern Chinese history begins with the Taiping Rebellion. The great tradition of China's two thousand years of imperial history came to an end in the political, social, and intellectual turmoil that prevailed in Chinese affairs from the latter half of the last century to the Revolution of 1911. In this period of crisis the first major break with the past was brought on in the middle of the nineteenth century by the Taiping Rebellion, a vast uprising that, though unsuccessful in the end, contained, in the beliefs it propagated and the organization it established, elements so alien to China's tradition that they indicate to us in retrospect the first internal manifestation of the effect of an outer and inner crisis in Chinese traditional society.

Even the name given the rebellious movement by its leaders had its special appeal in the expression of a new slogan that differed basically from the dynastic titles assumed by the founders of new dynasties in the past. *T'aip'ing T'ien-kuo,* "The Heavenly Kingdom of Great Peace," as it is usually translated, was to be a kingdom that secured a new kind of "peace"—the everlasting fulfillment of God's will on earth, and—in an implied meaning of the word "Taiping"—of justice and equality for all.[1]

An extraordinary combination of individual and general factors characterizes the Taiping Rebellion and sets it off from the past: a fanatical religious faith derived from Christianity, which clashed with traditional Chinese culture; a system that combined primitive equality of the members of a revolutionary sect supported by a common treasury with the absolute power of a ruthless, self-indulgent leadership, and that combined equality and separation of the sexes and complete chastity among the followers with the possession of large harems by the rulers; a lead-

[1] For the translation of T'aip'ing T'ien-kuo as "Heavenly Kingdom of Great Equality," see Lo, *Shih-kang,* pp. 52-53. For the previous history of the term "Taiping" see Vincent Y. C. Shih, *The Taiping Ideology: Its Sources, Interpretations, and Influence* (Seattle, forthcoming).

3

ership headed by a man who was clearly mentally ill and made up of others who used crude religious hoaxes to assert authority—these were new and most unusual characteristics that demonstrated how different the Taipings were from all earlier rebels in Chinese history. If to these special phenomena are added the drama of the shifting fortunes of battle in a major civil war, the savage infighting among the rebel leaders, and the vast destruction and loss of life caused by fourteen years of fighting, the Taiping Rebellion becomes a spectacle of new extremes in China and one of the most extraordinary stories of all history.

If the Taiping Rebellion was a new beginning in Chinese history, it arose in a setting that still contained the familiar elements characteristic of periods of dynastic decline and rebellious uprisings in the past. Grave corruption in government, heavy overtaxation of the farmers, high rent, desertion of the land by the peasants, the increase of a roaming population, banditry and general insecurity, the increasing importance of secret societies, the formation of local self-defense units that took matters into their own hands, and frequent small-scale warfare which led to uprisings against government authority—these had been the conditions for dynastic changes by rebellion or foreign conquest throughout imperial history. These same conditions existed under the Ch'ing dynasty in the first part of the nineteenth century, conditions that boded well for the success of any leader who could use them to defeat the government forces and re-establish the political order under a new dynasty.

While the setting was similar to that of earlier rebellions, the Taiping Rebellion itself and its goal were basically different from former dynastic upheavals. The Taipings attacked not only the ruling dynasty—they attacked the traditional social order itself. And this wider attack gave their rebellion a character totally different from that of rebellious movements of the past.

It had been the strength of the Chinese system that its periods of crisis affected the political order only. After the fall of a dynasty and a shorter or longer period of crisis in the battle of contending leaders, a new political beginning was made under a new dynastic rule; but the social system remained essentially intact throughout. The strength and stability of the Chinese social order was indeed demonstrated by its ability to survive not only the fall of dynasties but even prolonged political disorder.

This system was based on the acceptance of Confucian social and political beliefs, which sanctioned dynastic authority and under which the educated elite, the gentry, who preserved and handed down these beliefs, played a dual role as officials of the government and as the leading stratum of society. Whatever rebel leader from within or military conqueror from without tried in periods of chaos to establish a new dynasty, he needed the services of the educated Chinese gentry to re-establish a functioning administrative system and maintain control over society.

The survival of the social system through the many political crises of Chinese past imperial history and the ever continued success in the rebuilding of the political structure in this traditional Chinese society testify to the strength and relative autonomy of the social order, which the dynastic state affected only to a limited degree. Imperial administration was always limited in scope, just as the government's administrative staff was limited in number. The educated, the gentry, held a monopoly on office, but most of them did not serve the state. Instead of becoming government officials, they remained at home in their own districts and provinces where, on their own responsibility and not under any orders or instructions from the government, they carried on functions of public service that took the place of government administration.[2] Arbitration of conflicts, management of public works, the handling of public welfare problems, the education of the next generation of gentry, these were among the services rendered by that large majority of the gentry who did not hold official position. These services, expected from the gentry as an obligation connected with their privileged positions in society, were also the main source of income for most of them.[3] The government approved of and counted on these services of the gentry, which were not only a necessary counterpart to the administrative actions of the officials but were also in some cases connected with them. The government officials handled the taxes but received some assistance from the gentry in collecting them and sometimes levied additional taxes to reimburse the gentry for some of its services. The government reserved to itself all military authority but in emergencies it tolerated and even encouraged gentry leadership of local military forces. The line between the affairs that the government handled through its officials and those that were handled by the gentry on their own was thus fluid and shifted

[2] See Chung-li Chang, *The Chinese Gentry* (Seattle: University of Washington Press, 1955).
[3] See Chung-li Chang, *The Income of the Chinese Gentry* (Seattle: University of Washington Press, 1962).

according to the situation. But the general division between the functions of the government officials and those carried out by the gentry as leaders of society remained characteristic of the relationship of state and society in imperial China.[4]

There was thus in imperial time a distinction between a small number of crucial matters handled by the government and the large number of public affairs handled outside the government structure by the leaders of society. This division of jurisdictional authority no dynasty could have changed without attacking the Confucian system itself and thus undermining the very basis on which the cooperation of the Confucian gentry depended. Though applied in its own autonomous area, the gentry's authority for maintaining order in society was based on the same beliefs that sanctioned the dynastic authority of the government and was carried on by the same group who as officials served the government.

The beliefs on which this authority was based were not shaken by the downfall of a dynasty. In fact the Confucian code worked as a check on the dynastic government and provided an explanation for the fall and rise of dynasties, while maintaining its claim as the basis for the only possible social order. During all the political upheavals of the past the social order continued and provided the elastic recuperative power that enabled Chinese imperial society to survive many internal and external political crises. In times of political chaos, when the dynastic government no longer functioned, the gentry's management of day-to-day affairs under the moral code not only remained valid, but the prestige which they held enabled the gentry to take over many of the functions of the dynastic government, especially those of tax collection and military defense. Sometimes members of the gentry themselves assumed new military and political leadership, or upstarts, seizing power during a time of crisis, depended on the services of the educated to establish their own political and military organization. It was thus from the social foundation that the Chinese political order was rebuilt after each dynastic change. After the failure of any one dynastic government, the gentry remained the stratum from which the new conqueror could recruit a staff willing to serve as long as the gentry's role in society and the state was accepted. Until the nineteenth century there had been attacks only against a government in power—attacks permitted by the Confucian

[4] See Franz Michael, "Regionalism in Nineteenth-Century China," introduction to Stanley Spector, *Li Hung-chang and the Huai Army* (Seattle: University of Washington Press, 1964).

teachings—but no attacks against these Confucian teachings, the Confucian gentry, and the Confucian society itself.[5]

The first major challenge to this dualistic system came from the Taipings, who sought not only to destroy the dynasty but also to replace the Confucian ethics with their own religious teachings and to end the traditional autonomy of the moral and social order. By their attempt to incorporate the teachings of their beliefs and the management of all public affairs in their governmental structure, the Taipings sought to introduce a monist order in which the state would be all. This set the Taipings not only against the government but against the defenders of the existing social order itself, the gentry, and all those who believed in the Confucian system.

In the nineteenth century, when the Ch'ing government showed all the symptoms of approaching collapse, the social leadership of the gentry was still strong enough to maintain the social order and defend it against attack. In defending the social order against the Taiping attack, the gentry had no choice but to defend the dynasty as well. The hold of the Confucian beliefs over Chinese society and the strength of the gentry's leadership were demonstrated in the defeat of the Taipings, not by the armies of the government but by newly formed forces under gentry leadership which took over when the dynasty failed. It was the resistance of these new armies that defeated the Taiping Rebellion and in so doing saved the dynasty. In fact, had the Taiping Rebellion challenged only the heavenly mandate of the ruling house, it might well have succeeded, for the time seemed ripe for a dynastic change in China, if not yet for the overthrow of traditional beliefs and the traditional social order.

The decline of organization and government, which had contributed to the downfall of previous dynasties and which undermined the position of the Ch'ing dynasty in the nineteenth century, had its reasons in the imperial system itself. Since the dynastic government had to respect the gentry's special position as guardians of the Confucian political philosophy and moral code and as managers of social affairs, the dynasties faced a vital problem of control over the very group on whose services they depended. There was the danger that the officials, who were themselves members of the gentry, could, with the support of this social group, gain an autonomy that might become fatal to the dynastic government.

[5] Buddhism, which had been a rival educational system in earlier centuries, had been unsuccessful in challenging the Confucian monopoly.

Each dynasty faced, therefore, the problem of controlling the educated elite and preventing it from misusing its power against the interest of dynastic authority. The measures taken by each dynasty to strengthen its authority were more or less the same, and eventually there developed a system that reached its highest point of sophistication under the Ch'ing.

Official control over the gentry's management of social affairs was very limited. It could only be exercised with regard to those gentry functions that were carried out with government approval and cooperation. But in this cooperation between officials and gentry each side depended on the other, and relative strength depended on the given situation. In times of crisis the officials might depend more on the gentry's action in collecting funds and establishing military defense corps than the members of the gentry on official approval. Even in times of peace the government had to depend so much on the gentry's services that it had little direct means of control.

The main means used to maintain government power over the gentry was the imperial examination system, fully developed since Sung times. Through it the government could determine entrance into gentry status, which now depended on the degrees given in the examinations. By limiting the number of candidates that could pass the examinations, the government could limit the number of gentry. In fact the number of degree-holders in each district was about equal to the number needed to carry on the public functions the gentry performed. The group was large enough to handle local affairs and yet not so large as to become dangerous to the government. The control of the examinations, however, permitted the government also to determine the content of the examinations and to emphasize that aspect of Confucian teaching which stressed discipline and loyalty to the dynasty. Through the educational officials the government also maintained a supervision over the gentry in each area. The educational officials were selected from the area in which they were to serve, an exception to the general rule that no official should serve in his home area. It was the very task of the educational officials to maintain close connections with the local gentry and thus form a link between the administration and the social leadership. Through their management of the examinations, their control of stipends, and their disciplinary authority, the educational officials maintained the government's control over the scholar-gentry, and at the same time transmitted the gentry's views and feelings to the government. Through its educational officials and the management of the examination system, the government exercised some control over the gentry, a control which was, however, at best indirect and tenuous.

If its influence over the nonofficial gentry remained indirect, the government established a direct system of control over the officials with the aim of preventing them from building their own power on the basis of cooperation with their fellow gentry. It had become a government practice not to permit any official to serve in his home district or province, where he would have close relations with the local gentry. He came as a stranger to the locale where he held office and did not have enough time to grow roots and establish a working agreement with the local gentry leaders. Officials were not permitted to remain in any such position more than three years at most, so that they could not become too closely identified with the interests of the administrative areas they served.

More important, however, was the system of mutual checks and division of functions and authority that characterized the official system. Each official on the higher regional level and also in the military organization was extraordinarily circumscribed in his authority and handicapped in his activity by a plurality of administrative organizations in which the functions of officials often overlapped and were not always clearly defined, a situation that fostered a spirit of competition and administrative rivalry. Since any false move could be reported to the court by superiors and competitors, the whole system led to a stifling of initiative and personal effort. It aimed at securing the government against ambitious members of the organization and chilled the spirit of all officials. It discouraged initiative, energy, and ambition and created a situation in which each officeholder was concerned with avoiding any risky move and maintaining the good relations with his superiors and other officials so important for promotion and survival in office. In this system there was little room for bold innovation, and each official could only attempt to maintain and improve his position within the existing order. The system, which aimed at protecting government authority and security, stressed the continuation of routine and was not the most propitious form of administration for efficient government.

It was this trend that under each new dynasty led after a period of the full development of given possibilities to stagnation and demoralization. Since advance was possible only within a system that could not expand, officials could only improve their position at the expense of others or by imposing a greater burden on the taxpaying population. To get a larger share one had to take from the funds that were to serve the public and to cover up through one's connections. This practice was always bound to lead to corruption, a corruption in which each member of the government organization had to participate. The phenomena of corruption and vast overtaxation that accompanied the decline of each dynasty can therefore be traced to the limitations of the system itself.

Overtaxation forced many small farmers into debt and eventually caused them to lose their land, while some of the officials and gentry were able to buy up property. This property, privileged as it was, did not have to carry the same tax burden as that of the common farming population. The tax burden on the working farmers was thus further increased, while high rent paid to landlords aggravated the lot of the tenant farmers.

Heavy taxes and high rent and lack of protection from a corrupt officialdom caused many farmers to leave their land and join roving groups of dispossessed people who became bandits. Indeed in each period of dynastic decline, large-scale banditry prevailed in many parts of the country. Sometimes this banditry required military action and appeared in the official records of the dynasty, but beyond these major incidents there was a general state of insecurity. Bandit groups that established themselves in the hills and other less accessible areas were a constant threat to the settled communities.

Against this threat there was insufficient protection from the officials. Only large-scale trouble justified a call for troops by the local officials. And the troops themselves were no longer a protection. Since the military forces had been incorporated into the administrative organization by the dynasty in order to prevent military officials from becoming autonomous in their power, the military organizations were exposed to the same corruptive influences as the rest of the administration. Like other officials, military officers were shifted from post to post, were limited in their authority, and had no clear chain of command. Position and advancement depended on influence and connections; and the natural result of this system was bribery and corruption. In each such crisis the records speak of officers pocketing the pay of the soldiers, and of units vastly under strength and without training. The frequent desertions by soldiers who did not receive their pay were not only ignored by the officers but actually welcomed by some who in this way found it easier to misappropriate the deserters' pay. When inspections were made, the ranks were filled by men hired for the occasion—beggars or coolies or farmers. As a result, the officers were corrupt and the troops demoralized. Each campaign was a new opportunity for graft by the officers and an occasion for the troops to live off the land. In fact the armies were feared by the population, and their coming was dreaded as much as a raid by bandits.

Since the corrupt officialdom and the equally corrupt military forces no longer provided protection, the people of the villages and towns began to establish their own defense units. This development ran counter to the policy of the dynastic government, which considered its monopoly of military organization one of the main safeguards against rebellion. It was the rule that soldiers were professionals and that ordinary people were not permitted to carry arms. But in times of decline, when its own forces had become ineffective, the government had to permit or even encourage the arming of such local forces for defense and maintenance of order. It was a dangerous expedient to surrender the main weapon of power to local forces, and the risk was recognized by the court, which attempted to limit the use of such extra-regular local forces to a specific occasion of desperate need and to dissolve them as soon as the emergency had passed. But once accepted, such local defense units could not easily be abolished, especially when the need for them remained. Once in existence, these local corps became important factors in local politics. To maintain themselves, they had to have financial support to buy weapons and other equipment and to provide for their upkeep, and they had the power to obtain such support. Special contributions changed to regular levies, and special income was derived from levying duties on trade, and, frequently, from illegal activities such as gambling and prostitution. To prevent clashes and difficulties with these units, the officials had to close their eyes to these financial activities and had to permit their development into regular local financial and political enterprises.

These military units thus became the most important political forces of their localities. They took up the fight for local issues in which their communities were involved. From the defense of their villages against banditry they moved on to battles against neighboring forces over local interests. Issues between villages over water rights, over property, over women, over ethnic or religious controversies were settled by arms. In peaceful times, the local magistrate had been the arbiter in these conflicts. If the local gentry leaders had acted as intermediaries, they had done so with the approval and backing of the official. Now the issue was settled by force or the threat of force. Local defense corps and bandit organizations came to fight with each other for local control, and the line between them became ever more difficult to draw. In the small-scale warfare that ensued the officials often remained neutral; or they supported one side and so gave it a mantle of legality, automatically classing the opponent as an outlaw or bandit. As long as local clashes did not lead to large-scale trouble but could be hushed up, the official more often than not was unwilling to interfere and was inclined to accept the dictates of the stronger side or maintain a neutral attitude. Official authority therefore declined, and local leadership arose that controlled its own local forces and collected its own funds to maintain its authority and protection over a submissive area.

Administrative officials could, however, maintain a neutral position only so long as the issues and battles were minor and so long as they themselves retained the major share of the tax revenues and general control and authority in the areas under their jurisdiction. There was a very precarious line between the autonomy of local forces and a challenge to all government authority. A single local corps consisting of some hundred men could not easily attempt open rebellion. It was not strong enough to oppose the troops that the officials could still muster, and it had to guard against the rival local forces that a skillful official could employ as counterforces against it. Such an official policy of "divide and rule" became impossible whenever a number of local corps of one area succeeded in banding together to form a regional force, and a stage of open rebellion was reached.

During such times of crisis, much of the leadership of local organization came from the gentry. But there was also another type of organization and another type of leadership that became important during such periods—the secret societies and their leaders.

Secret societies led many of the uprisings that occurred all through imperial history. Based on the mutual aid and protection of their members, the secret societies had a type of organization that was easily transformed into a military and political structure. The secrecy of their membership and leadership made these societies the ideal vehicle for conspiracy and political uprisings against the government.

What the secret societies had to contribute was their militant political organization. They were formed as brotherhoods of the persecuted and of those who had no voice or power in the existing political and social structure. They formed underground political organizations, rival and potentially hostile to the existing state organization. Their members were sworn to aid each other in distress, to give refuge to members who were in hiding from the officials, and to support each other in conflicts with outsiders as well as with the government. Loyalty to society brothers was the first obligation, but above the brotherhood of equal members was a hierarchy of officials of the society who could enforce absolute authority and discipline. The societies were secret orders of all those who had no other way to defend themselves against the pressures of the state and the privileged social leaders. They flourished especially in the rural villages and among the peasants but frequently included within their membership lower scholar-gentry.

Their jointly held popular beliefs, derived from Taoist and Buddhist tradition, unified the members of the secret societies. From these religious and philosophical schools they took their concepts of brotherhood and equality and a system of rites and magic, which they used to enforce their belief that supernatural powers gave them support. These ideas ran counter to the tenets of state Confucianism, but they formed no clearly defined rival ideology.

Secret societies in China had developed over the last centuries into two differing types of organization. The secret societies in the provinces of North China were called religious societies and placed much more emphasis on religious beliefs and practices derived from Buddhist tenets. There was also a much greater unity of control under a centralized system in which all branches were under the direction of one group of leaders. In south and central China the relations between different local society branches remained much looser. All branch societies belonged to an over-all roof organization called the Triad, but local leadership remained autonomous. There was also less stress on religious beliefs. It was therefore perhaps easier in the south to establish new organizations similar to the existing secret societies, especially if such an organization introduced a strong ideological appeal that the existing societies did not have. In the south as in the north the secret societies provided centers of unrest and a potential framework to unite local armed groups under a larger regional leadership, but the Triad organization in the south lacked the compactness and most of all the ideological appeal necessary for a rebellion. The existing societies therefore provided a model after which a rebellious organization could be patterned instead of being themselves the vehicles through which it could be carried out.[6]

[6] At the fall of the Ming dynasty, secret societies carried on the fight for Ming pretenders to the throne against the new Manchu rulers. The secret-society organizations that carried on during the rule of the Manchu dynasty continued to hold a vague allegiance to the idea of a Chinese Ming ruler as against the emperors of the alien Manchu dynasty. There was not much reality in their Ming

All these elements of crisis and of new beginnings appeared during the nineteenth century and formed a serious threat to the survival of the Ch'ing dynasty. Besides these general phenomena of the cyclical crisis, a number of special factors aggravated the problem for the Ch'ing government. One of these special factors was the pressure of a rapidly growing population on the limited resources of agricultural land. The population, which has been roughly estimated as 100,000,000 at the start of the dynasty, had increased to about 300,000,000 by the beginning of the nineteenth century. The population thus increased threefold while the square mileage of cultivated land and the quantity of agricultural production grew only very little. This increasing disproportion between population and cultivated land emerges clearly from the records of the Ch'ing dynasty. (See Table 1.)

The reasons for the rapid population growth during the preceding two hundred years or so, which has its parallel in other parts of the world in industrial as well as agricultural countries, remains still a matter of speculation. In China the period of comparative peace and orderly government secured by the Ch'ing dynasty during the first century after the complete conquest of the country has been given as one explanation for the population increase. No rebellions large enough to affect the population figures occurred before the nineteenth century. No epidemics or natural catastrophes caused large loss of life. But there was also no economic change that would have provided the resources to feed so many more people. It has been said that new crops introduced from abroad, such as the sweet potato and the peanut, increased the food available and that such increases could not be deduced from the records of taxable land, since such crops were planted on hilly and mountainous land not used for the main crops and not registered for taxation. But even if these additional food crops made some difference, the over-all problem of a rapid population increase was one of the most critical issues faced by the Ch'ing dynasty, and in effect by all subsequent Chinese governments.

Another new factor that added to the crisis was the currency and fiscal problem created by the impact of the West. Since the eighteenth century, Western trade had grown considerably through the system of controlled exchange between the foreign merchants and the licensed Chinese firms, the Cohong, at Canton. This trade at first had not had

---

loyalism, but their continued opposition to the Manchu dynasty could be brought to life through any conditions favoring rebellion. Secret societies played, therefore, a part in the uprisings of the troubled years of the nineteenth century and later became the basis of Sun Yat-sen's revolutionary movement.

TABLE 1

OFFICIAL CENSUS OF POPULATION AND CULTIVATED LAND, 1661-1833

Year	Population*	Cultivated Land † (in *mou*)	Land-Population Ratio (*mou* per capita)
1661	19,137,652 ‡	549,357,640	—
1685	20,341,738 ‡	607,843,001	—
1724	25,510,115 ‡	683,791,427	—
1753	183,678,259	708,114,288	3.8
1766	208,095,796	741,449,550	3.5
1812	333,700,560	791,525,100	2.4
1833	398,942,360	737,512,900	1.8

* From year-end entries in *Ch'ing-shih-lu* or *Tung-hua-lu*.
† From sections on land system in *Huang-ch'ao wen-hsien t'ung-k'ao* and *Huang-ch'ao hsü wen-hsien t'ung-k'ao*.
‡ Taxable population only (*ting*).
Note: The reliability of the Chinese official figures on cultivated land and population has been questioned and under each category there are indeed serious doubts about the accuracy of these figures. The most obvious impossibility is the discrepancy between the population figures for the years 1724 and 1753 as given in the chart. This discrepancy is easily understood if one considers the change in the tax system that occurred during this time. In early Ch'ing time one of the major taxes was a head tax, and it was therefore not in the interest of the taxpaying families to admit the existence of more taxable adults than were already registered by the officials. It is quite an indication of the weakness of the governmental authority that it was unable to overcome this resistance to any true recording of the population for tax purposes. When this head tax was amalgamated with the land tax in all the key provinces in the 1720's, there was no longer any reason to conceal the number of members of each family, and the official census figure suddenly swelled to many times its former total. The figures from 1753 on must therefore be regarded as much more reliable than those of the earlier decades. But aside from the break in the figures, the steady increase in population is apparent from both the earlier and later figures.

A different problem exists with regard to the figures on cultivated land. It was in the interest neither of the taxpaying farmers nor of the local officials responsible for the transmission of taxes to admit the existence of all the taxable land under cultivation, and it is generally assumed that these figures remained somewhat below reality. But the steady increase of the land reported indicates that new land brought under cultivation could not be concealed altogether and had eventually to be included in the tax record; and it can actually be assumed that the land record was not too far beehind the reality. (See Supplement to Chang, *The Income of the Chinese Gentry*, pp. 294-95.) But even if both the population and the land figures are, as some suspect, below the reality, these figures indicate quite clearly the growing discrepancy between population increase and cultivated land. Since the existing technique of land cultivation did not change, there was thus a serious problem of overpopulation, which added another element to the cyclical problems in producing the crisis of the nineteenth century.

a substantial effect on the over-all Chinese economy. Under the Ch'ing dynasty, trade, including frontier trade, had been favored more than previously, but its total amount had remained negligible in relation to the total substance of the Chinese economy. By the turn of the eighteenth century, however, the Canton trade began to have a serious impact on the Chinese economy, not so much because of the quantity of goods involved as because of the imbalance of the trade. By that time there had been added to the legitimate trade, under which Chinese goods such as tea, silk, and porcelain had been exported and cotton goods from India as well as some other Western products had been imported, a vast illegitimate trade in foreign opium. By the beginning of the nineteenth century, the value of this new import had become much higher than the value of all the legitimate trade. Formerly in the regular trade the value of the exports had been much higher than that of the imports, and the balance had to be covered through an import of silver into China, but the amount was negligible in relation to the total Chinese economy. Through the import of opium the imbalance was not only reversed, but the outflow of Chinese silver that resulted became serious enough to upset the internal Chinese fiscal system.

The Chinese internal currency system was based on silver and copper —silver to be used for tax payment, for the payment of salaries by the government, and for all calculations of the official treasury; copper to be used for local buying and selling, especially in the local agricultural markets. As a result of the outflow of silver, the internal value of silver to copper was changed from 1:2 to 1:3. This greatly aggravated the financial problems of the Chinese farming population, whose tax and rent payments were calculated in silver but whose income was based on devaluated copper.

The general causes of cyclical decline and the special effects of population increase and the economic impact of Western trade and opium smuggling created the conditions that resulted in the crisis of the Ch'ing dynasty in the nineteenth century. The Ch'ing government had become corrupt and inefficient. Overtaxation, high rents, and population pressure had forced people off the land, and banditry had increased. Local defense organizations had taken over in many parts of the country where official protection was no longer available. Secret societies had become active in organizing local unrest. The government was financially weakened through graft and the great costs of military campaigns. The military adventures under the Ch'ien-lung emperor in the second half of the eighteenth century, which had expanded the Chinese position in central Asia, had depleted the treasury reserves; and during the same time the vastly expanded system of presents, bribes, and graft had cut into government revenues. After the death of the Ch'ien-lung emperor, his chief political adviser, Ho Shen, was tried on charges of corruption, sentenced to death, and the immense fortune which he had accumulated was confiscated. But the malaise of the system was not cured. By the turn of the century, local outbreaks had occurred in several parts of the country. In the first decades of the nineteenth century, the uprising of the White Lotus Society covered much of the territory of central China. In the southwest there had been trouble with the Miao tribes, who reacted against Chinese seizure of their lands and extortion by local officials. In the 1830's small-scale local uprisings occurred in many provinces all over the country, and banditry increased. To deal with the trouble, officials had permitted or actively sponsored local self-defense corps, and in many instances local authority had shifted into the hands of the leaders of these local forces.

This was the necessary result of the decline of the regular Manchu military forces. The Manchu banners had already lost their military value during the eighteenth century. The life of an idle elite had corrupted their morale. Their pay remained the same and could not have easily been increased under the fixed government budget system. In a steady, slow inflation, prices had risen, so that the real pay of the troops had declined. The number of paid soldiers in the banners also remained the same, while the banner population increased. Occasional handouts by the government had not changed the situation, and the banner families had become privileged paupers, whose value as a fighting force, for the most part, had become negligible.[7]

The Chinese professional troops, the *lü-ying* or "green-banner" battalions, had been affected by the general corruption and demoralization. Their salaries, which were low to begin with, were often pocketed by the officers, and the underpaid soldiers lived off the land. Most of the units were considerably under strength, since vacancies created by death or desertion were not filled, and the officers kept the pay of the nonexistent soldiers. When inspections were made, stand-ins were hired for the occasion. Training was negligible and equipment was lacking; the army had become a typical part of the corrupted bureaucratic organization, totally unprepared to deal with any major emergency.

The weakness of the military forces was demonstrated during the time of the great external crisis which the dynasty faced with the first attack from the West. The Opium War (1839-42) had demonstrated the total inadequacy of the Manchu military forces for defense against outside attack. The fighting had been limited to the areas of Canton and the lower Yangtze, and in both regions local corps, led by gentry, had

---

[7] See Michael, "Regionalism in Nineteenth-Century China."

taken part in it. The weakness of the government forces demonstrated during the war and the humiliation of the defeat had done further damage to the prestige of the dynasty in China.

The Opium War and the Treaty of Nanking had had other effects on the internal Chinese development, especially in the south. One of the geographical and political units of China was formed by the area known as Liang-Kuang, the two provinces of Kwangtung and Kwangsi, Eastern and Western Kuang. In this region the Taiping Rebellion originated. Special geographic features set this region apart from other parts of China. Its ethnic, social, economic, and political complexities aggravated the problems created by the general conditions of economic decline and breakdown of political order in all of China. In these special local expressions of over-all problems can be found the immediate causes of the Taiping Rebellion.

Canton was the principal city of Kwangtung province. It was the political and military headquarters of the area and its center of communications and commerce. Canton's network of waterways was the outlet for three major rivers, the West River, the North River, and the East River, which bound the area together. The North River and East River connected the hinterland of Kwangtung province itself with the port of Canton; the West River, much longer than the other two, flowed through the province of Kwangsi and gave this province its outlet toward Kwangtung and the city of Canton. The two provinces were separated from other parts of China by natural borders of mountains and formed in themselves an economic unit. Kwangsi province was then the hinterland of Kwangtung and therefore felt all the repercussions of events that occurred in Canton.

During the Opium War, Canton had seen most of the fighting, and the changes brought about by the Treaty of Nanking had destroyed the trade monopoly formerly held by the merchants of the city. The end of the monopoly of trade and the growing competition of the new treaty ports, especially Shanghai, affected the trade routes and upset the existing transportation system. Groups of porters and of boat people were affected. After breaking down official resistance to their demands, the British also attacked the pirates in the delta of Canton who had made regular trade hazardous. The defeated pirates were driven upriver into the hinterland of Kwangtung and Kwangsi and added a further element of insecurity to a region already suffering from economic dislocation and local conflict.

Once internal decline and foreign attack had destroyed the equilibrium that had been maintained by the government, the problems that arose in the two southern provinces were perhaps more complex than in most other parts of China. Kwangtung province, and still more, Kwangsi were settled by a composite population. Most of the Chinese population consisted of two groups, the Punti and the Hakka. The Punti were descendants of the early Chinese settlers who had reached the area first and made up the majority of the population. The Hakka were a later group of Chinese settlers who had migrated to the south as a result of the invasions of north and central China by peoples from central Asia. Each, the Punti and the Hakka, had maintained their special customs and dialects. They were settled in different villages, and their differing customs and traditions often led to communal rivalries and clashes.[8]

In addition to these Chinese population groups, a large number of tribal people lived in the two provinces, especially in Kwangsi. People like the Miao, Yao, and the Lolo who had made up the pre-Chinese population of the area had been pressed back by the Chinese settlement to less desirable land and mountainous regions. These tribal people had a latent hostility against the Chinese officials and farmers who had taken land and imposed taxes. At times, when the pressure had become too harsh or when the Chinese authorities seemed weakened, the tribes attemped to strike back, and Kwangsi province especially had been the scene of a number of Miao rebellions. When Miao strength was in ascendance, their leading families had ruled over and taxed Chinese farmers, and their local military and political tradition had by no means been inferior to that of the Chinese.

In addition to these diverse ethnic groups, there were occupational groupings that created communities with special traditions and interests. The boat people, who lived on their boats and monopolized the traffic on the rivers, formed communities of their own. The miners and the charcoal burners in the mountains formed tight groups organized under their own leadership.

The diversity of ethnic composition and of occupational groupings made the province the favorite ground for the establishment of secret societies. All over the province branches of the secret societies were established which protected the members of the different interest groups and often gave these groups a political coherence. Some of the activities of these societies were as illegal as they were profitable. Kwangtung and

[8] There were villages of people of other Chinese groups, such as the Min; most of these people lived in Fukien province, but some of them had migrated into Kwangtung.

Kwangsi were salt-producing areas, and salt was a government monopoly. Salt-smuggling was one of the major activities of such local organizations. The more government authority declined, the stronger these local underground organizations of different kinds became. The provincial accounts of the early part of the nineteenth century are full of reports on smuggling, banditry, piracy, and rebellious activities of secret societies.[9]

This was the setting in which the Taiping uprising took place. When official authority declined and corruption increased, and when the government troops had become demoralized and ineffective, local organizations took over to defend the many legitimate and illegitimate interests of their members. Kwangtung and Kwangsi provinces became the scene of small-scale warfare between rival groups. There was a basic conflict between the Punti and Hakka villages. Both sides were armed, and in the clashes between local corps and other local forces the officials could either side with one group against the other or remain neutral altogether, hoping that the local unrest would not lead to the banding together of larger forces and rebellious outbreaks that would challenge the authority of the officials themselves.[10]

The origin of the Taiping Rebellion can be found in these conditions of decline that characterized the end of a dynastic cycle, aggravated by special factors of population growth and the new Western impact. The rebellion's geographical starting point in the southeast can be explained by the complicated ethnic and social conditions of that area, which sharpened any local conflict. However, both the cause of the rebellion and its goals differed basically from those of the upheavals in earlier periods of crisis. The new faith preached by the Taiping leaders and the system they tried to establish marked a radical departure from the past.

[9] See Laai Yi-faai, Franz Michael, and John C. Sherman, "The Use of Maps in Social Research: A Case Study in South China," *The Geographical Review*, LII, No. 1 (1962), 92-111.

[10] A contemporary Western missionary writer dealing with the background of the Taiping Rebellion describes the growing local autonomy, village warfare, and the decline of the authority of the officials as follows: "In China, where the distance to the district town or nearest Mandarin office is often very great, perhaps twenty or thirty miles, and where a lawsuit generally results in a mere spending of large sums of money to the benefit of the Mandarins and their servants, the method of settling any disputes between themselves by means of appointed, or generally acknowledged headmen, is in most instances resorted to, and very often war between different villages is resolved upon, carried on for months, and peace finally concluded without any interference on the side of the Mandarins who at the present time have lost a great part of their influence among the native population." Hamberg, p. 3.

Part I

The Origin of the Taipings
and Their Rise in Kwangsi

Hung Hsiu-ch'üan and the Organization of the God Worshippers

THE prophet and head of the Taiping Rebellion was Hung Hsiu-ch'üan, a man of simple origin. Hung was born on January 1, 1814,[1] in the village of Fu-yüan-shui in Hua-hsien, Kwangtung province. He came from a Hakka family which, four generations before Hung was born, had moved to Hua-hsien from Chia-ying-chou, a Hakka district in eastern Kwangtung at the border of Fukien province. Hung's father, Hung Ching-yang, was a small farmer who worked his own fields, first in Fu-yüan-shui and later in Kuan-lu-pu in the same district, a Hakka village of some four hundred people to which the family moved during Hung

---

[1] The exact date of Hung's birth is the tenth day of the twelfth month of Chia-ch'ing 18, which corresponds to January 1, 1814, in the Western calendar. Some Western authors have given the date as 1813 (Meadows, p. 74; Brine, p. 64; Hail, p. 33). These writers seem to have relied on Hamberg, p. 5, where that date is given. The explanation for Hamberg's mistake may be that Chia-ch'ing 18 corresponds for the most part to 1813. The correct date was worked out by Chien Yu-wen in *Shou-i-shih*, p. 52. Chien computed the date from the Chinese dates of Hung's early activities recorded in the Taiping document, the "Taiping Heavenly Chronicle" (document 17). Several Chinese historians have compounded Hamberg's error by deducing from his wrong date of 1813 that Hung was born in Chia-ch'ing 17. Lo, *Shih-kang*, p. 38; Kuo, *Jih-chih*, I, 3. For further discussion, see Chien, *Shou-i-shih*, pp. 51-54, and his latest work, *T'ai-p'ing T'ien-kuo ch'üan-shih*, I, 1-4.

Hsiu-ch'üan's childhood. Hung had two elder brothers, Hung Jen-fa and Hung Jen-ta,[2] who helped their father with the work on the farm.

Hung Hsiu-ch'üan was said to have been a very intelligent child, and his family had great hopes that the youngest son would be able to acquire the learning and the academic degrees that alone opened the way to a better life in traditional China, not only for the scholar himself but also for his family and relatives. The privileges and opportunities enjoyed by members of the scholar-gentry and especially by those who succeeded in entering upon an official career enabled them to advance and support their relatives and friends, who were therefore willing to make great sacrifices to help a promising child acquire the learning that was the source of all this fortune. Hung Hsiu-ch'üan was sent to school at the age of seven and was said to have made rapid progress. In 1827, at the age of fifteen *sui,* he began to participate in the official examinations. But though he passed the preliminary examinations, he failed in the main examination in Canton, the examination for the *sheng-yüan* degree that would have admitted him to the privileged status of the gentry.

In view of the difficulty of the examination, the large number of candidates—sometimes over a thousand—and the small quota of about a dozen who were permitted to pass in these examinations, the failure was not surprising. But with so much at stake it can easily be understood that the candidates labored under great nervous strain. Those who failed tried again whenever the examination was held, and Hung Hsiu-ch'üan tried several times to pass the examination, the last time in 1843, but he never succeeded. During all this time when he was preparing for the examination, he, like many other student candidates, supported himself by teaching school in his village. He was, then, one of the unsuccessful scholars who were disappointed and frustrated—the marginal group from which in periods of crisis the leaders or supporters of rebellious movements often came. Men who had not succeeded under the existing system could easily become hostile to it; in their futile attempts to obtain a degree they had gained enough education to organize or direct a political uprising.

[2] Hung Hsiu-ch'üan's clan name was Hung Jen-k'un, giving him the same first part of the personal name as his brothers according to the Chinese tradition. His childhood name was Hung Huo-hsiu. He used the name Hsiu-ch'üan only after 1837. See documents 2 and 17. Some secondary sources giving relatively full accounts of the early part of the Taiping Rebellion and the early life of Hung Hsiu-ch'üan are Chien, *Shou-i-shih;* Chien, *Ch'üan-shih;* Chien, *Chin-t'ien;* Lo, *Nien-p'u;* and Hamberg.

When Hung failed in another attempt in 1837, he became critically ill. The humiliation of his failure and the realization of the disappointment he had become to his family and neighbors must have been hard to take, and this experience, together with the nervous strain of the examination itself, brought on a serious breakdown. He was carried home from Canton and remained delirious for several days, during which time his family regarded him as mad and feared for his life.[3] At times he was unable to recognize others. He talked irrationally and had fits of rage during which he could be restrained only with difficulty. When Hung recovered from his illness, those who knew him felt that his personality as well as his appearance had changed. "He was careful in his conduct, friendly and open in his demeanor, his body increased in height and size, his pace became firm and imposing, his views enlarged and liberal." [4] Hung also started to take an active interest in political affairs, both local and national, and obviously regarded himself as a man with a mission. He began to assume authority in his native district, deposed on his own authority an "Inspector of the Ground" named Moo, used a whip of nine rods for lashing evildoers, and became generally feared.[5] He claimed later that his knowledge of the problem of opium import and of the Opium War made him even then a confirmed enemy of opium-smoking and of the government for its policy of permitting the trade.[6] In his words:

> Each year they [the Manchus] transform tens of millions of China's silver and gold into opium and extract several millions from the fat and marrow of the Chinese people and turn it into rouge and powder. . . . How could the rich not become poor? How could the poor abide by the law? [7]

[3] In the Taiping accounts Hung's illness lasted for forty days. As analyzed by Kuo T'ing-i in *Jih-chih*, I, 14-27, and by Chien Yu-wen in *Shou-i-shih*, pp. 70-79, and *Ch'üan-shih*, I, 22-32, the actual period of illness was probably only four days. Cf. the Taiping document "A Hero's Return to the Truth" (document 205). As pointed out by Teng, p. 53, the "forty days" of Jesus Christ's fasting is frequently mentioned in *Good Words to Admonish the Age*, and so Hung's illness was later declared to have lasted the same length of time.

[4] Hamberg, p. 14. A short diagnosis of Hung's mental illness can be found in an article by P. M. Yap, "The Mental Illness of Hung Hsiu-ch'üan, Leader of the Taiping Rebellion," *Far Eastern Quarterly*, XIII (May 1954), 287-304. This study by a psychiatrist is based, however, only on the limited material available in English. A fuller medical case study could probably be made from Hung's writings and poetry in this documentary collection.

[5] Hamberg, pp. 40-41.

[6] See document 15.

[7] Document 205, "A Hero's Return to the Truth."

Several odes that he composed in these years immediately after this illness show Hung's expansive mind and new notions of grandeur and express his vague ambitions to conquer the land and become a ruler.[8] These odes, though, do not yet contain the elements of Christian teaching that were soon to give Hung's restless mind a new focus.[9] Hung, even in his new condition, made a last attempt to pass the examination in 1843 and failed again. And shortly afterwards there came to his attention a Christian tract which seemed to him to provide an explanation of his own experiences and which gave a new direction to his thinking, affected as it was by his illness.

This tract had actually come into his hands seven years earlier, in 1836, while he was in Canton for the examination. It was given to him on the street by a Chinese Christian convert, named Liang A-fa, and the title of the tract, which was in Chinese, was "Good Words to Admonish the Age." The tract admonished the reader to believe in God and Jesus Christ, to obey the Ten Commandments and never to worship demons.[10]

[8] See documents 4 and 5.

[9] There may have been more such examples of Hung's pre-Christian expressions of the new powers he felt and the new aspirations he possessed, but such other odes may have been later revised. According to Hamberg, p. 29, Hung continued to rewrite his odes and other pieces, even those written later, "to all of which he, however, afterwards made considerable additions, and most of which are contained in the 'Imperial declaration of Thai-p'hing,' afterwards printed at Nanking."

[10] The date on which Hung received this Christian tract varies in different writings. One possible date is 1833 because it is maintained that this was the year Liang A-fa went to Canton to distribute the book to examination candidates. Meadows, p. 75; Mackie, p. 61; Boardman, p. 12. Another possible date is 1837, based on the confession made by the Kan Wang, Hung Jen-kan in 1864. Lo, *Nien-p'u*; Teng, p. 52. The date of 1836 accepted here can be seen in Hamberg, p. 8; the Taiping document, "Hung Hsiu-ch'üan's Background," document 1; Chien, *Shou-i-shih*, p. 68; Chien, *Ch'üan-shih*, I, 20; Lo, *Shih-kang*, p. 39. Kuo T'ing-i in *Jih-chih*, I, 12-14, has pointed out the following: (1) Numerous data offer overwhelming odds against the date 1833. Liang A-fa did compile and distribute the book in 1833, but Hung did not necessarily have to receive it in that year, nor to have received it directly from Liang. (2) Hamberg's book was based on Hung Jen-kan's narration, which was made twelve years earlier than Hung Jen-kan's confession. Hung Jen-kan should have been fresher on the dates at that time. The 1836 date has now become even less doubtful with the discovery of the document "Hung Hsiu-ch'üan's Background," document 1. (3) The year 1837 as mentioned in the confession might have been an unintentional mistake on Hung Jen-kan's part, or it might have been made intentionally in order to show that Hung's ascent to heaven during his illness in 1837 had nothing to do with the Christian tract, since there would then be no time in between for Hung Hsiu-ch'üan to study the book.

Hung took the pamphlet, but at the time paid little attention to it. Now, in 1843, shortly after he had failed again in what was his last attempt at the examination, a cousin of his, Li Ching-fang, while looking through Hung's bookcase found the Christian pamphlet, read it, and immediately told Hung about its extraordinary content. Hung, who now read the pamphlet carefully, found in it not only a doctrine that he was willing to accept but also what he believed to be an explanation of his own experience. His illness, which must have been embarrassing to him in spite of his new self-assurance, based on his delusions, could now be ascribed to a religious experience.

Hung had the fantastic notion that he had been chosen by the Christian God, of whom he now learned, for a special mission to defeat evil, which was represented by devils and demons, and to bring about God's rule on earth. His illness now became for him the turning point in his life, the time he had met God and been given his new task. When he had been ill and delirious, he had simply left this world and had been up in heaven where he had met God and Jesus Christ, who taught him the doctrine and gave him his assignment. On God's command, he had battled the demons, and his wild behavior during the delirious seizures viewed by his family and friends had been simply the signs of the battle he had carried on in that mysterious other world, of which he could now give glorious accounts. His behavior during his illness could therefore be readily explained through this fantastic story of his ascent to the heaven about which he had read in the pamphlet and which he now embellished by the fantasy of his story.[11] And the mission which he now believed to have received, to return to earth, fight the demons, and bring man back to the worship of the true God gave a purpose to his new ambitions. Hung had thus found the basic elements of a system of teachings into which he could pour his own vague ideas of his mission and which provided the framework for the delusions of grandeur created by his illness. Hung's interpretation of these Christian teachings formed the basis of what became the ideology of the Taiping Rebellion.

Hung immediately accepted the religious doctrine as given in the pamphlet and embellished it with his own story. He and his cousin baptized each other in the way prescribed in the pamphlet. Hung then

---

[11] Even the six-year delay in this interpretation could be explained by Hung's account that God had indicated to him in heaven that after his return to earth he would only slowly awaken to the truth and that a book would tell him the truth as it had now indeed come to pass. See document 17.

wrote another poem that dealt with these newly found ideas of God, Christ, atonement, heaven and hell, repentance, and the worship of God,[12] and began to preach these concepts to his family, his friends, and the villagers.

The ideas Hung received from the tract itself were later enlarged by his reading of the Bible and a few months' instruction with a Protestant missionary, the Reverend Issachar T. Roberts in Canton. Hung went to Canton in March of 1847 to study with the Reverend Roberts, an American Southern Baptist, but left again when he was unable to find means of support, possibly because two other students of Roberts intrigued against him. Hung left without having received formal baptism. Hung's original limited understanding of Christianity cannot have been greatly affected by this exposure to Christian teaching, as can be seen from the writings in which he put down his beliefs and which were made public later as official proclamations of his Taiping movement.[13]

Since Hung believed that he himself had been in heaven, he could be his own witness to prove the fancies of his imagination. Hung believed in a God as the creator of all things, a God whom man must worship and serve; but it was a very personified God, with whom Hung had a very personal relationship. This God was an imposing figure with a golden beard who sat in heaven like an emperor in a dignified posture, in a black dragon robe, with a high brimmed hat, hands on knees, and who was surrounded by his heavenly family and court. It was a God who expressed his problems in personal conversation and who had feelings of great sadness about the state of the world. In spite of God's wrath and the flood, in spite of Christ's sacrifice, men continued to serve the demons. In the fight against these demons, who looked very much like the demons of Chinese folk tales, God now enlisted Hung's services.[14]

It is only natural that Hung's views of God and heaven were also colored by his Chinese ideas on the family. God had a heavenly wife, and Jesus Christ, who as God's son played his part in the family, had also his own heavenly wife. When Hung was in Heaven, Jesus' wife, a kindhearted woman, was like a mother to Hung, and exerted her modifying influence on Christ when He was angry with Hung for not learning his biblical lessons well. Altogether heaven was a beautiful place with

[12] See document 6.
[13] See especially documents 10 and 17.
[14] See document 17.

beautiful maidens and angels, with heavenly music and a heavenly wife for Hung, who was understandably reluctant to follow God's command and go back to earth for his mission, though he had eventually to obey.[15]

This personified image of the Christian God and of heaven had its counterpart in Hung's personification of evil. The reason for God's sadness was the success of the demons in taking over the earth and misguiding the people. Even heaven had been penetrated by these demons, of whom the serpent god was the worst and most powerful.

Christianity to Hung was a battle between God and the devil, and this battle was in Hung's mind a very personal one. It was his mission to fight for God and to kill the demons or send them to hell. God had been exasperated before when he sent the flood and when his Son, Christ, had descended to earth to redeem the sins of man. When he was received in heaven, Hung learned that he was God's son too, a younger brother of Jesus Christ, and therefore charged to take his role in the battle. His raving during his illness was now interpreted by Hung as his battle with the demons in heaven so dramatically described by him for his followers. And now on earth it was his task to bring the people back to the worship of God and to slay the demons. The demons were all those who refused to accept God's will as now interpreted and repre-sented by Hung—especially the Manchus. This simplified righteousness was a very suitable ideology for a rebellious movement.

Essentially Hung's preaching was an appeal to believers to worship God the creator, on whose favor and grace all things depended, and thus to receive God's care in this world and go to heaven afterwards—and to fight the demons that stood in the way of the fulfillment of God's kingdom.[16] In addition to this basic appeal to all to worship God the creator and to attack the demons, Hung's writings contained, however, a complex mixture of ideas taken from Chinese tradition.[17] Hung had indeed little understanding of Christian teaching or theology, of such problems as original sin and redemption, or of the teachings of Christ in the New Testament. Hung stressed the story of the Old Testament, of the creation, the flood, and of God's anger with man, a story which he interpreted literally and which he related to Chinese history. Up to the time of the Three Dynasties, the people had worshipped God, but

[15] See document 17.
[16] See document 10.
[17] For the different elements that contributed to Taiping ideology, see Vincent Shih's forthcoming book, "The Taiping Ideology: Its Sources, Interpretations, and Influence."

then they had been led astray. Buddhism and Taoism, which he must have hated as competitive ideologies for rebellion, were false teachings of the devil, and Confucianism itself, though not without value, had misled the people. Though he used Confucian references at first to support his teaching, Hung eliminated some of these later.[18] And psychologically most interesting is his later embellishment of the story of his experience in heaven where Confucius was taken to task by God for having misled the people and was given a beating, obviously a great satisfaction to Hung, the luckless candidate in the Confucian examination.[19] To the mixture of the Bible and Chinese history was added Hung's story of his ascent to Heaven and of his mission to establish God's kingdom. The promise he gave was that behind him was the supernatural power of God that would bring success in a miraculous way.

Among Hung's first converts were his cousin Hung Jen-kan, who was later to play an important role in the Taiping movement, and Hung Hsiu-ch'üan's close friend and fellow teacher, Feng Yün-shan, who came from a nearby village, Ho-lo-ti, in the same district. To demonstrate his faith, Hung Hsiu-ch'üan removed the idols from his and his colleagues' schoolrooms and together with Hung Jen-kan composed a poem to recognize the occasion.[20] When asked by the elders of their village to compose the customary poems in praise of the local gods at the occasion of the lantern festival early in 1844, the two Hungs refused and when criticized for this disrespectful attitude, wrote instead a verse to confess their new faith.[21]

This attack against tradition cost Hung his position as schoolteacher, and with it his income. This may have been the primary reason that he and his friend Feng Yün-shan left their home villages and started on a career as traveling preachers.[22] The two (with two other friends who soon turned back) set out on April 2, 1844, and traveled through several regions of Kwangtung province on the border of Kwangsi, regions that were known to have many branches of the Triad Society.[23] They also covered the border areas inhabited by Yao tribal people and

[18] See comment on documents 10 and 17.
[19] See document 17.
[20] See document 17.
[21] See document 8.
[22] See Hamberg, p. 26.
[23] Kuo T'ing-i stresses this point as an indication that Hung chose this area in the hope of finding there a following of his own. See *Jih-chih*, I, 37, 112.

then moved into Kwangsi, where they settled down in the village of Kuei-hsien with some relatives of Hung's.[24] They preached and seemed to have gained some followers; but when the son of his host was arrested, possibly because of suspicions aroused by Hung Hsiu-ch'üan's activities, the feelings toward Hung changed. Hung decided to leave but was implored to stay until the arrested man had been released, while Feng and two other relatives went on their way back. Feng remained, however, in a place called Hsün-chou, while Hung Hsiu-ch'üan eventually returned to his home village in Kwangtung in September, 1844.[25]

It was Feng Yün-shan who succeeded in setting up a new society that made an organized group of the adherents of the preaching of Hung Hsiu-ch'üan and of Feng himself, and the core of the later rebellious movement. Feng continued his preaching in several villages in the neighborhood, and established himself in Tzu-ching-shan (Thistle Mountain), a strategic mountain area in southern Kwangsi. There Feng founded the *Pai-Shang-ti-hui*, or God Worshippers Society, a formal organization of the followers of the new faith with branches in many villages.

The God Worshippers Society had some of the characteristics of traditional Chinese secret societies. Its members were held together by a bond of loyalty in the defense of their interests against outsiders and by the general spirit of brotherhood that prevailed among the members of all Chinese secret societies. But the belief that united the members of the new society differed fundamentally from the vague Buddhist, Taoist, and Confucian concepts used by the traditional societies. The members of the God Worshippers Society accepted a new religious faith, a faith quite contrary to all tradition of Chinese imperial society, a faith in a personal God and his guidance for one's personal salvation as well as in all matters of daily life and in the larger problems of economic, social, and political affairs. It was this faith that enabled the God Worshippers to accept some of the most revolutionary changes in their personal lives and in their social and political order.

This religious organization was established by Feng Yün-shan in the absence of Hung Hsiu-ch'üan whose alleged religious experiences could all the more effectively be referred to by Feng, the preacher of the new faith. However Christian the new faith may have been, there can be little doubt of the sincerity of the God Worshippers. In the record

[24] See document 17.
[25] See document 17.

preserved of their simple prayers to be offered on ordinary and special occasions can be found genuine religious feeling and great trust in God, whose blessing is sought at the beginning and end of each day, at birth, marriage, and death, and in the ordinary affairs of life. There was as yet very little of the political doctrine in which religious teachings were later to be used by the Taiping leaders to give their authority and power divine sanction. To help the inarticulate and uneducated members of the group, special forms of prayers for each occasion were written down, so that the faithful had only to have their names included on the form and then the paper was burned as in Buddhist practice.[26]

But from the outset the political reality of the intervillage fighting gave the branches of the God Worshippers Society their militant character. In most cases, conversions were not of individuals alone but of whole families and clans or of whole occupational groups, such as charcoal burners and miners. The various local groups of the God Worshippers founded regular congregations within the villages, large enough to form local military units which could defend themselves against other such local forces. Often a whole village or occupational group would form such a congregation, and these local groups sometimes numbered several hundred.

What gave this God Worshippers Society its special militant character was the fact that it was formed among Hakka by Hakka leaders. Once the society was established and its many branches were functioning, the Hakka found in it an organizational protection in their fight against the Punti. Large groups of Hakka, already in conflict with their non-Hakka neighbors, joined the rapidly growing society. In the villages where they predominated, the Hakka congregations took over local control and forced others to join. The conflict between Hakka and non-Hakka was thus transformed into one between the God Worshippers Society and opposing militant organizations. In the words of one of the later Taiping leaders:

> For several years after the members began worshipping God, no apparent move was made. In the twenty-seventh and twenty-eighth years of Tao-kuang (1847-48), however, bandits in Kwangsi were ravaging the country everywhere, disturbing cities and towns, and the various inhabitants organized themselves into local corps [*t'uan-lien*]. The local-corps members and the God-worshippers were distinguished from one another. The God-worshippers would form themselves into one group, and the local-

[26] See document 24, comment.

corps men would form themselves into another group. Each party pursued its own course and endeavored to surpass the other, and the pressure finally led to the uprising. At the outset of the uprising, there would be both local-corps men and God-worshippers in one and the same village, and there were also attacks by one village on another. Therefore the members gathered themselves together.[27]

Branches (*fen-hui*) of the God Worshippers Society were established wherever there were enough members, and were therefore scattered widely. They were more numerous in Kuei-hsien, where some of Hung Hsiu-ch'üan's relatives lived and where Hung and Feng had visited in 1844, and in the district of Kuei-p'ing, where Feng had centered his efforts around his headquarters at Tzu-ching-shan.

Tzu-ching-shan was a mountain area that could easily be defended. It could only be approached from two sides, the west and the south, and had a small number of villages connected by goat trails. This area could not easily be penetrated by official authority and military forces, and had been pretty much on its own. Each of the small villages had formed its own organization, a *pao*, under the authority of a local *pao* chief. The isolation of this area had, however, its own disadvantages, since it could be easily blockaded, and the leaders trapped. An ideal gathering point to assemble the members of the various groups for an open outbreak was in the small town of Chin-t'ien at the foot of the mountain area.

In August, 1847, Hung Hsiu-ch'üan went to Thistle Mountain and joined Feng Yün-shan in the leadership of the God Worshippers Society, which Feng had established and which by this time had grown to a following of over two thousand converts, mostly peasants and miners. Together the two expanded the organization and its program. In the preceding years Feng had used Hung's poems, odes, and essays, together with his own understanding of the biblical story, as the basis for the God Worshippers' religious creed. Now Hung wrote a record of his preaching activities, and his writings at this time clearly indicate that in his mind the preaching of his religious experiences and ideas was to be used to realize his political aspirations.[28] The demons that had to be fought were not only the evil spirits of the supernatural world but were now also the Manchus and their supporters who had misled the people, and the movement thus took on a rebellious character.

While traveling in nearby tribal territory, Hung increased his reputa-

[27] See document 382, "The Confession of Li Hsiu-ch'eng."
[28] See documents 10 and 17.

tion by smashing some of the statues of the local deities.[29] Since descriptions of the local beliefs indicate that the myths and customs attacked by Hung were derived from tribal tradition and were anathema to the Chinese, Hung's attack upon the demon worshippers must have been quite acceptable to the Chinese population and to the Chinese magistrates, who were not aware of the more dangerous content of Hung's preaching.

At that time, Hung was already using the term T'ai-p'ing, which was later to be bestowed on his rebellious movement, and called himself the *Chün Wang*, or Noble King, indicating the political character of his group and the role he himself assumed. He also stated that he and his followers "wrote a memorial asking the Heavenly Father, the Supreme Lord and Great God, to select for them a firm stronghold where they could settle themselves." [30]

Hung's writings of this time are full of allusions to the heroes of Chinese history. This appeal to history is another indication that he himself planned to play a historical role, in fact a greater one than the role played by the figures alluded to.[31] These historical allusions are used as examples to demonstrate how failure and success had depended in the past upon whether or not God's precepts had been followed.[32]

The religious doctrine which Hung preached was therefore now taking on more of its political character. The strange mixture of concepts that formed Hung's religious teachings lent itself easily to such political application. In the direct and simple interpretation of the biblical story and its miracles, which he embellished with his own fantasies, Hung saw proof of God's political interest in the state of mankind and in the establishment of his rule on earth. The battle against evil that had started with the Flood and had been continued by Jesus Christ was now

---

[29] See documents 14 and 17.

[30] See document 17.

[31] See documents 10 and others.

[32] The reader cannot escape the impression that Hung used these writings not only to express his religious convictions and political mission but also to display his knowledge of all the historical data and classical references with which he had filled his mind in preparation for the examinations in which he had failed. A few years later, when these essays and poems were re-edited, most of the historical allusions disappeared, and the Taiping doctrine acquired by that time more and more the character of a break with Chinese historical tradition. Some of the few references that remained were disparaging remarks on the rebel leaders of late Ming, Li Tzu-ch'eng and Huang Chao, indicating that what Hung propagated was not a traditional rebellion but a religious movement that broke with tradition.

in the hands of Hung, who carried out God's command. He had to organize the faithful, to establish on earth the Heavenly Kingdom of Great Peace, the T'ai-p'ing T'ien-kuo.

There was no grasp of the deeper theological meaning of Christian teachings, of the problems of original sin and redemption, or of the Holy Ghost and of the Trinity. The Holy Ghost became simply God's voice and was later to be used by the most powerful of Hung's lieutenants to assume command through trances in which he claimed that God's voice spoke through him. And in analogy to Christ's role of redeemer of sin, this man claimed to be the redeemer of illness for mankind, after having suffered a prolonged illness himself.

This literal interpretation of the Christian doctrine provided the authority of command for the Taiping leaders. The rules of the Ten Commandments which were set by Hung into poems[33] were used as a system of discipline for the God Worshippers community and enforced like a code. But the real basis of the political system that was established was the concept of the Christian community as one great family whose members were all children of God.[34] This concept fitted into the Chinese tradition as well, and provided a justification for the new order that was to be organized. Since Hung had found in heaven a replica of the Chinese family system, complete with wives and sisters-in-law for everyone, it was not difficult for him to fit himself into this system as the younger brother of Jesus Christ and to lead the large family of the faithful on earth. This family concept may help to explain the principle of the common treasury—the family property—which the Taipings were to establish, and the Taiping idea of the followers as equal children of God, brothers and sisters all, who were to live in complete chastity until God's purpose was accomplished, when they could live happily together as husbands and wives ever after.

Hung's preaching thus provided the framework of an ideology for a rebellious movement and as such was a most suitable and extraordinary basis for the Taiping Rebellion, but beyond that his fantasies and the interpretation given to them by his lieutenants cannot be formulated into a logical or coherent system, and his own story indicates that the symptoms of insanity which began with his illness in 1837 increased during the following years. Yet under the conditions of chaos and local crisis his claim of divine guidance carried conviction with his followers.

[33] See document 24.
[34] See document 10.

The new family system of the kingdom of God that he proclaimed seemed to them to promise a better world, and instilled in them a religious fervor that lifted their organization above the level of a troop banded together for local fighting to that of a disciplined army, ready for a rebellious movement.

At first, however, the God Worshippers had to deal with the opposition of rival local organizations. The gazetteer of the area recounts some of the clashes between the gentry-led local corps and the God Worshippers that occurred before the Taiping uprising in which the local bandits had connections with a member of the gentry who covered up their raids and disposed of the stolen goods. In 1847, when in the district of the early Taiping concentration in Kuei-hsien a local corps was first started, the leader of this local corps, a member of the gentry, had connections with bandits. The magistrate therefore considered this local corps quite unreliable, and the more respectable people of the community remained aloof. After the death of its first leader, the local corps did fight against pirates and bandits who were becoming more numerous. But no clear line was drawn between legitimate defense and illegal activities.

When Feng Yün-shan organized the God Worshipper units and was accused by a local gentry before the magistrate, the latter therefore did not act. This unwillingness of an official to take sides in clashes between the Punti and Hakka or between the local corps and the God Worshippers, favored the leadership of the God Worshippers in their preparations for local uprisings.

The officials, obviously regarding the God Worshippers as another force for local self-defense, were very slow in taking any action. When Feng Yün-shan first organized the local groups of followers in the districts of Kuei-p'ing and Kuei-hsien, he was twice taken prisoner by the leader of the local corps. On the first occasion, in December, 1847, his own group of God Worshippers freed him by force. In January, 1848, the leader of the local corps petitioned the local magistrate to arrest Feng, but the magistrate, following his policy of neutrality, declined to act. The local-corps leader then took Feng prisoner again with the help of his troops and sent him this time to the magistrate, accusing him of planning a rebellion.

The repeated capture of Feng indicates that he was regarded as the true organizer of the God Worshippers Society and that Hung, its religious leader, was of less interest to the local military leader. When

Feng was taken and detained by the magistrate, together with another Taiping leader, Lu Liu, Hung Hsiu-ch'üan left for Canton to petition the governor-general for Feng's release.[35] Hung hoped to use the imperial promise of tolerance toward Christianity for this purpose. However, the governor-general, Ch'i-ying, had left for Peking, and Hung started back to Kwangsi. In the meantime, Lu Liu died in prison, but Feng was released by the magistrate in exchange for a monetary payment, which was collected by the God Worshippers to buy him off. The only limitation placed on his freedom by the magistrate was that Feng should return to his home province, Kwangtung.

When Hung returned to Kwangsi and found that Feng Yün-shan had been sent back to Hua-hsien in Kwangtung, he himself left for Kwangtung to meet his friend there again. The arrest and banishment of Feng and the temporary absence of Hung Hsiu-ch'üan created a problem of leadership for the God Worshippers in the districts of Kuei-p'ing and Kuei-hsien. The absence of the main organizer and the spiritual leader of the movement provided an opportunity for new leaders to emerge, men who did not derive their authority from a close allegiance to Hung Hsiu-ch'üan.

There must have been a strange atmosphere in the camp of the God Worshippers while their regular leaders were gone. At prayer sessions people came forth and began to speak with tongues. Most of the people who thus spoke up were incoherent, and arguments seemed to have arisen whether it was God or the devil who spoke through the persons who were thus possessed. But this method of speaking in tongues was used by two men to assert their authority.[36]

The man who took over the leadership in this way was Yang Hsiu-ch'ing, from Hsin-ts'un village near Chin-t'ien. Yang came from a family of farmers who had originally emigrated from Kwangtung province. From the descriptions of his colleagues, his biography in an imperial intelligence report,[37] and from the history of the rebellion itself, Yang emerges as a shrewd and ruthless man, who eventually used every means to concentrate all power in his hands. He had lost his parents at an early age[38] and had become a charcoal burner[39] and seems to have established

[35] Hung's dismay at his friend's capture was expressed in another poem. See document 16.
[36] See Hamberg, pp. 45-46.
[37] See Chang, *Tse-ch'ing*.
[38] See document 50.
[39] See document 382.

himself as a leader of a group of charcoal burners and miners who joined the God Worshippers. He must have had some education, since it is reported that he was at one time a clerk in a government office. It was also said that he had been a servant and that he later organized convoys for transporting merchandise through the area. If this is true, he had control over a group of men and enough power to guarantee the secure passage of goods through a bandit-infested area. The government intelligence report that gives this information also claims that Yang was supposed to have shared the profits of this convoy system with Hung Hsiu-ch'üan. All these statements may be true, but cannot be verified.[40] From the Taiping records, we know that Yang was the maternal uncle of a local patron of Hung and Feng.[41]

Yang is mentioned in these records for the first time in April, 1848, as assuming a position of authority during the absence of Hung and Feng from the headquarters area. According to his own account, he had been taken ill and had been deaf and mute for about two months. Then suddenly he spoke up in the meetings. He had trances, simulated or perhaps genuine seizures, in which he claimed to be possessed by the Holy Ghost, representing the person of God the Father, who through Yang instructed the God Worshippers as to what they should do. Since neither Hung nor Yang nor the group of God Worshippers had a clear understanding of the concept of the Holy Ghost, Yang's performances were fully accepted and gave him the divine sanction of his leadership which was effective in this group of religious fanatics. But while Hung must have been genuinely convinced of his own ascent to Heaven and of his divine mission, Yang's actions seem to indicate that he was playing a part.

Together with Yang, another leader came into prominence. This was Hsiao Ch'ao-kuei from Wu-hsüan in Kwangsi, who had been a farmer in the area of Thistle Mountain.[42] Hsiao seems to have co-operated closely with Yang Hsiu-ch'ing and may have been a relative of his.[43] Hsiao established himself as a leader in the same way as Yang had done —by having trances. He claimed to represent Jesus Christ, whose spirit spoke through him to the God Worshippers. In October, 1848, he was

[40] See Yang's biography in Chang, *Tse-ch'ing*.
[41] See also Chien, *Shou-i-shih*, pp. 153-54; Chien, *Ch'üan-shih*, I, 134-36; Lo, *Shih-kao*, p. 175; Chien, *Chin-t'ien*, pp. 28-29.
[42] See document 50.
[43] See Chien, *Shou-i-shih*, p. 154; Chien, *Chin-t'ien*, p. 29; Chien, *Ch'üan-shih*, I, 136-37.

reported to have had his first seizure.[44] In April, 1849, Yang had another trance or, in the Taiping parlance, "The Heavenly Father again descended to the world." This occurred at Kuei-hsien, where Yang also asserted his authority in this role.

Between the two of them, Yang and Hsiao thus took command of the God Worshippers and tried to impress them with the necessity of obeying their divine leaders. They took the precaution always to include Hung in their story, referring to him as the "sovereign" who had ascended to heaven and received his mission from God, but their own authority was directly derived from God and Jesus Christ and therefore obviously potentially above that of Hung, "the younger brother" of Jesus Christ. When Hung and Feng returned to the area of Kuei-p'ing in the summer of 1849, they had to take note of this new type of leadership based on trances. According to a report, they investigated the trances and repudiated those that they declared to have been the inspirations of the devil, but recognized Yang's and Hsiao's performances as true manifestations of God's and Jesus' appearances on earth and in this way sanctioned the leading role of these two ambitious men.[45]

The Rising at Chin-t'ien

When Hung and Feng rejoined the God Worshippers in the districts of Kuei-hsien and Kuei-p'ing, the organization had grown strong enough to prepare for the open rebellious uprising that the leaders had contemplated for some time. Now clashes with the local corps grew more intense. In February of 1850, the local corps fought, defeated, and captured a bandit leader of the Kuei-p'ing district named Ch'en A-kuei. On the way home from this campaign, the victorious local-corps troops passed through villages of God Worshippers in the area of Chin-t'ien, manhandled the villagers, and threatened to kill them because they were God Worshippers. This threat was used by Feng Yün-shan in what seems, according to local history, to have been the first open summons to rebellion addressed to the God Worshippers by one of their leaders. Feng argued that there was no choice but to rebel, for otherwise the God Worshippers would be suppressed and killed by their enemies. It

[44] See document 23.
[45] For the description of the trances of Yang and Hsiao and the speaking in tongues by members of the God Worshippers congregation and for Hung's action in trying to judge these trances, see Chien, *Shou-i-shih*, pp. 168-69; Chien, *Ch'üan-shih*, I, 172-74; and Hamberg, pp. 45-47.

was a small group of some 130 people who gathered at the home of one of their leaders, Wei Ch'ang-hui, a rich owner of a pawnshop and land, and a man of some education.[46] Wei belonged to a large clan, which joined the God Worshippers Society and strengthened Wei's prominent role in the group. From the outset, therefore, Wei was one of the prominent leaders of the God Worshippers Society, though his authority was not derived from any supernatural sanction, as was that of Yang and Hsiao, and of Hung himself.

The gathering at Wei's home was reported by the local corps to the district magistrate, who ordered the God Worshippers to disperse. The group seems to have obeyed temporarily, but gathered again when some of the local-corps men kidnapped a concubine from a Hakka family. This time the gathering grew to include some 300 people who would not by themselves have been a sufficient threat to the authorities had they been dealt with immediately. But the officials were slow in attributing to the God Worshippers a more serious role than that of troublemakers and rivals of other local defense units, and thus the God Worshippers had time to bring up their forces by calling in groups from other communities of the area.

When they began to gather their followers, the God Worshippers' movement and organization were seriously threatened by a strange division of their forces which can only be understood as a conflict and power struggle in the leadership. In May, 1850, Yang Hsiu-ch'ing, who before the return of Hung and Feng had through his trances asserted himself as the highest authority, fell ill and withdrew from all activity. According to the account by the leaders of the rebels, Yang's illness lasted until November, a period of six months. As had happened once before, he became deaf and dumb and "pus came out of his ears and water from his eyes." Yang thus became incapacitated and had been given up, as he complains in his later description of his ordeal.[47] Later on, he claimed that he had undergone this illness and the earlier one

---

[46] According to Li Hsiu-ch'eng's confession, document 382, Wei Ch'ang-hui "was a native of Chin-t'ien in Kuei-p'ing, and had the academic title of *chien-sheng* through purchase. He was engaged in public affairs, and was generally acquainted with yamen routine." According to the local gazetteer, however, it was Wei's father who had purchased the academic title of *chien-sheng*, and when there was a celebration of this occasion in the family, the regular gentry ridiculed the affair.

[47] See document 50.

for the sake of others; God, in his anger that Hung Hsiu-ch'üan had not yet been heeded in his mission to establish God's kingdom on earth, was ready to punish man with illness and disease. Yang had suffered his illness to redeem all others and thus had become the "redeemer from illness," a title which begins to appear about two years later among the titles describing Yang's role and status.[48]

In 1850, however, this illness became of immediate political importance; whether Yang actually had a disease or whether he faked an illness to cover up his wish to withdraw from co-operation is impossible to tell. We can only speculate about the reasons for Yang's action, which was followed by the departure of Hung and Feng, who left Chin-t'ien for Hua-chou in the neighboring district of P'ing-nan and stayed away from this primary center of the God Worshippers all during the critical time of the latter half of the year 1850. It is possible that Yang's withdrawal resulted in the refusal of some of Yang's adherents to participate in action for the common cause and that a tense situation at Chin-t'ien was the reason for Hung and Feng's departure.

Although they stayed away from Chin-t'ien, Hung and Feng proceeded with their plans for an uprising. That they had decided to go ahead can be seen from the fact that in June, 1850, Hung sent for the members of his family in Hua-hsien, Kwangtung, to join him in Kwangsi, where they would be safe from reprisals by government officials. In July the leaders of the God Worshippers called for a concentration of the forces of all branches at Chin-t'ien.[49] The original group there had already been joined by a larger group of Hakka, more than 3,000 strong, who had been driven from their homes by a local conflict with Punti and had joined the God Worshippers at Po-pai. When this group crossed the river at Kuei-p'ing and joined the God Worshippers' camp, the group at Chin-t'ien became formidable. It was then joined by other groups from P'ing-nan, Kuei-hsien, Wu-hsüan, and Lu-ch'uan and became in a short time a force estimated at 10,000 to 30,000 people. This concentration was obviously too large to be dealt with by the local corps or by a local official without the help of regular army units. The uprising thus became a problem for the provincial administration and the regular military forces, and soon for the central government.

[48] See documents 47, 48, and 50.
[49] It is not clear whether the call went out from Hung or from the leaders at Chin-t'ien or both.

The various groups that assembled at Chin-t'ien were very uneven in strength and were brought together by a number of local leaders.[50] One group came from Kuei-p'ing under the leadership of a man called Su Shih-chiu. Another local leader, Lai Chiu, brought the God Worshippers from all the localities of Yü-lin prefecture. Another group from Kuei-hsien had been well organized before they marched to Chin-t'ien and had already on the way increased their number from the original 1,000 to more than 4,000 people and had brought their own cannon. They were led by Shih Ta-k'ai, a Hakka from Kuei-hsien who had studied for the examination but had failed. Like Hung, Shih was therefore a man with some education who was frustrated by his failure in his attempt at a regular career. Shih was to become one of the chief leaders of the movement.[51]

The groups that gathered at Chin-t'ien consisted mostly of Hakka who had joined the God Worshippers in part as a protection in their conflict with the Punti. The movement seems, however, to have included also some followers who were Punti, and there may well have been a conflict between the Hakka and the Punti to be overcome as the movement became broader in its purpose. Since all of the major leaders and most of the followers must have been Hakka, it was necessary to reassure the Punti that there would be no discrimination against them in the rebellious movement. This problem is still reflected in an account which was written in 1860 at Nanking on the orders of Hung Hsiu-ch'üan. Hung, trying to reassert the original principles of the movement, referred to this problem in the words: "Whether Hakka or Punti, they are all treated alike." [52]

The movement was also joined by several bandit units, the most important of which was a gang of several thousand pirates under a well-known leader, Lo Ta-kang. In contrast to other bandit and pirate chiefs who soon left the movement because they were unwilling to accept the

[50] Some of them are only mentioned in the report of the original forming of the camp and do not reappear in any later account of Taiping actions. The most detailed information on this formation of a military camp by the God Worshippers comes from Chien Yu-wen's *Shou-i-shih*, pp. 190-91, and Chien, *Ch'üan-shih*, I, 205-9. Chien uses the *Lu-ch'uan hsien-chih*, which was not accessible to the author.

[51] See also document 320.

[52] See document 2. This statement, which must have been meaningless in 1860, can only be explained as Hung's recollection of the problem that arose at the beginning of the formation of the camp at Chin-t'ien.

strict moral code and discipline of the God Worshippers, Lo Ta-kang became a faithful follower and one of the leading figures in the movement.[53] Among the groups who joined were also people of the Miao tribes and other local tribal groups. Their motive in joining the rebellion must have been their bitterness over official extortion and over their economic troubles. They had been the very targets of Hung Hsiu-ch'üan's idol-smashing campaign, and those who joined must have been fully converted to Hung's teaching. It was a considerable force that gathered at Chin-t'ien to form a military camp (*t'uan-ying*).

It was all the more remarkable that the two primary leaders of the movement, Hung and Feng, remained absent from the main theater of operations. Whether Yang's illness and his withdrawal from all action with the effect it had on Yang's own following was so embarrassing to Hung and Feng in their attempt to centralize and organize the uprising that they left, or whether they wanted to broaden the movement, the two stayed away from Chin-t'ien at the time of the formation of the camp there. They remained in Hua-chou in the neighboring district of P'ing-nan, where they stayed in the house of Hu I-kuang, a member of a wealthy family who held the academic degree of military *sheng-yüan* and was therefore a member of the lesser gentry.[54] Hu was a friend of Hung and especially of Feng, who formerly had been a teacher in Hu's home. At this place, Hung and Feng gathered another, obviously smaller, military force.

At the outset, there were thus two military concentrations. The main one at the headquarters in Chin-t'ien was during Yang's illness under the control of Wei Ch'ang-hui, Hsiao Ch'ao-kuei, Shih Ta-k'ai, and Ch'in Jih-kang, also a native of Hua-hsien, who was "an ordinary laborer by trade." [55] Of these, Hsiao was the only one whose authority was based on what he claimed to be divine revelation. But there was also Yang, who was inactive but whose presence had to be taken account of by the others. The other concentration was at Hua-chou, directly under Hung and Feng and their host, Hu I-kuang.

Both these concentrations were now attacked by local government

[53] See Yi-faai Laai. "River Strategy: A Phase of the Taiping's Military Development," *Oriens*, V, No. 2, 1952.

[54] See Lo, *Shih-kao*, p. 187; Chien, *Shou-i-shih*, p. 186, referring to the Hsün-chou gazetteer, 56:20a, calls Hu a military *sheng-yüan*. See also Chien. *Ch'üan-shih*, I, 199-200.

[55] See document 382.

troops. At the end of September, 1850, forces under the prefect of Hsün-chou and a district magistrate of Kuei-p'ing attacked the concentration at Chin-t'ien but were repulsed. At the beginning of November, government troops in P'ing-nan district surrounded the concentration under Hung and Feng at Hua-chou. The situation became critical, and the God Worshippers at this place and their leaders seem to have been in great danger. At this moment Yang Hsiu-ch'ing suddenly recovered from his illness and claimed to have been informed of Hung's trouble by the Heavenly Father. He led the forces from Chin-t'ien in an attack against the government troops at P'ing-nan, broke the encirclement, and saved Hung and Feng.[56] Yang thus saved the leader of the movement and demonstrated his quality as a military leader. At the same time he claimed that his action had been the result of his own divine guidance. He had thus become the main military commander of the concentration at Chin-t'ien; but the lack of clarification of his role vis-à-vis Hung and Feng may have been the reason that even after this military cooperation the two units did not join.

Though the forces remained separate, Yang had obviously succeeded in assuring his supremacy in the management of the Chin-t'ien concentration. It must have been necessary to yield this position to him as a price for his cooperation and possibly also for that of the groups of charcoal burners and miners who were under his authority and whose special skills—such as the miners' knowledge of explosives and their experience as sappers—were essential for military success. When, in January, 1851, the two groups finally combined their forces at the village of Ts'ai-ts'un in Kuei-p'ing district, Yang became the commander of the central corps and the chief of staff and therefore the most powerful military leader of the movement.

The united force won a decisive victory over government troops and then returned to Chin-t'ien, where on January 11, 1851, Hung Hsiu-ch'üan, on his thirty-eighth birthday, declared the formation of a new dynasty, the T'ai-p'ing T'ien-kuo, The Heavenly Kingdom of Great Peace. Hung himself assumed the title of T'ien Wang, or Heavenly King, and now issued orders from Chin-t'ien under this name.[57]

During the year 1851 the Taipings remained in the southeast part of

---

[56] See documents 50 and 382; also Hamberg, p. 52.
[57] See documents 23 and 385. See also Chien, *Shou-i-shih,* pp. 203-7, and Chien, *Ch'üan-shih,* I, 223-29.

Kwangsi and fought a number of local battles with government forces and also with pirates who were fighting on the government side.[58] These pirates were members of the Triad Society. They had at first joined the Taipings, but when they found out about the strict enforcement of the rules which the Taiping leaders had imposed on their followers, they broke away from the Taipings, and, as was the practice of the time, became—in name—government forces. Only the pirate leader Lo Ta-kang and his band stayed with the Taipings and accepted their religious beliefs. The knowledge of boats and navigation which these men brought to the Taiping forces proved to be of advantage in the coming campaigns.[59]

During this time the Taiping military organization began to take shape. What had been a group of villagers who had accepted the religious teachings of Hung Hsiu-ch'üan and had banded together, first in defense of their communities and then under the exciting promise of a new order, now became soldiers of a unified, disciplined military force. The Taiping movement was forged into an indoctrinated army, the tool with which the Taiping leaders hoped to conquer the country and establish their rule. As the model for their army, the Taiping leaders used the classical *Chou-li* system, a utopian organization ascribed to the Duke of Chou, the founder of the Chou dynasty. In this system, the civilian and military organizations were combined. The people were farmer-soldiers who did their productive work for society and took up arms when the need arose. Their military officers were also their magistrates, and military and civilian aspects of government were not separated.

This highly centralized, disciplined system of government, which dif-

[58] During most of the year 1851 the Taipings were fighting a number of smaller battles in the area of the districts of Kuei-p'ing, P'ing-nan, Wu-hsüan, and Hsiang-chou. Mo-ts'un in Kuei-p'ing, and Tung-hsiang in Wu-hsüan were their major military centers, and Tzu-ching-shan was their main base. See Hsün-chou gazetteer, 56:15-46.

[59] See Yi-faai Laai, "The Part Played by the Pirates of Kwangtung and Kwangsi Provinces in the Taiping Insurrection" (Ph.D. dissertation, University of California, 1949). Lo and his pirate forces cannot have had too great an influence on the Taiping military command, since the Taipings later became outmaneuvered in battles on lakes and rivers by the forces under Tseng Kuo-fan. Already in this first year the Taiping situation was weakened by the defection of the main pirate leaders Chang Chao, alias "Big-headed Goat," T'ien Fang, alias "Great Carp," and others who left the Taiping armies and, fighting for the government, helped to block the Taiping advance to the east on the water routes. See document 50; also Hamberg, pp. 54-56.

fered basically from both the imperial Chinese system and from the feudal order which preceded the imperial time, never existed in this form. Although the classical text of the *Chou-li* may have described in part some institutions of the early Chou period, it is now believed to have been composed during the period of the Warring States.[60] It was used on several occasions during imperial history to give the authority of antiquity to drastic changes in the political system attempted by reformers. Wang Mang, a revolutionary and political reformer of Han times, referred to it in his attempt to set up a highly centralized government which was to provide a much greater area of control for the state than had been secured under the imperial system. The *Chou-li* was also referred to by Wang An-shih, the statesman and political reformer of Sung time, to give some of his reform measures the backing of classical authority.

The Taipings followed these precedents when they made use of the prestige of this text in giving the aura of classical sanction to their organizational measures. What they did was to apply to their combined military and political organization the *Chou-li's* nomenclature for official ranks, and to use its division and size of units as a model for their own forces. The basic unit of the Taiping army was the squad of twenty-five men. Each squad was led by a sergeant (*liang-ssu-ma*), under whom there were five corporals and twenty men, each corporal being in charge of four men. Five squads were combined into one platoon under a lieutenant, and five platoons into a company under a captain, five companies into a battalion under a colonel, and five battalions into an army corps, which was the largest unit of the Taiping army and was headed by a corps general. The size of an army corps was theoretically 13,156 men and officers, the size of the units and the titles of the officers being the same as those described in the *Chou-li*.

The officers within this new army were appointed and shifted from command to command, so that the Taiping leaders had full disciplinary control over the organization. It seems to have been the policy to bring together in each squad men from different places, another measure de-

[60] See Bernhard Karlgren, "The Early History of the Chou Li and Tso Chuan Texts," *The Museum of Far Eastern Antiquities*, Bulletin No. 3 (Stockholm, 1931), pp. 1-59. For this as well as other references the author is obliged to A. F. P. Hulsewé, who in "China im Altertum," in Propyläen Weltgeschichte, II, *Hochkulturen des Mittleren und Östlichen Asien*, p. 483, describes the Chou Li as "ein idealisiertes und systematisiertes Bild der Organization eines Herrscherhofs am Ausgang der Feudalzeit."

signed to prevent any autonomy of the unit or its commanders.[61] It can be assumed that from the very beginning it was the policy of the Taiping leaders, in the creation of their army, to distribute their followers in such a way as to destroy the cohesion of the village groups.

Besides organizing their followers into military units, the Taiping leaders separated men and women into different units. The women were organized in the same type of units under their own officers who had the same titles as the men. The units for men and women were in separate camps, and no contact was permitted. The enforcement of separation of the sexes was of obvious importance in maintaining discipline in a mobile force. This measure was, however, established on the basis of religious doctrine. Men and women were brothers and sisters, sexual relations were sinful, and chastity was God's commandment. Even married couples were forbidden to have sexual relations. Those who disobeyed were to be beheaded.

The Taiping leaders never applied this measure consistently. It was applied first to the mobile Taiping military force, and later to the population of the cities of Wu-ch'ang and Nanking after their capture by the Taipings. Like the army, the whole population of these cities was divided into camps for men and women. But the Taipings could not apply this radical measure to the population of all the villages and towns that their forces held, and did not attempt to. The acceptance of the Ten Commandments with the rules against adultery, to which were added strict prescriptions against prostitution, indicate that they also applied standards of morality based on normal marital relations. There was no explanation of this difference in standards, nor was the distinction in standards ever stated. The Taiping leaders themselves were free from all such limitations and in fact established harems of their own.[62] The division of the Taiping followers into camps for men and women was therefore in practice a matter of military discipline, notwithstanding the attempt to justify it through a doctrine of absolute chastity. This becomes apparent also from the promise which the Taiping leaders made that

[61] For a later period, we have a captured roster of such a Taiping unit, which indicates that the men of one squad came from ten different provinces. See Chang, *Tse-ch'ing*, for this roster taken by Tseng's troops.

[62] Hung Hsiu-ch'üan seems to have selected women for his harem at the very beginning of the uprising. There is a report that a year later at Yung-an he already had a harem of fifteen women with him. See Hung Ta-ch'üan's confession, document 37. Of the other leaders, such as Yang Hsiu-ch'ing, we only know for certain that they had large harems at Nanking.

after the conquest of the empire and the defeat of the "demons," the families would be reunited.[63]

When the women's units were first established, they were used for labor and possibly in some cases for actual front-line fighting. There are some government reports that mention the appearance of such troops in combat.[64] These battle units were reportedly made up in the main of women from the Miao tribes, who were hardier than the Chinese.[65] Most women's units were, however, assigned to other duties, and we read of weaving battalions and other work units.

This military organization of the Taipings which was at first formed at Chin-t'ien consisted according to government reports of between 285 and 300 squads, or a total of about 7,000 men, a listing that may or may not have included the women's camp.[66] The establishment of this military organization was believed to have been the work of Hung himself, who during the beginning of the campaign issued all important orders under his name and was personally in command. It can be assumed that he had the help of Feng Yün-shan, the original organizer of the God Worshippers and Hung's main lieutenant. However, the fact that the main camp at Chin-t'ien was under the command of Yang Hsiu-ch'ing during the critical time before the official proclamation of the rebellion may support the argument that Yang, whose gifts of organization and command were later clearly demonstrated, was the actual creator of the organization that was afterwards simply confirmed by Hung. In Hung's first proclamation at Chin-t'ien in January, 1851, he exhorted his followers to obey the heavenly commandments, ordered that men and women be quartered separately, forbade his followers to harass the people of the area, preached harmony and obedience to the leaders, and asked for united effort and courage in battle. During this whole time, however, Yang Hsiu-ch'ing and Hsiao Ch'ao-kuei used their trances to strengthen their own position of authority by expressing the same exhortations that Hung had stated in his proclamations.

As important as the creation of a disciplined military organization of armed people who were all brothers and sisters was the establishment of the common treasury. Before the gathering at Chin-t'ien, many of the God Worshippers had already lost their land and other immobile prop-

[63] See document 50.
[64] See Chang, *Tse-ch'ing*.
[65] These women had never been crippled by the Chinese custom of footbinding, a custom which, however, had never been applied by the Hakka women either.
[66] See Chang, *Tse-ch'ing*.

erty, or had converted it into cash and had handed it over to the common treasury of their militant group. Some of the Hakka had, as we know, been driven from their land by the hostile Punti and had thus become homeless refugees. Whether under the threat of such expulsion or because of the call to the assembly at Chin-t'ien, the followers all liquidated their holdings so that all their possessions could be carried with them. It was thus as much a practical measure of a mobile force as an ideological demand based on the principles of brotherhood which led to the establishment of a common treasury into which all handed their belongings and from which they all received their daily needs.[67]

But the practical origin of this principle does not detract from its prime importance for the Taiping movement. The principle that all property should be held in common by the brothers and sisters and that each would be given from the common fund according to his or her needs gave the Taiping movement its special character. This principle, too, was based on the idea that all the Taipings, as children of God, formed a large family and that all property belonged to the head of the family, the Heavenly Father, whose representative was the T'ien Wang, the younger brother of Jesus Christ. A primitive communist view was therefore made plausible as an analogy to the Chinese family tradition, transferring the bonds of the smaller traditional Chinese family to the family of brothers and sisters in the Christian community. The application of this principle of the common treasury to the ownership of all land by the Heavenly King was expressed later in the Taiping land law[68] and was a logical outgrowth of this concept of a family under God, the basic ideological and political principle accepted at the outset of the organization of the movement at Chin-t'ien. This system also permitted the leaders, who had direct access and control over the common treasury, to use a greater share for themselves and to live eventually a life of luxury in the palaces of Nanking. From the beginning, the group of secondary leaders that formed around Hung Hsiu-ch'üan, consisting of men of different origins, shared the authority. These men were set apart from the rest of the followers and were "more equal than the others." Together with their prophet, Hung Hsiu-ch'üan himself, they formed among themselves a special brotherhood, the group of seven "brothers" mentioned in several of the Taiping proclamations of this time and later. Though all the Taipings were children of God, these seven "brothers" by impli-

---

[67] See Hamberg, pp. 52-53.
[68] See document 46.

cation were in a different category. Hung himself was God's son and the younger brother of Jesus Christ, and now the other leaders were brothers of Hung and shared in his intimate relationship with God the Father. The list of brothers mentioned in the proclamations begins with Jesus and Hung and then lists the Taiping leaders, Yang, Hsiao, Feng, Wei, and Shih, who share in this way in the highest authority over their followers. It is easy to see that this special relationship of the collective brothers could lead to a grim and bitter power struggle. The original strength of this feeling of brotherhood, however, is still echoed in the letter which Shih Ta-k'ai sent to Hung Hsiu-ch'üan in 1857, after strife and assassination had divided the leadership and destroyed it. In the letter Shih melancholily recalls the original strength and unity of this brotherhood.[69]

The coming struggle was already indicated in the different sources of authority claimed by the members of this brotherhood. Hung, the prophet of the movement, had through his ascent to heaven and the revelation that he was God's younger son, entrusted with the mission of establishing God's kingdom, the only direct claim to belonging to God's immediate family. For him to admit the others as his brothers was already a reduction of his standing and raised an issue that remained crucial in the coming power struggle. Among the others, only Yang and Hsiao had the direct authority of their trances, which could be used to strengthen their position within the group. Hung's primary position as leader of the movement could not be challenged in view of his part in starting it, the authority he derived from his ascent to heaven, and the fanatical self-assurance caused by his mania and conveyed to his followers. Yang, with his impersonations of the voice of God and his assumed role as redeemer from sickness—an analogy to Jesus—could invoke a higher source of authority but remained in person subordinate. Hsiao, as the voice of Jesus, was theoretically third in line, while the others had no such divine sanction. It is therefore understandable that during the first period at Chin-t'ien and the marches back and forth to Tung-hsing and the village of Mo in 1851, the commands given by the T'ien Wang were supplemented by the orders of the "Heavenly Father" and "Jesus," given through the mouths of Yang and Hsiao. At Tung-hsing for instance, "Jesus ordered the followers to keep the heavenly commandments, to obey the orders of the leaders, to live harmoniously with all brothers, not to loot, not to run away in battle, and not to retain property," and

[69] See document 212.

he promised that the followers would later receive high titles and threatened execution to all who disobeyed. And when at the village of Mo, "Jesus" scolded the people for their selfishness, the "Heavenly Father" hurried to give them a similar sermon the same evening.

The uncertainty of the order of authority was overcome when, on August 15, 1851, Hung Hsiu-ch'üan, the T'ien Wang, issued a proclamation that established a system of command and a division of authority among the leaders.[70] The army was divided into advance, central, and rear units, and each of the leaders was given command over his own army unit and the title "commander" (*chu-chiang*). Hsiao and Shih were given the command of the advance guards, and Wei and Feng of the rear armies, while Yang was appointed commander of the central army and of the imperial guard, a position all the more crucial since Hung himself stayed with the central army. The main Taiping force was thus organized as a disciplined army under leaders who were potential rivals for power, but who had each been given his position of command.

Not all of the groups that joined were amalgamated at the outset into this army under the five commanders. Some bandit and pirate units seem to have become attached to the Taipings as subsidiary forces rather than being merged into the Taipings' own army.[71] Quite plausible and significant is the story of the eight chiefs of the Triad Society who wanted to join the Taiping movement with their bands. Hung demanded from them and their followers the acceptance of the Taiping religious beliefs and code, which was to be taught to them by sixteen Taiping tutors. When one of these tutors retained the money given by the bandit chieftain instead of handing it over to the common treasury, he was executed. This example gave the eight chiefs an uncomfortable feeling and they left the Taipings complaining that these laws were too strict.[72]

The Taipings took their ideology and the necessity to adhere to it so seriously that they used it to explain military defeat and success. One

[70] See document 23.

[71] According to one account, two women bandit chiefs who joined the rebellion with some 2,000 followers were placed by Hung at a distance from the main force to serve as an outpost on each flank. This distinction between the integrated main force of the Taiping followers and attached units under special leaders can be readily explained if we regard the attached units as organized bandits or secret-society groups under their own leaders who were willing to cooperate with the rebellion but not accept its beliefs. This form of autonomous cooperation could only be temporary.

[72] See Hamberg, pp. 54-55.

of the groups of Taiping adherents failed to break through the government forces on its way to join the concentration at Chin-t'ien. This group from southern Kwangtung came too late to cross the West River after the defection of the pirates, who went over to the government side and blocked their passage. It was a sizable force that was thus cut off from the main body of the Taipings and then destroyed. The Taiping explanation of the failure of this unit was that they had not adhered to the religious precepts, especially the rules of chastity, since they had promised those fighting in the first line that after victory they would be given women as a reward for their fighting valor.

At Chin-t'ien, the Taiping movement had thus become organized as a group of fanatical believers in a new faith, aiming at establishing their order in China. They formed an integrated military force and established a common treasury, under a leadership that shared control of the group under the over-all direction of Hung Hsiu-ch'üan, the Heavenly King. Among the top leaders themselves, however, a struggle for power had already started in which Yang Hsiu-ch'ing was emerging as the most important figure.

Part II

The Organization at Yung-an
and the March to Nanking

Yung-an and the New Structure of Leadership

THE concentration at Chin-t'ien had brought the Taipings together and had enabled them to create the beginnings of their organization. A brotherhood of leaders had emerged, with Yang already the most important figure but with Hung Hsiu-ch'üan still in actual control. Hung personally issued the orders and edicts on the Taiping system and made the decisions on moving the camp.[1] Under his name appeared also the most important edict on the division of the army and the assignment of commands.

From Chin-t'ien, the Taipings moved east to Wu-hsüan, Hsiang-chou, and returned again to Hsin-hsü at Kuei-p'ing, where with their control of Thistle Mountain they could maintain their position against the Ch'ing government armies. In the fall they burned Hsin-hsü and moved east. At Kuan-ts'un in P'ing-nan district, they inflicted a great defeat on the government troops, which retreated to P'ing-nan city. The Taipings then moved on to T'eng-hsien and went from there to the city of Yung-an, and captured it.

At Yung-an, the Taipings halted and took time out to organize their movement more fully. Here they spent all the time from September 25,

[1] See document 23; see also Kuo, *Jih-chih*, I, 129-30, who lists the edicts issued on the march and concludes that during this stage Hung still made the main decisions.

1851, to April 5, 1852.[2] Yung-an, a city built in the hills, was neither very prosperous nor in a strategically advantageous position, and it has been argued that the Taipings chose it for their temporary base simply because of its auspicious name, Yung-an, or "Everlasting Peace." [3] However that may be, the Taipings needed time to recoup and reorganize the losses they had suffered in the battles they had fought and to reorganize their forces, incorporating the many new recruits they had gained. More important still may have been the necessity of a new indoctrination of their followers and the need for clarifying the chain of command among the Taiping leaders.

While the marching orders had been given in the name of Hung, the Heavenly King, both Yang and Hsiao in their trances also had given orders and "instructed the multitude." Their orders had mainly dealt with discipline, courage in battle, and the duty of handing over all property. Violators of these rules of discipline and persons who had fled in battle were threatened with execution. It was Yang who, representing the Heavenly Father, had one follower executed for disobedience, deception, and cowardice, the first such execution reported in the Taiping documents.[4] Several times Yang tried to intimidate the followers in his trances by reminding them that God, whom Yang represented, knew everything and that it was of no use and indeed dangerous to try to conceal action or thought: "If you deceive Heaven, do not think that Heaven does not know," and "When killing the demons, if one does not go forth while another advances into battle, in truth you must not think that Heaven does not know this." [5]

The claim of omniscience could of course best be maintained if Yang could reveal during his trances important happenings that were unknown to the others. To do this he had to have a well-functioning and secret information system. It can be surmised that his own group of charcoal-

[2] See Kuo, *Jih-chih,* I, 133-52.

[3] See Lo, *Shih-kang,* p. 52. Yung-an was the administrative capital of a *chou* included in the prefecture of P'ing-le. It is bordered on the west by Wu-hsüan and Hsiang-chou, on the south by P'ing-nan and T'eng-hsien, on the east by Chao-p'ing, and on the north by Li-p'u and the prefectural city of P'ing-le. To the west of the city wall, there is the Meng-shan mountain range.

[4] See document 23, which deals with the T'ien Wang's edicts during this time, as well as with the selection of the stories of trances by Yang and Hsiao made by the T'ien Wang. This document clearly indicates the growing authority of Yang and Hsiao, and ends with the edict that establishes the positions of the top Taiping leaders.

[5] See document 23.

burners and possibly men of his former convoy organization were a useful nucleus around which he may have formed his personal staff of informers. This information he could then use to surprise the other Taiping leaders and the followers with the revelations of his trances, thus creating the fear of the all-knowing God and of Yang, his mouthpiece. Yang's chance came at Yung-an, where he obtained information about the attempted treason of one follower who had brought some new recruits to the camp but who, on the way, had made a treasonable pact with government officers. This traitor had promised government officials that he would in a prearranged way open a gate of the Taiping camp and assist the government forces in a surprise attack and capture. After his arrival at the camp, this man had tried to gain other supporters, and his negotiations had obviously been overheard. These facts Yang revealed in a dramatic trance session, speaking as the all-knowing God. The session was at Yang's house to which Yang had called the other leaders, Wei, Feng, Shih, and other officials for a conference. Yang, in his trance, ordered the traitor arrested. Then the leaders proceeded to Hung's house to report. Here Wei interrogated the culprit, who, however, did not confess. After returning to his own house, Yang again called the leaders, this time including Hung, to come to his house, where all, including Hung, had to kneel before Yang impersonating the Heavenly Father. The traitor was brought before Yang—the Heavenly Father—and, being confronted with a detailed description of his actions, broke down and admitted his guilt. This coup of unveiling a plot which, if successful, might very well have meant the end of the uprising, established Yang's authority among the greatly relieved and shaken leaders.[6]

By this time Yang Hsiu-ch'ing had already been formally given the leading executive position in the Taiping organization. It had obviously become necessary for Hung Hsiu-ch'üan, the T'ien Wang, to give some more definite ranks and titles to his leaders and followers of the movement. The critical military situation at Yung-an where the Taipings were being surrounded by a growing government force made it all the more necessary to strengthen the fighting spirit by a promise of great rewards. This Hung himself tried to do in his proclamation of the twelfth day of the tenth month when he warned his followers of the devil's path and the demons who tried to delude them, and promised rewards on earth and in heaven. Those who died in battle would ascend to heaven and would also receive hereditary titles. To those who lived

[6] See document 22.

he promised enjoyment of the fruits of victory once the campaign had been successful and a capital had been set up for the Heavenly Kingdom on earth which, in the leaders' minds, may already have been the city of Nanking.[7] "When we arrive at the Heavenly Court [Nanking]," he proclaimed, "all those meritorious officials who together with us conquered the hills and rivers shall on the higher level be invested with the titles of chancellor, senior secretary, commander, general, or imperial guard, or at the least with the title of corps general. These titles shall be handed down through successive generations, and, in dragon robe and horn-encrusted girdle, those [who bear the titles] will be permitted to attend the Heavenly Court. I sincerely inform you that since we are all fortunate in being sons and daughters of the Heavenly Father, and also fortunate in being brothers and sisters of the Heavenly Elder Brother, in this world we shall display majesty beyond compare and in heaven we shall enjoy interminable felicity. . . ." [8]

What was necessary, however, was not only the promise of ranks and positions to boost the morale of the leaders and followers but an immediate decision on organization and authority to give satisfaction to Yang Hsiu-ch'ing and Hsiao Ch'ao-kuei, who through their trances pressed for larger authority, and to guarantee the position of the other leaders of the movement. On December 17, 1851, the T'ien Wang issued an edict which contained a new system of organization and authority for the Taipings.[9] In the first part, Hung Hsiu-ch'üan, the T'ien Wang, or Heavenly King, had to redefine his own position, which was no longer to be as exalted as it seems to have been in the beginning. He proclaimed, "Only the Heavenly Father, the Supreme Lord and Great God, is the one true God. . . . Besides the Heavenly Father, the Supreme Lord and Great God, there is no one who can usurp the address 'Supreme' or usurp the address 'God.' Henceforth, all soldiers and officers may address me as 'Sovereign,' and that is all; it is not appropriate to call me 'Supreme,' lest you should offend the Heavenly Father. The Heavenly Father is the Holy Heavenly Father and the Heavenly Elder Brother is the Holy Saviour. The Heavenly Father and the Heavenly Elder Brother alone are holy. Henceforth, all soldiers and officers may address me as 'Sovereign,' and that is all; it is not appropriate to call me 'Holy,' lest you offend the Heavenly Father and the Heavenly Elder Brother. . . ." In

[7] See note 44.
[8] See document 23.
[9] See document 23.

these words Hung Hsiu-ch'üan drew then a clear distinction between God and Jesus Christ, who were supreme and holy—divine qualities which did not apply to Hung himself in spite of his claim of being the younger brother of Jesus. He placed himself on a more equal level with the other leaders of the movement[10] and by implication strengthened the position of Yang and also of Hsiao when the latter claimed to speak with the voices of the Heavenly Father and of Jesus Christ.

Having established this principle, the T'ien Wang proceeded then in his proclamation to invest the group of leaders with new titles in the following way: "Now I specially invest the left minister of state and first chief of staff as the Tung Wang [East King], to be in charge of the various nations in the east; I invest the right minister of state and second chief of staff as the Hsi Wang [West King], to be in charge of the various nations in the west; I invest the front guide and first deputy chief of staff as the Nan Wang [South King], to be in charge of the various nations in the south; I invest the rear protector and second deputy chief of staff as the Pei Wang [North King], to be in charge of the various nations in the north; I further invest brother Shih Ta-k'ai as the I Wang [Assistant King], to aid in sustaining the Heavenly Court." He added, "the above invested princes shall all be under the superintendence of the Tung Wang (*i-shang so-feng ko wang chü tung-wang chieh chih*)." He further added, "in addition, I proclaim that the Queen shall be addressed as *niang-niang*, and that the imperial concubine of the first rank shall be addressed as *wang-niang*. Respect this." [11]

This important proclamation established the main structure of the Taiping organization. All the important Taiping leaders were now *wangs*, or kings. Hung himself as the T'ien Wang was now the "Sovereign" and remained the head of the movement. The titles of the other kings taken from the four cardinal directions had their traditional symbolic meanings and were used in the Chinese order of precedence, but may have had additional meaning as an implied promise of a future geographical

---

[10] These other leaders were, however, also deprived of their previous designations as "princely fathers" to be brothers all. The proclamation reads: "The Heavenly Father, the supreme Lord and Great God, is our Holy Father and our Spiritual Father. Formerly I have ordered you to address the various chiefs of staff, the left and right ministers of state, and the front guide and rear protectors as 'princely fathers,' which was an indulgence to conform with improper practices of the mortal world. According to the true Way, this was somewhat offensive to the Heavenly Father, for the Heavenly Father is alone the Father." Document 23.

[11] See document 23.

division of conquered territory. The fifth king had to be added to mark Shih Ta-k'ai's leading position.

The promise implied in the title of their own share of the future kingdom can also be deduced from the fact that each of the kings was permitted his own administrative staff. What provided a central direction over these different administrations was that the Tung Wang and his staff were clearly placed in control of the whole administration. All official matters were to be directed and controlled by him.

This central controlling position of Yang had in practice existed before this appointment. A proclamation issued a month earlier had decreed that reports on merits and misconduct during battles were to be made through a chain of command upwards from the sergeants through the lieutenants, the captains, the colonels and corps generals, the corps superintendents, the corps commandants, and the chancellors, who had to pass them on to the chief of staff—namely Yang—who in turn would memorialize the Heavenly Court—namely Hung—for action and would then send the respective orders down the same chain of command.[12] The proclamation thus indicates that promotion and demotion had already been in the hands of Yang, who a month later was formally invested with the central administrative position.

This final victory of Yang was a real change compared with the original system of leadership of the army units established at Chin-t'ien. When the army command had been divided among the five commanding generals with Hsiao and Shih holding command over the advance guard, Yang over the center, and Wei and Feng over the rear, each had been responsible for his unit. When a year later, in 1852, the original Taiping decrees and proclamations were edited and published together by the Taiping leaders, this proclamation carried the addition: "These were the arrangements formerly used when on the march or in bivouac; henceforth, however, obey the orders of the general, the Tung Wang."[13]

The new organizational system established at Yung-an under the Tung Wang's central administrative leadership provided also for a number of other high positions and titles. Some chief lieutenants of the T'ien Wang received the titles of chancellor and senior secretary. These secondary leaders had different relationships with the top group. Some, such as Ch'in Jih-kang, Meng Te-en, and Hu I-kuang, were men who had brought groups of followers to the concentration at Chin-t'ien, and al-

---

[12] See document 23, November 17, 1857.
[13] See document 23.

though they did not become members of the top group of the brotherly kings, they were given leading officer positions and commands in the integrated armies. They and a number of men in junior positions formed a general administrative staff that must have been under the orders of the Heavenly King himself, orders which were, however, no longer given without the Tung Wang's advice.

In addition to this general staff, there were officials who were personally attached to one or the other of the five new kings, being relatives or close friends. Indeed, it must be assumed that each of the key leaders, Yang, Hsiao, Feng, Wei, and Shih, had from the beginning his own group of personal lieutenants and immediate followers. They formed a staff organization for each of these different leaders. These men also received titles, and when the top leaders were made kings their respective staffs were organized into offices and departments with graded ranks for the officials in the same way and with the same designations as had been given to the general staff of the Taiping central court. A complete account of this system exists only for the later period after the conquest of Nanking when the organization was fully developed. By that time the staff listed for each of the kings and the major central officials varied in size from several hundred to several thousand people. But while their staffs may have grown in size during the campaign and at Nanking, each of the kings must have already had his own staff at Yung-an. Two of the kings were killed in battles on the march from Yung-an to Nanking, and we know from the record that they had had complete staffs that were dispersed after their deaths.[14]

The proliferation of individual staffs indicated an element of "federation" among the top leaders that may have implied a promise of an eventual division of the spoils. The central control of the movement was, however, clearly established not only by the integrated army but also by the commanding position of the Tung Wang, through whose hands all reports and edicts were to go and who had in practice the real power of decision. The conflict between this actual power of one man and the concept of collective leadership of the several kings was, however, not eliminated but remained inherent in the system, and could thus lead to the savage power struggle that erupted a few years later after the movement had established its capital at Nanking.

Yang Hsiu-ch'ing's new role as the actual executive head of the Taiping forces found immediate expression in the new type of proclama-

[14] See Chang, *Tse-ch'ing*.

tions issued at Yung-an. From now on many of the proclamations, and especially the most important military and political statements, were issued by Yang himself or by Yang and his friend and supporter, Hsiao Ch'ao-kuei. Now Yang and Hsiao took it upon themselves to retell the Christian story to their followers as if it were their discovery, and together they issued strong appeals not only to their followers but to the Chinese people to rise against the Manchu oppressors. In three main proclamations[15] Yang and Hsiao asserted their own authority and then described the evils of Manchu rule to excite the sentiment of rebellion.

Yang's and Hsiao's authority for leadership was based on the fact that they themselves became more and more identified with God and Jesus Christ, whose spokesmen they claimed to be.[16] From the time of the Old Testament to the incidents of their own trances, there is one continuous demonstration of God's power. Through their proclamations, Yang and Hsiao try to instill into the Taipings the fear of God, whose "great anger" has been manifested ever and ever again. It was his "great anger" with man's evil-doings that caused God to send the flood. In "great anger" he rescued his people from Egypt. In "great anger" with mankind's delusions, he sent his son Jesus Christ, and it was again in anger that he gave the T'ien Wang his mission to save mankind now. And since that was not enough, God and Jesus came down themselves to enjoin and exhort the Taiping followers to do their duty. Fear of God and of his "great anger" is therefore to frighten the people, while a glorious life on earth and heavenly bliss hereafter are their rewards if they see the light and fight for the cause.

This religious thundering is combined with an appeal to Chinese racist hatred of the Manchus. The "Manchu demons" are attacked not so

---

[15] See document 28.

[16] Since religious authority was the basis for power in this fanatical movement, the new importance of Yang Hsiu-ch'ing and his cohort Hsiao Ch'ao-kuei found its expression in a reordering of the religious revelations. When Yang issued "The Book of Heavenly Decrees and Proclamations" (document 23, probably reissued in 1863; see the comment), he began the religious story with the event that signified his own assumption of authority. The story begins with the "Heavenly Father's" descent to earth, in April, 1848, the first time that Yang played his role as God's mouthpiece. The second event described was Hsiao Ch'ao-kuei's debut as the spokesman of Jesus Christ, and only then does the story introduce the T'ien Wang's personal role and his sponsorship by the Heavenly Father. The personal experience of the T'ien Wang remains still unique and gives this leader his exalted position. But Yang and Hsiao in their special roles represent clearly a higher authority, an authority that is fitted into the history as given by the Bible.

much because they are non-believers but because they are really barbarians. They are beasts who are vilified in strong language for their de-
spoliation of China. They have usurped the throne, have enslaved the
Chinese, ravaged their women, and forced vulgar habits on the Chinese
people. The Chinese must be ashamed for having suffered all this. "Can
the Chinese still deem themselves men?" The Manchus indeed are no
better than swine and dogs, and a great reward is promised to anyone
who captures or cuts off the head of the Manchu emperor, "the Tartar
dog, Hsien-feng."

  This appeal to rise in anger at China's shame and kill the "demons of
the eight banners" was directed not only to the Taiping followers but
also to the members of the newly-formed local corps and to the members
of the secret societies who were reminded of their old loyalty to the
Ming dynasty as against the Manchu invaders. The appeal is thus really
to a Chinese racist sentiment. The Heavenly Father and his agents will
establish a new type of Chinese empire to take the place of the prolonged misrule of the Manchu barbarians, a kingdom in which all as
children of God are members of one family. For good measure, Buddhism, the doctrinal rival, is attacked as well, and all loyalty belongs to
God and his commands. "Those who obey Heaven will be richly rewarded; those who disobey Heaven will be publicly executed." This
then is the content of the call to rebellion by Yang and Hsiao, a call
that integrates the religious teachings of the God Worshippers with a
racist Chinese political program and asserts the authority of these two
key leaders of the movement.

  The political attack against the Manchu dynasty contained in these
proclamations by the Taiping leaders had a broader appeal among the
discontented than the religious doctrine of Hung Hsiu-ch'üan had had.
A number of the secret-society groups that had gathered followers in the
southern provinces were anti-government but not inclined to accept the
Taipings' religious doctrine or to submit to Taiping discipline. To them
the political part of the manifestoes coming out of Yung-an and later issued by the Taipings during their victorious march to the Yangtze and
to Nanking was a welcome expression of their own political goals. There
are among the documents that have been ascribed to the Taipings several that contain only the political attack against the Manchu rulers
without the religious doctrine that was the basis of the Taiping movement. It cannot be said with certainty whether these proclamations
originated from the Taipings themselves or were issued by some of the

leaders of secret societies who were not a part of the Taiping organization. It is quite possible indeed that such secret-society leaders made use of Taiping proclamations, eliminating all the religious teachings and retaining only the political and racial appeals. They may have also issued proclamations of their own, exploiting the appeal of the Taiping Rebellion for their own ends. Whether they are mutilated Taiping statements or whether they are imitations, these proclamations reflect the spirit of rebellion that was radiating from Yung-an and was later spread by the Taipings on their march.[17]

For their own followers, however, the Taiping leaders established at Yung-an a rigid system of discipline and of indoctrination. The new organization that had been set up with the elaborate staffs of the Heavenly King, the East King, and the other kings provided an administrative hierarchy whose ranks and titles were specified in detail and taken very seriously. A code of etiquette was developed. All the Taiping leaders and their family members were given royal aristocratic titles, and a whole system was worked out providing the forms in which the leaders were to address each other.[18]

To give their government also the aura surrounding the traditional Chinese dynasties and copying their claim of ruling the heavens as well as mankind, the Taiping leaders issued at Yung-an their first own calendar.[19] They also issued, probably at that time, the Trimetrical Classic, composed in imitation of the popular Chinese primer of the same title, which was to be used for a simple form of preaching and memorizing the Taiping religious teachings.[20]

Of greater immediate importance, however, than these symbols of their dynastic claims and the self-assumed respectability of their aristocratic ranks and titles were the rules and regulations decreed for the Taiping army. These rules covered all situations in camp, on the march, and during battle.

[17] See documents 31, 32, and others.
[18] See document 25.
[19] See document 47. The Taiping calendar was first prepared by Feng Yün-shan during his imprisonment early in 1848. However, the publication and application of the Taiping calendar began at Yung-an. The government forces besieging Yung-an reported capturing a copy of the Taiping calendar of the second year of the Taipings, the earliest Taiping calendar known to have existed. For a detailed discussion of the calendar, see among others, Kuo, *Li-fa-k'ao,* especially pp. 27-32; Hsieh Hsing-yao, "T'ai-p'ing T'ien-kuo Li-fa-k'ao, "*Lun-ts'ung,* pp. 14-117, especially pp. 16-18; and Lo, *K'ao-cheng-chi,* pp. 97-137.
[20] See document 29.

The organization of the army, established first at Chin-t'ien, was now perfected. The units of the army had been organized according to a pattern based on the *Chou-li*.[21] The system was based on units of twenty-five men, which we may call squads, which were organized into battalions, companies, and regiments under an army corps.[22] This organizational plan must have been prepared in 1850 before the Taiping rising at Chin-t'ien.[23] But it can be assumed that the stay at Yung-an was used to expand and strengthen the organization and to relate it to the new structure of leadership. The total number of the force at Chin-t'ien, which has been estimated at from 10,000 to 30,000 men, was too small to account for five army corps at full strength, if each of the five leaders under Hung commanded his own force.[24] It must be assumed that though each of the kings had his command, the armies were not their own personal forces and that each of the kings was simply given a unit to command and may have shared the command with one of his kingly brothers.[25]

Yang must have been from the beginning not only in direct command of the central force, but commander of all armies, which from the start formed a unified organization. Now, however, this authority was confirmed and formalized under the new regulations issued at Yung-an by the T'ien Wang. It was this integration of the new army under unified command that gave the Taiping forces their formidable strength. This strength was maintained by a carefully worked out system of rules and regulations that dealt in great detail with all situations in camp, on

[21] See document 26.

[22] The corps had 5 regiments, each regiment 5 companies, each company 5 battalions, and each battalion 4 squads. There were, nominally at least, 10,000 privates, 2,500 corporals, 500 sergeants, 125 lieutenants, 25 captains, 5 colonels, and 1 corps general in each army unit, a total of 13,156 officers and men.

[23] See Kuo, *Jih-chih*, II, Appendix, 194-95. See also the soldier's roster in Chang, *Tse-ch'ing*, which indicates that the military organization existed at least as early as July, 1850.

[24] Document 23 states somewhat confusingly that the following army commands were established: Forward Army commanded by Hsiao Ch'ao-kuei, Left Army by Shih Ta-k'ai, Center Army by Yang Hsiu-ch'ing, Right Army by Feng Yün-shan, and Rear Army by Wei Ch'ang-hui. But the document also states that the Forward and Left armies were combined, and so were the Right and Rear armies. This may indicate that at that time there were actually only three armies.

[25] That the units themselves were made up of men coming from different localities also indicates that the Taiping army was an integrated force and not a combination of personal forces. This explains the special role played from this time on by Yang Hsiu-ch'ing as commander in chief and his authority over the other kings.

the march, and during battle.[26] On the basis of these rules, the Taipings established an extraordinarily strict discipline, which, from the accounts we have, seems to have been rigidly enforced. Men who threatened to desert or retreat in battle or who hesitated to attack were immediately killed by their officers, and capital punishment was the penalty applied to violations of a number of other disciplinary rules.

If the Taipings used fear to maintain the strictest discipline in their armies, they sought to spread the same fear of their power and respect for their authority among the population of the regions that they were to reach on their march. Those who surrendered and accepted the Taiping rule were to be spared and well treated, and severe rules of discipline were to prevent the Taiping soldiers from committing any act of aggression against the people or their belongings. But all people in towns or villages who resisted were demons and were to be destroyed. In some places where they had met resistance, the Taipings indeed slaughtered the whole population of the towns they took. This system and policy is well attested to by one of the best Western observers of the time. Thomas Taylor Meadows, an interpreter in the British Civil Service stationed in China, gives this account of the discipline and behavior of the Taiping armies on the march from Yung-an to Nanking:

> The men received a fixed pay, said not to be very high, but to be issued with a punctuality quite unknown in the Manchoo armies. A strict discipline is maintained, and all informants concur as to the circumstance that officers rigidly carry out in battle the military rule of cutting down all who fly, all who hesitate to advance to the attack. In two or three cities where the inhabitants turned out to resist their entrance, they put every living being to the sword, man, woman, and child; but in other cases, where deputations of elders have waited on the leaders to render submission, the troops have not been allowed to enter.[27]

The rules of strict discipline, of quick promotion and demotion according to merit in battle, formed the armies into a tool that could be used by an able commander and strategic leader. It is impossible to determine today how strategic plans were made and decisions arrived at, but it is quite clear that Yang Hsiu-ch'ing was the chief commander of the Taiping forces, responsible for whatever success and failure the

[26] See document 27.
[27] *Parliamentary Papers*, 1853, p. 6, in a letter from Thomas T. Meadows to Consul Alcock, dated March 26, 1853.

Taipings gained during these years. The strength of the organization under him and the respect in which the Taiping forces were held by their opponents can be seen from the evaluation given in the government intelligence account, which cared little for the Taipings' political system and their religious beliefs but thought highly of their military effectiveness.[28]

At Yung-an "the system of the sacred treasury" which had already been set up at Chin-t'ien became fully applied and generally enforced. When first established, the rules of this system provided that the members of the Taiping movement had to hand over all their personal belongings to a common pool from which the members received their food and clothing.[29] At Yung-an the T'ien Wang decreed: "Henceforth, it is commanded to all you soldiers and officers: whenever you kill the demons and take their cities, all captured gold and valuables, silks and satins, precious things, and so forth must not be kept privately secreted, but must all be delivered to the sacred treasury of the Heavenly Court. Offenders shall be punished."[30] And later, on the march at Ch'ang-sha, Hunan, in September, 1852, punishment for violation of this rule was again emphasized in the T'ien Wang's proclamation: "If you should continue to carry or keep valuables privately, once it is discovered you shall be beheaded and displayed to the public." The sacred treasury provided in return the regular food and clothing rations for each Taiping unit, and in addition paid out a small amount of cash to the soldiers and officers. This pay was called "Sabbath pay" and was ostensibly given to enable the Taiping followers to buy articles and offerings for worship. But the pay was graded according to the rank of the soldiers and officers, and may have served as a small regular pay for personal needs.[31]

The system of the sacred treasury was not only an instrument to maintain a disciplined military organization. It was an integral part of the new order which the Taipings were to establish. When the Taipings set up their government in Nanking, the concept of the sacred treasury became the economic basis of their political system.[32] It represented the idea of state property which was under the control of the leaders.

[28] See Chang, *Tse-ch'ing.*
[29] See previous section.
[30] See document 23.
[31] See also Meadows letter quoted above.
[32] See document 46, "The Land System of the Heavenly Dynasty," published later in 1853, and Lo, *Li-hsiang-kuo,* especially pp. 8-12, 38-41.

As in other such situations, though the system provided for the needs of the members of the movement, these needs varied according to the rank and position of the receiver. The Taiping leaders, their courts, and their harems could draw on the treasury for their needs and luxury supplies, and in this sense the institution was a measure elastic enough to cover up what must have been an extraordinary inequality. The common treasury made it possible for the leaders to live very well, while the followers had only the barest essentials, and often not enough.

The March to Nanking

While the Taipings organized their rebellion, the imperial government built up its defense. The defeats of several *lü-ying* units in the fighting in Kwangsi province had shown the seriousness of the situation. After the Taiping rising at Chin-t'ien and the first defeats of government forces, the government had appointed a special imperial commissioner to organize the campaign against the rebels. The first nominee was Lin Tse-hsü, the former imperial commissioner at Kwangtung at the time of the Opium War. Lin died on his way to the troubled province in November, 1850, and in his place Li Hsing-yüan, a former governor-general of Kiangnan and Kiangsi, who had been active in military affairs, was sent to deal with the rebellion. In May, 1851, he too died before he had been able to gain any results, and a new imperial commissioner, Sai-shang-a, a Manchu and a Grand Councillor, was appointed to conduct the campaign. Sai-shang-a went to Kwangsi and attempted to strangle the rebellion by concentrating all his available forces in a siege of the city of Yung-an. The *lü-ying* which he brought together for this operation were far superior in number to the Taiping forces.[33] But the *lü-ying* units were unpaid, poorly trained, and corrupt and had little fighting spirit. They were therefore a poor match for the fanatical, disciplined, and determined men of the Taiping army.

When the Taipings had completed the organization of their government and armies, and when they began to feel the shortage of food resulting from the siege, they decided to give up Yung-an and, in a well-planned attack, break through the surrounding government armies. On April 5, 1852, the Taiping forces attacked and broke through the

[33] The Taipings are believed to have numbered by that time some 40,000 to 50,000, of whom, however, little less than half could be counted as combat soldiers. The force which the government concentrated for the siege of Yung-an was belived to have been almost ten times that number.

government lines. Their attack was highly successful, and they inflicted severe losses on the government forces. According to their own account:

> In the *jen-tzu* year [1852], at Yung-an *chou*, our food supplies were almost exhausted nor was there even any red powder. The demons, several hundred thousand in number, rank upon rank, encircled the city from all directions. There was no avenue of escape. . . . We then moved the camps and broke through the encirclement; and because the Heavenly Father had changed our hearts, we, one and all, with utmost energy and disregard for our persons, struck through the iron passes and copper barriers, killing inumerable devilish demons, and directly arrived at the Kwangsi provincial capital.[34]

While the main Taiping forces broke through the siege intact and gained a substantial victory, the Taiping rear guard was scattered and suffered losses. One of the leaders, who had been with the rear guard, was captured by government forces. His story led to confusion on the government side and has become a puzzle to later historians. The captured man's name was Hung Ta-ch'üan, and his capture was reported to the court by the government commander as a great military success. Before Hung was executed, he was led to write his confession, which was sent to the imperial government. It was the practice of the time to give captured rebel leaders the opportunity to write before their death such a confession, which permitted the prisoner to include in the historical record his side of the story. At times, the confession may have included an appeal for clemency, but there was little hope, and so the satisfaction for the writer was that his story would survive him. For the government such a final accounting would provide valuable information.

There has been a question of the reliability of these confessions as they were sent by the officials on the spot to the government, and in particular about that of Hung Ta-ch'üan. It is understandable that a doomed man would want to exaggerate his role and importance. But it was also to the interest of the government's military commander to describe his prisoner as a highly important person in order to gain greater credit for the capture. For the commander who had been defeated by the Taipings and had not been able to prevent their breakthrough, it was especially important to show some success.

For these reasons Hung Ta-ch'üan's confession has been doubted by historians, and some have believed that the report of the capture and the confession itself were fabrications of the Manchu general. At the

[34] See document 50.

time some people even mistook the prisoner for Hung Hsiu-ch'üan, the T'ien Wang himself, because of the similarity in names, and this has added to the confusion. There is, however, no reason to doubt the existence of Hung Ta-ch'üan, his capture, and the authenticity of his confession.[35]

According to his story Hung Ta-chüan was an ambitious person of commoner origin who had failed in the examination, had become a monk, but had prepared himself through his reading of military and historical accounts for leadership of a rebellious uprising against the government that had denied him the career he sought. He had not shared the religious beliefs of the Taipings but had joined them in the hope that he could build up his own position. To the Taipings he was useful because of his knowledge and education. He claimed to have been in the T'ien Wang's entourage and his trusted adviser. He may have exaggerated in describing his part, but we know that the Taipings cooperated with and used a number of secret-society leaders, bandits, and adventurers who were not members of their religious organization and who were sometimes, as seems to have been the case with Hung Ta-ch'üan, given special titles that did not make them members of the Taiping system. At Yung-an, Taiping discipline was tightened, and an outsider would no longer have been treated with the same consideration as before, especially after Yang Hsiu-ch'ing had taken over. Hung Ta-ch'üan was relegated to the rear guard and may even have been abandoned to his fate. In his confession he claimed that his "signals were not attended to," but it is at least possible that this may have resulted from the confusion during the break-through and not necessarily from intended betrayal.[36]

From Yung-an the Taipings went on a campaign through Kwangsi and Hunan into the Yangtze valley. They besieged Kuei-lin, the capital of Kwangsi province, but gave up the siege after one month. During most of their march they avoided the strongly garrisoned cities and moved along the mountainous or hilly border areas of the provinces. They took the town of Ch'üan-chou and then moved into Hunan.

In Hunan they had not only to fight with the regular government troops, the *lü-ying*, but were also given battle by local defense corps led by gentry. Chiang Chung-yüan, a member of the gentry from Hsin-ning in Hunan, had organized a well-trained local corps to defend his home

---

[35] See Teng Ssu-yü, *New Light on the History of the Taiping Rebellion,* pp. 20-24, which deals with these different views.

[36] See document 37.

district against the Taipings. This local corps repelled the attack of a much larger Taiping force and inflicted heavy losses on the attacker.

The Taiping defeat had far-reaching consequences. The Taipings lost a substantial number of their well-indoctrinated and well-trained original followers, who could not be replaced; and they were forced to change their route. Instead of proceeding directly northward, they skirted the district and followed a new route toward the Yangtze. Instead of moving down along the Siang River and possibly using river transportation, they had to march through the western hilly and mountainous districts along the provincial boundary of Hunan. These were districts which had experienced a great deal of unrest in the preceding years. There had been considerable hardship for the tenants and small-owner farmers, and a number of small-scale uprisings had occurred, fomented by secret societies or local corps. Tenants had resisted the collection of rent, and in one case a group of local people under gentry leadership had interfered with the removal from the area of grain collected as tax in kind.[37] These outbreaks had been subdued, but the bitterness that remained and the conditions of economic stress made it easy for the Taipings to gain new recruits and supporters. Though the Taipings' defeat by Chiang Chung-yüan had delayed their progress, the slower overland march had therefore compensating advantages.

However, Chiang Chung-yüan's victory over the Taipings had a greater significance than the immediate military results. For the first time a new type of military force had successfully opposed the Taiping army. The victory by a local corps demonstrated to the government, as well as to the leading members of the gentry, the importance of local forces for the defense against the Taiping attack, which was directed against the social order as much as against the government. The contrast between Chiang's victory and the defeat of the regular troops taught a lesson which was instrumental in persuading the Manchu court to permit and encourage the establishment of local defense forces by the gentry. The gentry leaders of Hunan, on the other hand, saw in Chiang's victory an example which they could follow in defending Chinese tradition against the new ideology. The battle at Hsin-ning was therefore the first clash between the Taipings and the new type of local organization which was eventually to defeat them.

The Taiping march continued, however, and brought more victories. It also swelled the Taiping ranks until they grew from a military force

[37] See *Hunan t'ung-chih*, 89: 1b-3b.

of a few ten-thousands to a vast rebellious movement of over a million people. In order to increase their strength the Taipings used all the propaganda appeal that could be related to their movement. There were many aspects of the Taiping Rebellion that must have appealed to the population suffering from economic misery and the uncertainty of the time. To all those who had lost their property and livelihood and had become cut off from the regular life of a village economy, the main attraction of the Taipings must have been that they promised to take care of their followers. The principle of a common treasury that provided for one's daily needs must have seemed wonderful to all those whose immediate concern was to find enough to eat. How much that meant even at the beginning of the movement could still be seen from the testimony of one of the later Taiping leaders, Li Hsiu-ch'eng, the Chung Wang, who joined the ranks at the outset and rose to a position of high military leadership. After he was captured, Li described in his confession the conditions of the time and the reasons that caused him to join. He told of the life of poverty that he shared with his brother, the problem of food, and the appeal that the Taiping common treasury had to people like him.[38] It was this appeal of being fed by a common treasury that must have been more convincing to many of the new followers than the new doctrine, which was impressive as long as it was combined with the early successes of the Taiping campaign which the Taipings ascribed to God's miraculous support. How little the doctrine meant to most of the new followers that swelled the ranks of the movement during this march north is clearly indicated by the complete disappearance of the Taiping beliefs after the military defeat of the Taipings and the death of their leaders and of the hard core of the original God Worshipper group.

But the Taipings issued all along their route a number of proclamations to announce their political and religious ideas and aims and to gain popular support. They called for allegiance of the people of the area they invaded and warned against resistance.[39] They continuously repeated the story of the T'ien Wang's divine mission and of God's will and guidance. But they also denounced the Manchus as usurpers and oppressors and promised to better the lot of everyone. The people suffering under corrupt officials were to be freed from their plight, promised

[38] See document 382, "We were a poor family and lacked food, and therefore we followed him [the Hsi Wang]."

[39] We have a number of examples of their propaganda. Three of their most important proclamations were later combined in an official publication. See document 28.

tax exemption, and told that no injuries would come to them under the Taipings. To attract them to the Taiping cause the scholars were promised that civil service examinations would be held for them.[40] Such statements were usually sent into a city by agents before the arrival of the main body of the Taiping forces or posted right after the capture of the city.[41]

On their march the Taipings did not tarry too long when they could not overcome determined resistance. It was the speed of their movement that gained them success and awed their government enemies as well as the population. They failed to take Ch'ang-sha, which they invested from September to November, 1852, but succeeded on Tung-t'ing Lake in capturing a large fleet of several thousand boats, which enabled them to use water transportation on the lake and the Yangtze River for a rapid movement of their whole army.

Of the hundreds of thousands of discontented and impoverished people who joined the Taipings on their march through Hunan, not all came voluntarily. When the Taipings had captured Wu-ch'ang in January of 1853, practically the whole population was incorporated into their movement. They separated men and women into male and female camps and organized them within one month into newly created military units, which were taken along on the march toward Nanking, raising the Taiping number to at least half a million.[42] But many others came voluntarily because they had little to lose and much to gain. Many must have come from the villages and towns that the Taipings marched through; others belonged to local bandit and secret-society groups which were absorbed by the Taipings.[43]

From Wu-ch'ang, the Taipings moved down the Yangtze River in a rapid campaign toward Nanking.[44] They occupied Kiukiang on Feb-

[40] See documents 31, 32, 34, and 35.

[41] See document 36, which was posted in Nanking at the arrival of the Taiping forces there and stated briefly the Taiping belief in the basis of their power and the allegiance they demanded.

[42] See *Wu-ch'ang ping-hsien chi-lüeh* (writer unknown), collected in Hsiang, *Tzu-liao*, IV, 572; T'iao-fu tao-jen, *Chin-ling tsa-chi* (1856), also collected in *Tzu-liao*, IV, 610; Chang, *Tse-ch'ing*, *chüan* 11, "Number of Rebels."

[43] See a.o. Lo, *Shih-kang*, p. 60.

[44] The Taipings' decision to move from Wu-ch'ang down the Yangtze and take Nanking has been attributed by some to a proposal made by Ch'ien Chiang, a *chien-sheng* from Chekiang, who offered his services and advice. See document 33. Ch'ien Chiang's proposal included institutional reforms and the introduction of Western technical devices. When he failed to influence the Taipings, Ch'ien tried his luck on the government side. Since Ch'ien's other ideas were ignored, it

ruary 9, 1853, after attacking the town for a little over a week. It took them less than another week to occupy Anking, the capital of Anhwei and the main stronghold guarding the approach to Nanking. On March 19, 1853, they took the city of Nanking, which they made the capital of their government and kingdom.

When the Taipings gained Nanking, which they renamed T'ien-ching, the Heavenly Capital, the number of their followers had grown to over a million.[45] Of these, only a small number, perhaps 20,000, were original adherents of the movement from Kwangsi province. The rest had joined on the march. This rapid increase required constant reorganization and training of new military units. The original followers and members of the God Worshippers Society rose in rank and became the leaders of the movement whose rank and file was now made up of the discontented of most of the provinces of the central Yangtze area. The problem of the transformation of a sizable group of religious fanatics into a vast body of rebellious people and of creating a manageable organization must have been an exceedingly difficult and complex task. The man who had gained the central position of control, Yang Hsiu-ch'ing, was faced with a vast problem of authority and discipline, of

---

seems unlikely that his advice carried enough weight with the Taiping leaders to determine their decision to move down the Yangtze and make Nanking their capital. It is generally assumed that the plan to take Nanking was made by the Taipings even before their arrival at Wu-ch'ang. See Kuo, *Jih-chih*, I, 209; Lo and Shen, *Shih-wen-ch'ao*, pp. 139-43. It is of course easy to assume that the Taipings, once at Wu-ch'ang, should have been able to decide on the move toward Nanking without the advice of an outsider who wanted to sell his services by proposing the obvious. But the question when the Taipings decided on the move toward Nanking remains debatable. It could be argued that if the Taipings had already in Kwangsi decided to make their capital in Nanking, they would not have spent so much effort in the attempt to capture such cities as Kuei-lin and Ch'ang-sha. It can be assumed that when the decision to capture Nanking was made it was already the Taiping leaders' intention to make Nanking the capital. However, according to a story which Li Hsiu-ch'eng gives in his confession (document 382), there was, even after the capture of the city of Nanking, still disagreement whether the city should be made the capital or only garrisoned. According to this account the T'ien Wang wished to march on and "to take Honan as a base." At this point the captain of the Tung Wang's flagship spoke up and advised against moving to Honan, where there were no rivers suitable for navigation, and proposed instead to make Nanking the capital. According to Li Hsiu-ch'eng, it was this advice which convinced the Tung Wang, who apparently was the one to decide such matters, to stay in Nanking.

[45] The government intelligence report estimated a total of over three million. See Chang, *Tse-ch'ing, chüan* 11, "New Rebels."

training the followers and indoctrinating them in the faith of the movement and a belief in its leaders.

Yang's position had become stronger, and the contest for authority had been narrowed down as a result of the death of two of the original leaders in battle during the campaign. Already early on the march, at Ch'üan-chou, close to the Kwangsi-Kwangtung border, Feng Yün-shan, the Nan Wang, had lost his life in battle. Feng, who had been the original organizer of the God Worshippers and from the outset the most loyal supporter of Hung Hsiu-ch'üan and a sincere believer in the doctrine, might well have become the administrative head of the movement had he not been pushed aside by Yang Hsiu-ch'ing. He had, however, seemingly accepted Yang's authority and, according to one interpretation, could have played the role of harmonizing the conflicting attitudes and interests of the other leaders.[46] Feng must have remained, however, a potential rival and replacement for Yang, and his death left Hung Hsiu-ch'üan without the support of a personally loyal and experienced friend. This loss left Hung Hsiu-ch'üan in a position where he could more easily be manipulated by the shrewd and ruthless Yang.

The other casualty of the campaign was Hsiao Ch'ao-kuei, the Hsi Wang, Yang's intimate supporter, who was killed in the futile battle for Ch'ang-sha. Yang had been impersonating the voice of God to establish his authority, Hsiao had spoken as the voice of Jesus, and the two had obviously been a team, with Hsiao playing a supporting role to Yang in awing the followers into discipline and obedience. His death deprived Yang of the support Hsiao might have given in the final battle for leadership.

With a much greater number of followers and a much smaller body of leaders, the Taipings faced at Nanking the task of the final military campaign for the conquest of China and the problems of further planning and political organization of their conquests and of the government which they now had to establish.

[46] See Chien, *Shou-i-shih*, p. 301.

Part III

The Taipings at Nanking:
From the Establishment of Their
Government at the Capital to the
Assassination of Yang Hsiu-ch'ing
and Wei Ch'ang-hui
(March, 1853, to November, 1856)

Full Development at Nanking

WITH the capture of Nanking, the Taiping movement changed its strategic character. Up until that time the Taipings had been a mobile force whose success had in part depended on its mobility and the rapidity of its movement. The establishment of a capital and headquarters at Nanking meant that the core of the Taiping movement, its leadership and central army, became centered in a fixed position which could become the object of a planned and concentrated attack organized by the military leaders fighting for the imperial government. Not that the Taipings gave up their campaign against the dynasty and its capital at Peking. From Nanking they sent out armies to the north against Peking, and they also dispatched forces westward up the Yangtze to establish and expand their control over western China. But their headquarters had become stationary, and this basic transformation of the

72

Taiping Rebellion from a mobile to a stationary organization has been regarded by some as one of the crucial reasons for its eventual failure. The contrast between the early mobile and later stationary character of the Taiping Rebellion has been well recognized by contemporary observers and later historians. Meadows, writing at the time, said:

> We have now reached a point in the history of the Tae pings, where they ceased to move from place to place in one united body. Henceforth while occupying permanently an important position, extending over 50 miles of a large river in the heart of the country, they sent out from that position separate armies in different directions. It is the point where the Tae ping movement, in its military aspect, changed from what I have called the *locomotive* and *concentrated*, to what may, by way of contrast, be characterized as the *stationary* and *distributed* phase.[1]

The crucial significance of the Taipings' decision to settle at Nanking as a possible cause for the failure of the Taiping Rebellion has been expressed by Hail in his study of Tseng Kuo-fan and the Taiping Rebellion. Ascribing this decision to Hung Hsiu-ch'üan, Hail writes of him: "With a little more daring he could have made a clean sweep of it . . . the objective would have been reached, the Manchus hurled from power. One cannot help reflecting that the whole course of history might have been altered . . ."[2] Whether or not the Taipings might have succeeded in overrunning the capital if they had continued their mobile strategy of rapid advances by their whole force, the outcome would still have had to depend on their ability to organize a government and a new order that could maintain itself. There is no reason to assume that their efforts would have succeeded better at Peking than they did at Nanking, and it seems doubtful indeed that their attack against the whole Chinese social order and its beliefs would have found less opposition once the dynasty had been driven from its capital or brought to an end. One might even speculate that the military success of an over-all Taiping attack against Peking would have cleared the way for others to establish a government not based on the wild and radical Taiping doctrines but linked to Chinese tradition—a new dynasty perhaps better able to cope with the coming impact of the West. Or, such an all-out Taiping move, if it had failed, might have led to a much earlier ending of the Taiping Rebellion than did their decision to settle at Nanking and build their system there.

[1] Meadows, p. 174.
[2] Hail, p. 82.

As it was, the Taiping leaders proclaimed Nanking—usually known under its official Chinese name of Chin-ling—as their "Heavenly Capital," and there set up their government and developed their system of rule. That there may have been second thoughts on this decision can perhaps be inferred from the emphasis they placed on statements stressing the great advantages of Nanking as the most suitable site for a capital because of its strategic location in a wealthy region. Early in 1854 the Taipings published three series of essays dealing with important aspects of their political program.[3] These essays were written by scholars who had, by the accident of war or by their own choice, joined the Taipings at Nanking and now lent their pens to propagate three major themes stressed by the Taipings at the time.

Some historians have regarded these essays as examination papers, since some of the authors were participants in the examinations held then at Nanking to select scholars for the Taiping administrative staff. But others among the authors were already Taiping officials, and the papers may rather have been written for general propaganda purposes.[4] The largest number of such essays, forty-two, was written on the theme of the establishement of the Heavenly Capital in Chin-ling. These essays are of course all in favor of the selection of Nanking as the capital and stress its suitability for that purpose. The very repetitiveness of their phrasing and arguments indicates an official view that had to be given by all. This view is summed up in the words of Wu Jung-k'uan, one of the Taiping writers: "Chin-ling's city walls are strong and thick; Chin-ling's granaries are full and sufficient; Chin-ling's topographical conditions are like a crouching tiger and a coiling dragon; and Chin-ling's customs are elegant, simple and generous."

Non-Taiping reports seem to support the claim of the wealth of supplies and funds on which the Taipings could count in their first years at Nanking. In 1853, the amount of silver in the Taiping treasury at Nanking was reported to have been 18,000,000 taels.[5] This figure is all the more impressive since the imperial treasury at Peking at that time had been depleted by the expense of the rebellion to a sixth of the amount available in the Taiping coffers.[6] The Taiping granaries at

[3] See document 43.
[4] See discussion in comment on document 43.
[5] See Chang Chi-keng, "I-kao," in Hsiang, *Tzu-liao*, IV, 764.
[6] Lo, *Shih-kang*, p. 119. In 1814, the imperial treasury in Peking held 12,400,-000 taels. By 1850, it contained only 8,000,000 taels. By 1852, after two years of the Taiping Rebellion, the treasury reserves had been reduced to some 3,000,-000 taels of silver.

Nanking were reported to have held at the end of 1853 a total amount of 1,270,000 piculs of unhulled rice and 750,000 piculs of hulled rice, a sufficient amount to feed the Taiping forces and the Nanking population for many months.[7] When the American minister McLane visited Nanking at the end of May, 1854, E. C. Bridgman, a missionary who accompanied him, reported, "All the people we saw were well-clad, well-fed, and well-provided for in every way. They all seemed content, and in high spirits, as if sure of success."[8] The surrounding areas continued to supply the capital with grain, and the Yangtze River, as long as the Taipings controlled it, served as a main artery of communications on which innumerable boats traveled for the "one purpose of transporting provisions to Nanking."[9]

The choice of Nanking had therefore no immediate disadvantages, and until their river communications were destroyed in the battles in late 1854, the Taipings did not suffer from their loss of mobility. After establishing their capital at Nanking, the Taipings set out to accomplish the final defeat of the Manchu "demons" in Peking and to impose upon the country their system of beliefs and their social order. These purposes were the themes of two groups of essays that the Taiping leaders directed their scholarly retainers to compose.

The second series of essays published at Nanking in early 1854 were "Treatises on the Denouncement of the Demon's Den as the Criminals' Region."[10] Initiated by an edict of Hung Hsiu-ch'üan, the essays contained denunciations of the metropolitan area of the Ch-ing dynasty as the "demon's den" that had to be destroyed, and attacked the Manchus and their rule. It was a general propaganda attack against the enemy.

The third series of essays on the topic of "Affixing the Imperial Seal on Proclamations and Books for Publication" dealt with the establishment of a selected series of Taiping doctrinal writings.[11] The seal was to identify the books that had been approved by the Taiping leaders for publication, distribution, and use; unauthorized books were banned from circulation. In the words of one essayist: "In this world anyone who has books but fails to report for the affixing of the imperial seal before putting them into circulation will certainly be punished. By following this practice, heresies will not arise and the true Way will be propagated forever." The same writer even demanded that "all books by Confucius,

[7] See Chang, *Tse-ch'ing, chüan* 10; Hsiang, *Tzu-liao,* III, 278.
[8] See Fishbourne, p. 391.
[9] See document 88.
[10] See document 44.
[11] See document 45.

Mencius, the various philosophers, and the hundred schools, all the devilish books and heretical theories, must be burned and eliminated and no one permitted to buy, sell, possess, or read them, or punishment shall be levied."

In carrying out this policy of creating their own doctrinal literature, the Taipings fervently went about printing and publishing their texts. Their intention was to supplant all existing books with Taiping publications or to revise them and create their own versions. Already before their arrival at Nanking they had published their versions of *The Trimetrical Classic* and *Ode for Youth*[12] to take the place of existing books bearing these titles which had been popular Chinese schoolbooks for centuries. At Nanking they published their version of *The Thousand Character Essay*,[13] another popular rhyme book used as a kind of primer for Chinese school children. The revision was to purify the old popular text, so that "all ghostly words, strange, devilish, or false words will be expunged completely."[14] The Taipings also used Medhurst's Chinese pamphlet on "Important Observations Regarding Heavenly Principles," which they revised and published as one of the Taiping books.[15] The Taipings even revised the Chinese classics and some dynastic histories, such as the *San-kuo-chih,* but their revised versions have been lost.[16]

The most important texts that the Taipings printed, however, were their publications of the Old and New Testaments and of their own religious revelations. They printed the Old and New Testaments in separate publications and added their own story of Hung Hsiu-ch'üan's ascent to heaven and the Heavenly Father's manifestations as a third publication, "The Book of Heavenly Decrees and Proclamations," which they later called the True Testament.[17] The printing of the Old

---

[12] See documents 29 and 30.

[13] See document 51.

[14] See document 64.

[15] See document 49.

[16] On the revision of the Chinese classics, see Wang Shih-to, *Wang-hui-weng I-ping jih-chi* (Peking, 1936), Preface, p. 2a, and *chüan* 2, p. 10b; see also *NCH,* No. 174, November 26, 1853, p. 66, col. 4; the story was based on the information of a Taiping officer to Medhurst. According to Chang, *Tse-ch'ing, chüan* 2, biographies of Tseng Chao-yang and Ho Chen-ch'uan, Tseng and Ho were the scholars who revised the classics. Cf. also Lo, "Ching-chi-k'ao," pp. 20-24. On the revision of *San-kuo-chih,* see Shen Mou-liang, "Chiang-nan Ch'un-meng-an pi-chi," in Hsiang, *Tzu-liao,* IV, 436. According to document 208, "Imperial Regulations Governing Scholarly Ranks," published in 1861, a revision of the classics had been completed by that time by Hung Hsiu-ch'üan himself, but the revised versions were not yet published.

[17] See documents 40, 41, and 23.

and New Testaments aroused a great deal of attention among Westerners who learned, on visits to Nanking, of the large-scale printing
effort and were impressed with the fact that the books were circulated
free. Some of them had great hopes that the publication of the Bible
would establish the right Christian ideas among the Taipings and in
China.[18]

No notice was taken, however, at the time of Hung Hsiu-ch'üan's
annotations to the Old and New Testaments, which are indicative not
only of his lack of understanding but also of his totally disturbed state
of mind. They are often the incoherent, rambling, and unintelligible
remarks of a sick man who is trying to find his own role in the story of
the Scriptures. At one point Hung now seemed to believe that he had
been up in heaven all the time "born out of the belly of God's first wife,
that is, the Heavenly Mother, before heaven and earth existed." And
so he witnessed the descent of Jesus, the Elder Brother, to earth and,
before that, the time of Abraham, whom he now claims to have saved
and blessed. When Hung was ready to manifest himself and to descend
to earth as sovereign, he learned that he could not appear directly, but
had to "enter my mother's womb and descend into the world." Hung's
fantasies and his often completely incoherent remarks reveal, however,
the degree to which he had been brought to share his assumed role with
Yang Hsiu-ch'ing, the Tung Wang, whose name appears several times
in Hung's Bible annotations. The Tung Wang is the Holy Spirit whose
power is boundless, who foresees epidemics and restores men's souls. He
too is "God's beloved son" and "was born of the same mother as the
Elder Brother and myself." And in his confusion Hung tried to describe
the Trinity in a form in which the Tung Wang emerges as an unusual
combination of God, spirit, and God's son. Referring to the Biblical
command that you cannot have other gods, Hung says:

> The Holy Ghost is God. If there were another Holy Ghost, that would
> be having another deity. Therefore the wind of the Holy Ghost is the
> wind of the Holy Ghost, God. It is not that the wind is the Holy Ghost.
> The wind is the Tung Wang, the one who in heaven dispatches the
> winds. The Holy Ghost is himself the Holy Ghost. The wind is itself
> the wind. One and yet two, two and yet one. The son is born of the
> father. They were originally one body united in one, but the father is
> himself the father and the son is himself the son. They are both united
> and separated. It is like God now descending into the world, coming
> down as the Tung Wang. That which comes down as the Tung Wang

[18] See Fishbourne, p. 391.

is the Holy Ghost. The Tung Wang's original capacity is the wind. He is the comforter. The Father knew that the New Testament contains erroneous records; therefore he sent down the Tung Wang to manifest the proof that the Holy Ghost is God, that the wind is the Tung Wang. . . .[19]

And the confusion continues in rambling comments, which include a reference to the Hsi Wang sent down by Christ.

These and other references in Hung's annotations indicate the hold that the Tung Wang had taken even in the sick mind of Hung Hsiu-ch'üan as the leading figure in the Taiping religious as well as political hierarchy. This crude religious hoax described repeatedly in different versions can be understood only in the political context of the situation in Nanking. Through it, Yang Hsiu-ch'ing established himself as the highest ideological leader of the Taipings, being placed not only above Wei and Shih but also over Hung, the Heavenly King himself. As one of the group of original brothers—a younger brother—he was the T'ien Wang's inferior and had to support him, but as God's Holy Ghost, he was above the T'ien Wang and could command him and humiliate him whenever it served his purpose. In his own proclamation of the Taipings' religious doctrine,[20] which begins with the words, "I [Yang Hsiu-ch'ing], the Chief of Staff, have studied the fact that . . ." and continues with the biblical account of God's creation of the world, Yang speaks of himself as having been commanded by God to lead the people because "I have invariably been most cautious, sympathetic . . . just . . . equitable . . ." and ascribes to himself the omniscience of God. All officials and people should not have left "in their innermost souls . . . a particle of insincerity lest the Heavenly Father should discover and openly disclose it." This Big Brother role, with its claim of divine origin and divine revelation, must have obviously become more and more of a threat, not only to the other kings but to the T'ien Wang himself, and explains the merciless power struggle that followed.

The Tung Wang still praises the T'ien Wang as the "true Sovereign," to whom all have to be faithful and loyal, but he stresses mainly his own role as chief of staff and redeemer of the afflictions of the masses. His task as well as his titles have been conferred on him directly by the Heavenly Father, and he, "having respectfully received this command, came down into the world." He has been the one who rewarded all

[19] See document 41.
[20] See document 42.

those who had attained merit and he provided food, clothing, and shelter for all. To praise God and Jesus and the divine origin of Hung and himself, to promise rewards and to exhort all followers to be loyal and obedient, to place loyalty to the sovereign above that of any personal loyalties, he composed and made public a number of odes directed to all the followers. These odes, which were to strengthen morale and reaffirm the goals of the movement, demonstrate well Yang Hsiu-ch'ing's new position as the leading figure in the Taiping organization.

The most brazen move undertaken by Yang Hsiu-ch'ing to assert his authority among the Taiping leaders came at the end of 1853 when he used his trances to humiliate the T'ien Wang, interfere in his personal life, and take over from him all independent authority of decision-making. The "Book of Declarations of the Divine Will Made during the Heavenly Father's Descent to Earth"[21] describes one of the most grotesque examples of the use the Tung Wang made of his impersonation of the Heavenly Father and the Holy Ghost. With information gained apparently through his own harem women, before whom he first dealt with the topic in a trance, Yang denounced the T'ien Wang for the harshness of his treatment of the T'ien Wang's own women and his indulgence of his small son's misbehavior, under which the women seemed to have suffered. The Heavenly Father's command to change all this is first transmitted through the women to the other Taiping leaders. Then Yang has another trance in which, in the presence of the other leaders, Yang orders the T'ien Wang, who had hurried to the scene, to be beaten for his faults. The actual beating is not carried through after the T'ien Wang accepts the punishment and is willing to submit to it, but he has been publicly humiliated and the authority of the impersonator is unquestionably established. In the following conversations that Yang carries on, the farce is played to the end. We learn something of the conditions in the T'ien Wang's court from Yang's commands to the T'ien Wang not to kick his women because they may be pregnant, to discipline his little son, and not to execute people on the spot and in a temper lest innocents should suffer. Yang advises the T'ien Wang to leave decisions on capital punishment to himself, his minister, who thus gains authority over life and death. From this time on, the T'ien Wang seems to have been a figurehead, manipulated by the actual ruler of the movement, the Tung Wang, Yang Hsiu-ch'ing.

This role as doctrinal and actual government leader led the Tung

[21] See document 39.

Wang about a year later to restate the story of his part within the Taiping movement together with a number of new short odes in which he heaps high praise on the Taiping followers and commends them for their loyalty, devotion, and heroism. In "The Book on the Principles of the Heavenly Nature," [22] published by the Tung Wang's staff on his orders, cognizance is taken of the fact that the many new followers, who "have not been able to receive the Tung Wang's instructions personally, and hence are ignorant of the principles of Heaven's nature," have to be indoctrinated. And even some of the old followers "have not been able to cultivate goodness and uprightness." To all of them the Taipings' doctrine is retold in a version in which the Tung Wang is clearly the most important religious figure.

The Heavenly Father, the Supreme Lord and Great God, gives life, nourishes and protects all, and the Heavenly Elder Brother has given his life for mankind. But in China, under the influence of false religions and especially since the barbarians seized the country, people have worshipped the demons. In a number of popular sayings Yang's writers ridicule the superstition and beliefs of other religions and describe the religious revelations of the Taipings, retelling the story of the T'ien Wang's ascent to Heaven and the events of the rebellion as proof of the divine support given to the Taiping movement. But more and more the Tung Wang emerges as the most important doctrinal figure. Undergoing misery and bitterness to redeem the multitudes from sickness and to save the lives of the people, Yang Hsiu-ch'ing assumes a Christ-like character. At the same time, through his "golden mouth," he becomes God's voice and thus represents the Heavenly Father and the Holy Ghost, a Trinity in one, the most exalted of the Taiping leaders. He is the one responsible for all Taiping success; he is holy—in contrast to the other Wangs who are only eminent—and he is even listed occasionally ahead of the T'ien Wang, the Sovereign himself. There is no question in this document about who is the dominant figure in the Taiping movement.

The "younger brothers and sisters" to whom the Tung Wang directs the appeal of this story and of his odes were the elite of the actual fighting force of the Taiping movement. They were the old comrades who had participated in the campaign and who were now told to be proud of the hardships they had suffered, the mountains and rivers they

[22] See document 50.

had crossed, and the battles they had fought. This was their glory and a satisfaction in itself. They had now been promoted, given titles, and fitted into a whole hierarchy of ranks. But the victory had not yet been won, and therefore the "younger brothers and sisters" still had to exert themselves and should not deviate from their purpose, "since only by suffering extreme hardship can one enjoy complete happiness." And for anyone who "mistakenly steps onto the demon's road and abandons all halfway" there was still military discipline and severe punishment. The seriousness of this threat is brought home by the list of sample cases of crime and punishment that the document provides. These cases deal with anything from treason to the forbidden sexual relations between husband and wife and show also how dangerous it was to start quarrels with members of the all-powerful Tung Wang's staff. There are also examples of several bandit leaders who came to a bad end.

But the discipline, especially with regard to the separation of the sexes, must have been hard to maintain. By this time, the leaders themselves, including the Tung Wang, had acquired large harems, and the disparity between their behavior and life of luxury and the abstinence and frugality enforced on their followers must have created its problems. This may explain the emphasis the Tung Wang placed on the hardships he and the other leaders had suffered in their youth and at the beginnings of the campaign. The Tung Wang himself of course claimed to have endured great physical suffering when he underwent his illness to redeem others. And so the Taiping followers have to live a life of military discipline in which "licentiousness" is the "chief transgression." They are permitted to visit their families, but have "to converse before the door, stand a few steps apart, and speak in a loud voice." But the families of the followers were at least close, and this gave them, so the Taiping followers were told, an advantage over the imperial troops in their camps, who were far away from their families. As a final reward, the Taiping followers were promised that after victory was won, when "the seas and lands will be cleared, and the hills and rivers united under one command," this separation would end at last.

Then our younger brothers and sisters will be united with their families, and blood relations will again be together. . . . At the present time, the remaining demons have not yet been completely exterminated, and the time for the reunion of families has not yet arrived. . . . With peace and unity achieved, then our Heavenly Father, displaying his mercy, will reward us according to our merits. Wealth, nobility, and renown will then enable us brothers to celebrate the reunion of our families and enjoy the harmonious relations of husband and wife. Oh, how wonderful will that be!

With all these exhortations, however, the rule of the separation of the sexes must have been difficult to enforce and was in practice given up a year later.

The elite to whom Yang appealed in his odes did not give him the personal loyalty he tried to gain. According to the imperial intelligence reports "people laughed behind his back." [23] Yang was said to have acquired by that time the largest harem of the Taiping leaders and must have been hated by many of the women in the women's quarters at Nanking. It is known that several of them attempted to kill him.[24] Even the Taipings' own records contain a report of such an attempt to assassinate Yang Hsiu-ch'ing.[25] But Yang was in control of an excellent spy system, the "patrolmen" and "patrolwomen" in the cities and in the armies.[26] This secured his authority and enabled him to maintain strict discipline within the movement.[27] With the help of these spies, Yang was able to maintain internal order, collect information about enemies, and uncover and punish many offenders. A Western account of 1856 quotes a Chinese informant: "The insurgent chiefs, . . . by their spies sent all over the country, knew the state of affairs everywhere, and the strength and position of their foes in every quarter." [28]

The unquestioned authority of the Tung Wang at that time and the success of his military and political measures are still reflected years later, after the defeat of the Taipings, in the confession of one of the captured military commanders, Li Hsiu-ch'eng. Thinking back on the Taiping success, he wrote: "The law was so strict. Thus around the

[23] See Chang, *Tse-ch'ing, chüan* 1, biography of Yang.
[24] See Hsieh, "Chi-shih," in Hsiang, *Tzu-liao*, IV, 664.
[25] See document 79.
[26] See documents 143 and 149.
[27] Thus, when opium-makers were discovered by patrolmen, the offenders were decapitated. See document 59. The secret service system also discovered attempts at support to the government forces in capturing Nanking. See the statement by Wei Ch'ang-hui in his instructions to a certain Wu, corps commandant of a weaving corps. The roles of Wu and a *hsiu-ts'ai* named Chang Chi-keng in their attempt to help the government forces were described in Chang Ju-nan, "Chin-ling sheng-nan chi-lüeh," in Hsiang, *Tzu-liao*, IV, 699-702.
[28] *NCH*, No. 320, September 13, 1856, p. 27, col. 2.

year *kuei-ch'ou* [1853] operations were carried on with great success, and the people's minds were submissive. The Tung Wang's orders were strict, and the soldiers and people looked upon him with awe." [29]

The most important and most revolutionary of the laws issued by the Tung Wang's administration was the "Land System of the Heavenly Dynasty," a law issued early in 1854.[30] The Taiping land law, as it has commonly been known, is a remarkable document, utopian in character and revolutionary in scope. It contained more than its title indicated, for it provided not only a blueprint for the agricultural system that the Taipings envisaged, but it also gave the structure of the political system to be established under the Taiping rule.

Under this scheme the Taipings were to apply to the country in general the same system under which they had organized their own movement. The whole population was to be organized into military units of the same size and under officers who held the same titles and ranks as those of the mobile Taiping force. The difference was that while the original Taiping force had broken up the family and was made up of single men and women, the units of the general administration were made up of families. Twenty-five families formed the basic unit under the command of a local sergeant. Four such units, or one hundred families, were under the command of a lieutenant. Five of the hundred-family units were administered by a captain, five of the five-hundred-family units were administered by a colonel, and five of the twenty-five-hundred-family units were administered by a corps general. This unit of an army corps was the largest local administrative unit, comparable to the largest unit of the Taiping army. The army unit consisted of 13,156 men or women and officers; that of the local administrative unit of 13,156 families and officers. From the outset there was thus in theory a difference between the members of the Taiping movement themselves, which had been organized on the basis of separation of the sexes, and the population at large, which was organized on the basis of the family.

Not only the system but the titles of the officers were the same as in the Taiping army, the system and titles that had been derived from the *Chou-li,* the Chinese classical text that was believed to describe the system of the early Chou period of the twelfth century B.C. Now this system, which had provided the nomenclature and the unit division for

[29] See document 382.
[30] See document 46.

the structure of the movement, was meant to become the model for the new order of the whole society. At previous occasions, the *Chou-li* had been referred to by Chinese reformers who wanted to use the sanction of classical antiquity for their more or less radical innovations, but none of them had attempted to go as far as the Taipings did in their political and economic program. In their system the whole population was under the discipline and administration of military commanders who were at the same time military officers, administrators, and the doctrinal and religious leaders of their units, a system of total control of all life by the state which had no parallel in Chinese history. There had been precedents in Chinese political organization of combining military leadership and general administration in the hands of the same military-administrative officers.[31] But none of these earlier systems went beyond the military governmental system or aimed at merging all social functions and all intellectual life with that of the state. None of them therefore had the totalitarian character which the Taiping system, if applied, would have given to its state.

This character of the system was also clearly indicated by the land regulations from which this most important of the Taiping statutes took its name. These land regulations are, however, perhaps the most misunderstood part of the Taiping program. The Taiping movement did not have as its goal an agrarian revolution that would give the peasant the use of his land. The Taiping Rebellion was not, as has been held so often, a peasant rebellion in the sense that it was an uprising by peasants for peasant interests. Its leaders aimed at a political system in which the promises of their rewards for the new elite were rank and title and the good life for them and their descendants on this earth and happiness in heaven after death. The source of the rewards which they received for their services was the common treasury which provided for the needs of all—including those who had no special merits —and for the rewards of the meritorious.[32] The land system of the Heavenly Dynasty applied now this idea of a common treasury to the country as a whole.

What the law provided for was a division of the land among the

---

[31] The *tun-t'ien*, the agricultural garrisons established in earlier periods of Chinese history, the Wei and So system of the Ming, the banner system of the Manchus, all combined such military organization with general administration.

[32] See the Tung Wang's promises in document 50.

families according to the size of each family. But the land was not to be given to the families for private use; it was rather to be divided for better application of labor. The land was to be classified into nine grades according to quality, and each man, woman, and child was to be allotted a unit depending upon the quality of the land and the age of the person. Each person above sixteen years of age was to receive an amount of land equivalent to one *mou* of the first quality, and men and women were to be treated alike. Those under sixteen were to receive half this amount. The size of a unit of land given to a family would therefore depend on the number and age of its members. This distribution of land was not, however, to give the farmers and their families the free use of it for their own benefit. Each family was to retain only as much of the produce as it required to feed its members and to plant the new crops; "the remainder must be deposited in the public granary." Thus all surplus was to be taken by the unit's officer for the common treasury from which all expenses for the needs of the population were to be met. In the language of the document: "When all the people in the empire will not take anything as their own but submit all things to the Supreme Lord, then the Lord will make use of them, and in the universal family of the empire, every place will be equal and every individual well fed and clothed." [33] The law provides for the movement of people from places where the land is "deficient" to others where there is more, and expressly states, "All the fields throughout the empire, whether of abundant or deficient harvest, shall be taken as a whole . . ." and provides for removing the harvest from abundant areas to deficient areas of the country to provide for general equality.

It was the government and its officers who controlled all the surplus and distributed it according to needs and merits. This control, actually to be exercised by the Tung Wang, was theoretically in the hands of the T'ien Wang and descended from him through a prescribed chain of command. The sergeant, in charge of the basic unit of twenty-five families, managed the public treasury, kept records of production and disbursements, and determined what the people could keep for their food and seed and what they had to deliver to the treasury. He was the judge of all disputes within his unit; cases he could not settle were to be passed on to the lieutenant above him, and if necessary to the higher officers.

[33] See document 46.

The sergeant also held services on the Sabbath and supervised religious ceremonies, such as marriages and funerals. He was responsible for the education of the children. Every day all boys had to go to church, where the sergeant was to teach them to read the Old and New Testaments and the Taiping proclamations.

This system of administration, however, left no real authority to any of the local officers. Each officer was to report on the merits and demerits of the people under his command. These reports, beginning with those made by the sergeant, were to be passed along to the Tung Wang's staff and to the T'ien Wang himself, who in turn would issue edicts for promotion and demotion. There was no personal security because anyone could at any time be demoted or promoted. In this system the reward was promotion to higher and higher office. The punishment was death or demotion, and the lowest level to which one could be demoted was that of husbandman. The position of the laboring peasant was thus the lowest on the scale.

The Taiping land law was thus the basic document that combined the system of agricultural work, land use, and economic distribution with an organic law for the administrative organization and the religious worship to be enforced throughout the Taiping domain. The link between the political order and the Taiping religion was underlined. All officers had to worship the Heavenly Father each Sabbath and expound the holy books. Any officer neglecting this duty would be "reduced to husbandman."

This system, decreed from Nanking by the Taiping leaders, was revolutionary in its intent. It was a system of military discipline, of rewards and punishments, and of control of all economic, social, and intellectual life, which was to take the place of the Confucian system of social harmony. In the traditional Confucian society the ethics of human relations and of government had been in essence outside the control of government, a standard of reference which could, if necessary, be used to dispute the authority of the government, even that of the emperor himself. The educated men of imperial society, the gentry, could use the Confucian teachings as an outside authority to defend the social system as well as their own role as guardians of the code. The Taiping officers and followers had no such code of reference. Their leaders used the doctrinal control of the religious teachings to set up an absolute authority totally different from Chinese tradition.

Much has been made of the fact that the Taipings did not apply the stipulations of the land law.[34] In some of the areas they controlled—notably Anhwei, Kiangsu, Chekiang—the Taipings gave the local officers whom they appointed the titles prescribed in their organizational code, without, however, seeing to it that these local officers carried out all the functions of the system.[35] The apportionment of the land according to the land law, however, was never even attempted. The Taipings simply collected as much tax as they could from the local population and shipped the grain and cash to their capital, Nanking.[36] At first, in some cases, the Taipings may have freed tenants from payment of rent to the landlord but not from tax, and in later times they even supported the rent collection of landlords from whom they could more easily collect the high tax.

Although it was not actually applied, the Taiping land law, envisaging a completely controlled economy integrated into a totalitarian administrative system, was an extraordinary plan, and one may wonder about the thinking of the person or persons conceiving it. Its origin must be seen in the military organization of the Taiping movement itself and in the common treasury which the Taipings established at Chin-t'ien and Yung-an. At that time, Hung Hsiu-ch'üan himself, certainly Feng Yün-shan, and most likely Yang Hsiu-ch'ing must have had a major part in the establishment of this system by the Taiping leaders. Though extraordinary in character, this structure can still be explained as resulting more or less from military considerations. The merging of these institutional innovations into one system and the idea of applying this unified system to the whole of the Taiping realm as a new form of social and political life was, however, at least in concept, a social revolu-

[34] On the question of the actual application of the Taiping political, economic, and social program, see Lo, *Li-hsiang-kuo*, pp. 23-36; Lo, *Shih-kang*, pp. 90-96; Lo, *Ts'ung-k'ao*, pp. 103-7; Lo, *Shih-shih-k'ao*, pp. 186 ff.; Lo, *Shih-kao*, pp. 80 ff.; Chien Yu-wen, "T'ai-p'ing T'ien-kuo t'ien-cheng-k'ao," *Journal of Oriental Studies*, Vol. I, No. 1 (University of Hong Kong, January 1, 1954).

[35] See document 60 and Lo, *Li-hsiang-kuo*, pp. 23-26. See also document 61, which contains an order to apply for door-plates at Fan-ch'ang, Anhwei, and document 173, which gives an example of an actual door register of a family at Huang-kang, Hupeh. The population of Nanking was immediately after capture divided according to sex into two groups, which were then split up into groups of twenty-five, each lodged in a separate house provided with door registers. See document 170.

[36] See documents 53, 82, and 85, containing orders and memorials dealing with the collection of tax in money and kind, which indicate clearly that the Taipings used the traditional methods of tax collection. See also document 169, dealing with the tribute paid by people of occupied areas.

tion. The new land law was drafted at the time when all power was in the hands of Yang Hsiu-ch'ing and his staff, and it must therefore be accredited to him.

Yang, the Tung Wang, was also the obvious author of a series of regulations for the Taiping's military forces which was the basis of the effective operations of the Taiping army. These regulations, issued in 1855, under the title "The Elements of Military Tactics on Troop Operations," [37] go into great detail on actual military operations, on training, inspection, security measures, discipline, and drilling of troops. They prescribe that plans for military moves should be outlined on paper for distribution to the corps commanders prior to action and that plans should be made to prepare for any eventuality on the march and during battle. The regulations describe the organization of land and water forces. They deal with the signs and signals to be used for communication between the different military units, including the signals to be given in battle by means of such instruments as horns, drums, rattles, and flags. The regulations contain an elaborate disciplinary system enforced by military police. They deal with medical care for the wounded and sick, with military drill of the troops, and elaborate on specific techniques of warfare, going even into such details as a description of how to construct and use various types of booby-traps. The extraordinary versatility of Yang Hsiu-ch'ing's mind, his organizational talent, and his understanding of military problems are demonstrated in these regulations, which were the foundation for the organization and success of the Taiping armies and their strategies.

The documents that survive indicate the strong centralization of the system in the hands of Yang Hsiu-ch'ing. When major decisions were to be taken, the procedure was for Yang to lead the other two kings, Wei Ch'ang-hui and Shih Ta-k'ai in submitting a memorial to Hung Hsiu-ch'üan. Hung's rescripts to these memorials indicate that his approval was a formality; his occasional comments did not deal with the substance of the matter under discussion. Hung merely added a note of exhortation to an important memorial on troop movements submitted to him in this way.[38] A memorial on appointments to fill the increased number of administrative positions was approved by Hung with the comment: Imperially noted. That which you brothers have discussed is correct. Offices shall be invested in accordance with the list, and those invested shall

[37] See document 52.
[38] See document 58.

conscientiously administer heavenly affairs. Respect this!" [39] A very similar comment was added to Hung's approval of another memorial suggesting designs for the headgear to be worn by Hung, Yang, Wei, and Shih.[40] These memorials were presented in person by the three kings to the T'ien Wang. Yang's special position was indicated by the etiquette which permitted him to stand while the others knelt before Hung's throne. That the actual decision behind these formalities was made by Yang can be seen from the fact that appointment certificates were issued by Yang.[41] Indeed it was up to Yang to decide which issues he should dignify with such formal presentation to the T'ien Wang himself. Since his appointment as chief of staff all memorials had to be channeled through him. There seems to have been no check on his decision on which matters he should handle directly and which matters should have the formal approval of the T'ien Wang. As the intelligence report has it: "Memorials to Hung's court were few, but reports and petitions to Yang's court many." [42]

Within this administrative framework controlled by Yang, no moves could be made without his official approval, and his staff had the central authority over all supplies. Supplies derived from tax or tribute generally went first to Nanking and their distribution from the central stores was strictly regulated.[43]

This centralized control over army and administration was the basis for the initial success of the Taiping forces and for the hopes of establishing their government and program. But while Yang was in practice the head of the government and monopolized all power, the actual structure of government remained extremely complex and could become the basis for a challenge to Yang's authority and the power struggle that eventually ensued. When the framework of government had been created at Yung-an, each of the principal leaders had been permitted to

[39] See document 62.
[40] See document 63.
[41] See document 168.
[42] See Chang, *Tse-ch'ing, chüan* 7; Hsiang, *Tzu-liao*, III, 202.
[43] A lower officer had to petition a higher officer for appropriations of any amount. Documents 89, 107. A high officer such as a corps commandant had to request the approval of a senior secretary for his petition for military supplies before he could proceed to the yamens set up specifically for storage and distribution of supplies. Document 106. To obtain the use of a boat, proper official papers were also required. Document 108. Even a high official of the court of the Heavenly King, such as the chancellor of the Heavenly Department, had to make requests to the treasurer for supplies. Document 105.

form his own staff, and the Heavenly King himself had his own court administration and officialdom. Of the original five leaders who had become kings at Yung-an and who had each then been given his own administrative staff, only three were left, Yang, Wei, and Shih. The administrative staffs of Feng Yün-shan and Hsiao Ch'ao-kuei, the two leaders who had been killed in battle, had been dispersed among the others. By far the largest and most important staff belonged to Yang, whose officials were said to have numbered over 7,200.[44] Among them was a large number of personal attendants and guards, but 3,564 members of Yang's staff were reportedly of high rank, a number which alone indicates Yang's heavy work load and responsibility. They all could read and write and were thus capable of administrative work, and, significantly enough, all these officials and subordinates of Yang's staff were from Kwangsi province. Wei's staff, which was next in size, totaled some 3,000 members, less than half that of Yang's, and Shih had a smaller staff than Wei. But here the story did not end.

After the Taipings captured Nanking, two additional kings were created. The title of Wang was given to the two most important of the secondary leaders who had been with the movement since Chin-t'ien. Hu I-kuang was made the Yü Wang in 1853, but was demoted the same year; and Ch'in Jih-kang was made the Yen Wang, which title he retained until his death in battle in 1856. Each of these kings was given his own administrative staff, smaller than those of the other kings. In 1853 titles of nobility were also created, below the kings in rank but above and apart from the titles of the Taiping army and administrative staff. A few outstanding Taiping officers who had distinguished themselves were given the title of *hou* or count, and were raised above the staff officials into the privileged ranks of nobility. At the same time the relatives of the Wangs were also granted titles of nobility, such as *kuopai, kuo-tsung,* and *kuo-hsing,* meaning state uncles, state ancestors, and state brothers. The counts, as well as the state relatives, were not officials carrying out orders, but like the kings themselves had their own staffs. Each staff was selected by the titled leader himself and naturally consisted of persons especially attached to him (*so-shu*).

The multiplicity of administrative staffs may have made it easier for Yang Hsiu-ch'ing to weaken the authority of his most serious rivals by reducing their sphere of control. But the numerous administrative organizations brought into being could certainly not have simplified the

[44] See Chang, *Tse-ch'ing.*

problems of government. Following the traditional Chinese system, six ministries or departments were set up to deal with the various functions of government. This division into six departments was duplicated within each administrative staff from the T'ien Wang's staff down to the staffs of the counts and state relatives. Each of these staffs then consisted of six departments, to which were added a number of guards and servants. But the difference in importance of these various staffs could be deduced from their respective size, which in the case of the counts and state relatives could be as small as a few dozen. In this complex system Yang maintained his power by having all matters channeled through his staff, deciding most of them himself and preparing the decisions for those few matters that he selected for the T'ien Wang's formal approval.

To attract educated men for service in this administrative structure and to provide a basis for selection, the Taiping government posted notifications wherever its forces went, "summoning the virtuous." [45] In Nanking, Yang Hsiu-ch'ing introduced state examinations through which candidates for office in the Taiping government would be selected. The introduction of such examinations as the basis of government service was of course an imitation of the traditional Chinese system; but the content of the examinations indicated the contrast between the two systems. The Taipings based their questions on the acceptance and development of the themes of the Christian doctrine and the Taiping revelations which its followers had to affirm.[46] The first Taiping examination in Nanking was held in January, 1854, on the birthday of the T'ien Wang, and, at least in that year, more than one such examination was held in the capital on the birthdays of the various Wangs. One examination for women was also held during this period in Nanking.[47] In 1854, Taiping provincial examinations were also held in Anking, Anhwei, and Wu-ch'ang, Hupeh.[48]

To indicate that the new Taiping system was to replace the dynasty in its traditional role of relating the course of nature to mankind, the Taiping government issued new calendars, the first in 1853 and another the year after.[49] These calendars were issued for what was

[45] See document 76; see also document 73, a proclamation of Wei Ch'ang-hui seeking medical men who were promised high office and large salaries.

[46] See documents 166, 167.

[47] Shen Mou-liang, "Chiang-nan ch'un-meng-an pi-chi," in Hsiang, *Tzu-liao*, IV, 439.

[48] Chang, *Tse-ch'ing, chüan* 3; Hsiang, *Tzu-liao*, III, 111-12.

[49] See documents 47 and 48.

claimed to be the third and fourth year of the Taiping rule, which was thus counted as having started in 1850. The calendar was preceded by a memorial by Yang Hsiu-ch'ing and the other kings to the T'ien Wang and bears thus the stamp of the collective Taiping government under Yang's leadership. Actually, the system, which differed both from the traditional imperial as well as from the Western calendar, was most likely worked out in the earliest Taiping period by Feng Yün-shan,[50] but was now officially promulgated.

In the new capital the Taipings thus set up a new system of government, managed by Yang Hsiu-ch'ing, and based on a complex structure of bureaucracy and etiquette. A vast staff was accumulated under the courts of the T'ien Wang and the other kings, and each of the many offices was assigned its function and position.[51] The leaders and their staff were housed in palaces to be built in large construction programs by thousands of carpenters and workers collected from different towns occupied by the Taipings. The palaces and gardens to be built for the rulers were to be grandiose and extravagant,[52] an obvious indication of the interests and ambitions of the new Taiping leadership. Nanking was to be the fulfillment of the Taiping plan to establish their kingdom, but there remained still the task of destroying the Ch'ing dynasty and conquering the empire they had now begun to organize.

At Nanking, the Taipings divided their military forces into three major groups. The central army, under the direct command of Yang Hsiu-ch'ing as commander in chief, was stationed in and around Nanking. A section of this force under Wei Ch'ang-hui guarded the capital against government forces encamped close to Nanking near the Ming tombs. These imperial forces, called the Great Camp of Chiang-nan (*Chiang-nan Ta-ying*), were under the command of Imperial Commissioner Hsiang Yung, who had followed the Taipings with his troops all the way down the Yangtze River. Another section of the Taiping central army under Tseng Li-ch'ang as commander was stationed at Yang-chou to face the other great imperial force encamped there, the Great Camp of Chiang-pei (*Chiang-pei Ta-ying*), under the command of Ch'i-shan. Another unit of the Taiping central army under Lo Ta-kang and Wu Ju-hsiao guarded the city of Chen-chiang and its vicinity, while other

---

[50] See comment on document 47.
[51] See documents 124 to 163.
[52] See documents 69 and 92.

units defended Kua-chou, at the intersection of the Grand Canal and the Yangtze, and P'u-k'ou, the stronghold north of the Yangtze opposite Nanking. The central and main force of the Taipings was therefore stationed around the capital in a defensive position against the build-up of besieging government forces.

From this central defensive position the Taiping commander in chief, Yang Hsiu-ch'ing, sent out four attacking armies, two toward the north against Peking, and two up the Yangtze River into western China. According to the information given by some Taiping officers to E. C. Bridgman, the American missionary, in May, 1854, it was Yang Hsiu-ch'ing's strategic plan to form with these northern and western expeditionary forces a large pincer movement for the capture of the whole of northern and western China. According to Bridgman's description:

> They had four armies in the field, carrying on active aggressive operations: two of these had gone northward; they were designed to cooperate, and, after storming and destroying Peking, to turn westward and march through Shansi, Shensi, Kansuh, into Szechuen, where they are expected to meet their other two armies, which from Kiangsi and the Lake provinces are to move up the Great River and along through the regions on its southern bank.[53]

The northern expedition was under the command of two secondary Taiping leaders, Li K'ai-fang and Lin Feng-hsiang, who had led the Taiping vanguard toward Nanking and occupied Yangchow on April 1.[54] They left Yangchow on May 8, received at P'u-k'ou some reinforcements sent from Nanking, and advanced toward Ch'u-chou in Anhwei with

[53] *NCH*, No. 208, July 22, 1854, p. 204, col. 1. Bridgman had accompanied the American minister McLane on the visit to Nanking in May, 1854, on the "Susquehanna."

[54] Li K'ai-fang, a native of Lu-ch'uan, Kwangsi, had already been promoted to the position of corps superintendent in 1851 when the Taiping forces were still in Kwangsi. During the campaign in Hunan in 1852, he was successively promoted to corps commandant, general, and commander; and for his part in the capture of Han-yang and Wu-ch'ang in Hupeh, he was promoted to senior secretary and finally to the position of chief chancellor of the Earth Department. Lin Feng-hsiang, a native of Kuei-hsien, Kwangsi, was an imperial guard at Yung-an in 1852 and was promoted during the march through Hunan to general and later commander. In Hupeh he became senior secretary and then deputy chancellor of the Heaven Department. Upon the order of Yang Hsiu-ch'ing, Li and Lin handed over the command at Yangchow to Tseng Li-ch'ang and led the campaign northward. See Chang, *Tse-ch'ing, chüan* 2, biographies of Li K'ai-fang and Lin Feng-hsiang; Kuo, *Jih-chih*, II, Appendix, 34.

twenty-one army units, each consisting of several thousand men.[55] They added to their strength when they passed through the northern border area of Anhwei and Honan, an area in which there were numerous groups of local bandits and where the Nien had started a local rebellion.[56] Following the strategy of the early Taiping sweep through Hunan and the Yangtze valley, they moved rapidly through Anhwei and Honan without leaving behind garrisons or supply stations. At first they did not attempt to take a city if it was well defended. However, at Huai-ch'ing in Honan at the border of Shansi, with a force that was now reported to be between 70,000 and 80,000 men,[57] they decided to besiege this prefectural city, which they believed to contain rich military supplies. The battle lasted for two months, but the Taipings failed to capture the city and had to give up. The delay in their march and the lack of success of the battle of Huai-ch'ing is believed to have been a decisive turning point in the hopes of the northern expedition.[58] The Taipings suffered heavy losses in officers and shock troops, while the Manchu court at Peking gained time to prepare against the impending Taiping attack. The Taipings eventually penetrated Chihli via Shansi and reached the suburbs of Tientsin, but their strength had been spent and they were defeated. A relief army was sent early in 1854 but never caught up with the northern expedition. The troops were dispersed and destroyed. Lin Feng-hsiang was captured at Li-chen in Chihli on March 7, 1855, and Li K'ai-fang was taken at Feng-kuan-t'un in Shantung on March 31, 1855. This was the end of the northern expedition.

[55] Ma Chen-wen, *Yüeh-fei pei-fan chi-lüeh*, 2:7b. The exact size of the northern expeditionary force is uncertain. Some government accounts place it as low as a few thousand, e.g., *Chiao-p'ing Yüeh-fei fang-lüeh* (1872), 37:5, but this can hardly have been their real strength; cf. Kuo, *Jih-chih*, I, 248. The low figure may have possibly been that of the vanguard of the northern expeditionary force. Hail, p. 84, makes use of Sone Toshitora's data of 36 army units at 2,000 men each and arrives at a number of 75,000. *Hatsuzoku ranshi* (1879, collected in Tsūzoku Nijū-isshi, Tokyo, 1912), 1:14. Chien Yu-wen, "T'ai-p'ing T'ien-kuo pei-fa-chün chan-shih," *Ta-feng*, Nos. 93-99 (1940), gives a number of over 100,000, which seems rather high. The figure given by Hsieh Hsing-yao of several ten thousands based on a number of contemporary official and unofficial accounts seems most acceptable. See Hsieh's article on the northern expedition in *Ts'ung-shu, chi* 1.

[56] For the Nien Rebellion see Chiang Siang-tseh, *The Nien Rebellion* (Seattle: University of Washington Press, 1954).

[57] See Wang K'un, *Ni-tang huo-shu chi*, p. 387.

[58] See Hsieh Hsing-yao, article on the northern expedition in *Ts'ung-shu, chi* 1; Chien Yu-wen, "T'ai-p'ing T'ien-kuo pei-fa-chün chan-shih."

The western expeditionary forces left Nanking on May 19, 1853, eleven days after the start of the northern expedition from Yang-chou. On June 10 the western expedition recaptured the important city of Anking, lost earlier to the government forces, and then divided into several armies to drive up the Yangtze valley. One army, commanded by Hu I-kuang, set out north of the river to conquer Anhwei; and another, commanded by Lai Han-ying, advanced south of the Yangtze to conquer Kiangsi. A third mobile force, under the command of Tseng T'ien-yang, independently attacked cities to the south of the Yangtze River. The Anhwei army under Hu I-kuang got as far as Lu-chou, the new government capital of Anhwei, which was captured on January 14, 1854. The capture of Lu-chou was a major loss for the imperial government and led to the death of one of its ablest commanders. Chiang Chung-yüan, who as a result of the victories he had gained over the Taipings as leader of local corps had been made governor of the province, rushed with a small force to the defense of his capital, was defeated, wounded, and committed suicide by drowning, and the government thus lost its first successful commander of the new local forces in the battle against the Taipings.

The Taiping army south of the Yangtze, under Lai Han-ying, besieged Nan-ch'ang, the capital of Kiangsi, from June to September, 1853. When he failed to take the city, Lai was removed from his command, and the army moved into Hupeh and Hunan under two other leaders, Wei Chün and Shih Chen-hsiang. The high point of this campaign was the capture by the Taipings of Hsiang-t'an, Hunan, on April 24, 1854.

After a little over a year in Nanking, the Taipings' main expeditionary drives had therefore spent themselves. The northern expedition had failed. The western one had gained limited success, but had not succeeded in extending the Taiping rule to the upper Yangtze and western China. The Taiping water forces dominated the use of the Yangtze up into Hunan, and the area which the Taipings had occupied remained a source of recruitment, provisioning, and supply. But the original rapid Taiping drive had been transformed into a see-saw battle which gave the government forces time to recover from the shock of the first sweeping success of the Taipings, time for reorganization, and the build-up of new armies under new leadership that were to bring down the Taiping Rebellion.

The Turning of the Tide

After establishing their government at Nanking, the Taipings retained at first the military initiative. Though their military campaign against Peking had not been successful and their western campaign on the shores of the Yangtze River had met both successes and failures in the battles with the government troops, the Taipings steadily extended the territory they occupied and gained additional manpower and supplies from the Yangtze area. But while they struggled to consolidate their gains and establish their rule, their attack, hampered as it was by the confusion of their political and religious beliefs and their political order, was met by a counter force that represented not so much the declining government as the traditional leading group of Chinese society, the gentry, which now rose up in defense of the social order, which was as much under attack by the Taipings as was the government and the state. And before long, the incongruities of the political system of the Taipings led to an inner conflict—a violent and bloody power struggle which destroyed the unified central political and military command that had been established under the Tung Wang, Yang Hsiu-ch'ing.

The promoter and the leader of the new forces that were to defend the traditional social order against the Taipings was Tseng Kuo-fan (1811-72). He was a native of Hsiang-hsiang, Hunan, who had passed the highest examination and gained the *chin-shih* degree, and had served as an official in several central government agencies at the capital between 1843 and 1852. In the critical year of 1852, when the Taiping armies commanded the Yangtze River and threatened to overwhelm the central Yangtze provinces of Kiangsi, Hunan, and Hupeh, Tseng Kuo-fan had returned to his home in Hunan province to observe the traditional mourning period for the death of his mother. There the order of the emperor to supervise the organization of local corps in his home province of Hunan reached him.

The order was a sign of the despair of the imperial government, which was well aware of the corruption and decline of its traditional banner and *lü-ying* forces and hoped to gain a new means of defense against the Taiping danger by organizing local corps in the districts of the threatened provinces. In late 1852 and early 1853 a number of edicts were issued by the government appointing in all forty-three supervisors of local corps in the provinces of Hunan, Anhwei, Kiangsu, Chihli,

Honan, Shantung, Chekiang, Shansi, Kweichow, and Fukien.[59] Tseng Kuo-fan was one of those appointed.

What the government had in mind was the organization of small forces under gentry leadership, which could be relied upon to be loyal. These forces were to be set up in each district to contest the control of the districts by the Taiping forces. Such local autonomous forces had existed before. Under the Ch'ing, as under previous dynasties, they played their part in the defense against earlier rebellions and banditry. And in the first sweep of the Taiping attack, there had been the example of the local corps of Chiang Chung-yüan, which had successfully blocked the Taipings' march down the Kan valley and forced them to change their route.

Tseng Kuo-fan was at first determined to decline the mission. He had already prepared a memorial to the emperor requesting the completion of the observance of his mourning period, and refusing to take up the direction of military affairs. But before sending this memorial he learned of the loss of the city of Wu-ch'ang to the Taipings and of the danger to the province. Implored by his friends to help in the protection of their native places, Tseng Kuo-fan destroyed the memorial he had prepared and hurried to the city of Ch'ang-sha to undertake the military defense of his province and, as he well realized, of the civilization and cultural tradition in which he believed.[60] What Tseng Kuo-fan planned to organize was however a very different force from the one the government had in mind. Local corps forces of a few hundred men, organized on a local basis and for use within their home villages and district, were useful in defending their homes against local banditry. Such forces were of help as long as banditry was scattered, unorganized, and without a major political program. Tseng Kuo-fan well realized that the situation had passed the stage where local corps would be of help. What he undertook was the collection of existing units of local corps and the recruiting of new forces for the establishment of a larger, disciplined, and centrally directed new provincial army.

His army was the first such provincial army, the Hsiang-chün, the army of Hunan province, the core of the forces with which he planned

[59] For the edicts see *Hsien-feng tung-hua hsü-lu*, *chüan* 9, 10, 11, and 19. A full description of the establishment of the force by Tseng Kuo-fan can be found in Lo Erh-kang, *Hsiang-chün hsin-chih* (Hong Kong: Commercial Press, 1929).
[60] For the story of the dramatic events that surrounded Tseng Kuo-fan's decision to undertake the task of military organization, see Lo Erh-kang, *op. cit.*

and carried out the defeat of the Taiping Rebellion. He had to be cautious, however, in reporting to the Ch'ing government his plan of military organization. The establishment of such forces on an autonomous local basis, and the surrender of the dynasty's military power to such local corps was dangerous enough. Any such local military organization could move on from the defense of their area against bandits to a military takeover and defiance of the administration. In the small-scale local warfare that had preceded the Taiping Rebellion, there were numerous examples of local corps shifting from pro-government defense of the area to a defiant attitude, turning from forces at the side of the government maintaining peace and order to what the government would call banditry, but returning again to the government's side when properly enticed. The establishment of provincial armies was obviously in the last resort a threat to the dynasty's authority itself, and indeed, so it proved to be eventually. Tseng Kuo-fan did not fully state what he was doing. In his first memorial [61] he simply stated that he had enlisted from the countryside people from various districts and established in the provincial capital a large military corps, which was being trained. This force was to be centrally financed, since the people in the countryside were in no position to carry the financial burden. He proposed that the training regulations should follow those of Ch'i Chi-kuang of the Ming dynasty, and by this reference implied that he was building a personal army led by himself that could be used in campaigns outside its local area. He followed this up with other memorials. He stated that the local corpsmen could not be relied upon in critical moments and that it was better to recruit from these local corpsmen an official militia (*kuan-yung*), whose rations would be paid from public funds. Again he referred to the methods of Ch'i Chi-kuang and his organization,[62] and in a later memorial he admitted that he had organized official militiamen (*kuan-yung*) and not local corpsmen (*t'uan-ting*).[63]

In planning his new army Tseng Kuo-fan had then consciously departed from the government authorization. He realized that the local defense corps which had sprung up all over China were useful against local bandits and small raiding parties but were not large or strong enough to withstand the attack of larger organized armies such as the

---

[61] *Tseng, Tsou-kao,* 1:55 ff.
[62] *Tseng Wen-cheng-kung ch'üan-chi, Wen-chi, chüan* 4: "Hsiang-hsiang Chao-chung-tz'u chi."
[63] *Tseng, Tsou-kao,* 12:13 f.

Taipings commanded. The victory of Chiang Chung-yüan had been unusual; the success which this local corps gained against the much larger main Taiping force had been the result of brilliant leadership as well as of favorable strategic conditions. It could not be repeated, and by now the Taiping armies had grown further. They could not be stopped by local corps, but only by a mobile army that could be used for aggressive campaigns throughout a large area and would be strong enough to face the Taiping forces.

While organizing a large provincial army, however, Tseng Kuo-fan maintained some of the basic principles on which the successes of local corps had been based. Each local corps had been the personal army of its commander. In combining several existing local corps into a larger force, Tseng Kuo-fan retained the idea of personal loyalty of the soldiers to their commanders. The men were recruited mainly from the villages in the hilly and mountainous areas of Hsiang-hsiang and neighboring districts. Tseng preferred simple hardy peasants from the mountain areas to recruits from the towns, and he avoided the recruiting of the many transient people, the so-called roaming population, who could be found almost everywhere during these chaotic times.

Tseng's force was to be composed of units, each recruited, led, and paid for by its commander. The soldiers were recruited from rural districts and each unit consisted of men from the same neighborhood linked to each other by village ties and following their officers in personal loyalty. The commanders themselves were loyal to Tseng Kuo-fan, the chief organizer and leader of the force. In contrast to the traditional *lü-ying* army, which had been based on the principle of divided command, of transferring officers in turn to different units, Tseng's army was a personal army obedient to its commander, an army far more effective as a fighting force but in the long run far more dangerous to the government's central control. Tseng Kuo-fan selected not only his own commanders but also his own administrative staff to organize, equip, and finance the army and eventually manage the territory where his forces were stationed. While his military officers came almost exclusively from the district of Hsiang-hsiang in Hunan and a few neighboring districts, his political staff was selected from among the educated of a great number of provinces. It was this organization that became the main opponent of the Taipings. Among the administrators and strategists that Tseng Kuo-fan assembled were a number of future leaders of their own military and political organizations—men such as the Hunanese Tso

Tsung-t'ang and Li Hung-chang, from Anhwei province, who later was to become the leading organizer of the Anhwei army and of an important political organization of his own. The example of Tseng Kuo-fan was followed by other regional commanders in areas threatened by rebellions and banditry, until by the end of the century most provinces of China were dominated by regional forces under military organizations over whom the central government had only a minimal control. Tseng Kuo-fan's build-up of a regional force exemplified thus the growth of political power out of the social order and traditional leadership that occurred at the time of the weakening and decline of dynastic strength. But the organization of these regional forces was not, at least immediately, directed against the dynasty but against the common foe whose new political system threatened the social order as much as it threatened the dynasty.

The character of Tseng's force and his purpose of defending traditional Chinese society against the Taipings becomes apparent from the ideas Tseng expressed at the time. Tseng Kuo-fan himself came from a Hunan school of Confucianism that combined several trends of Confucian thinking including the prevailing trend of the Ch'ien-chia or Han school of thought with its stress on textual criticism and philological and institutional studies, and Sung Neo-Confucianism. However, Tseng placed more stress on the connection between practical affairs and Confucian thinking.[64] How much the fight against the Taipings was a fight for Chinese tradition is apparent from Tseng's proclamation issued in 1853 when he turned with his forces to battle the Taiping rebels.[65] In his proclamation Tseng reminded the population of the affected provinces of the calamities the Taipings had brought—how they had plundered the people, rich and poor, killed them when they resisted, forced them into battles and into labor service, committed atrocities against women refusing to unbind their feet, or boatmen refusing to serve them. But then Tseng turned to China's traditional teachings and the traditional relations of the Confucian order. The Taiping rebels had "stolen the ways of the foreign barbarians," had distorted the family relations by calling all people brothers and sisters, had declared that all land belonged to the Heavenly King and that all profit also belonged to him, had

[64] For Tseng Kuo-fan's Confucian thinking, see Hellmut Wilhelm, "The Background of Tseng Kuo-fan's Ideology," *Asiatische Studien*, III (1949), 91-100.

[65] See *Tseng Wen-cheng-kung ch'üan-chi, Wen-chi*, 3:1a-3a. A proclamation on the suppression of the Taiping rebels.

forced the scholars to give up the Confucian classics and to read instead the so-called teachings of Jesus. They wiped out the moral standards, the conduct of human relations, the classics, and the institutions that had existed in China for several thousand years. This, says Tseng, "is not only a tragedy for our Ch'ing dynasty but a great tragedy for the whole Chinese tradition (*ming-chiao*) and causes Confucius and Mencius to weep bitterly in the underworld. How could any educated person remain sitting, hands in sleeves, without doing something about it." In these words Tseng Kuo-fan called for the defense of the Confucian order by all the educated, the gentry, who were its guardians. For the people there was the reminder that the Taipings not only destroyed the Confucian temples—as former rebels in Chinese history had not done— but also the temples and images of local deities and of the Buddhists and Taoists, so that all the spirits of the gods were angry and would take their revenge. To right this wrong, Tseng Kuo-fan was under imperial orders to advance his troops by land and water, not only to ease the monarch's feeling but also to console Confucius and Mencius, to revenge the slaughter of a million people, and to erase the insult to the gods. With this appeal Tseng Kuo-fan asked for recruits, financial support, and the surrender of those who had been forced to join the Taipings. With this memorial expressing the spirit of the gentry leaders that organized the defense of Chinese tradition, Tseng Kuo-fan based his military campaign on the traditional beliefs for which he gained the support needed to defeat the Taiping attack and win the victory.

Tseng's army became a well-disciplined force, and it was paid well. The private soldiers were promised 4½ taels per month, almost double the pay given the regular government army forces, the *lü-ying*, and more than ten times the pay of coolie labor or farm hands. And if the pay of the soldiers of the Hunan army was not always regularly forthcoming, neither was that of the regular military forces; and from later reports we can gather that Tseng Kuo-fan in all his different moves to supply the funds for his military organization attempted to pay at least 60 per cent of the promised pay. If the back pay accumulated over too many months, unrest and mutiny among army units could be expected.[66]

The funds for Tseng Kuo-fan's army came mainly from sources over

---

[66] For the problem of competing with rival officials for maintaining a reasonable level of army pay, see the interesting memorial by Tseng Kuo-fan in Tseng, *Tsou-kao*, 20:23a-27b, a memorial of 1864 which describes one of the many battles for funds.

which the government had no direct control. At the outset the new force organized and led by gentry was also gentry-supported. Since personal contributions could, however, be increased if the contributors were given recognition and reward for their efforts, Tseng Kuo-fan asked and obtained from the imperial government the permission to sell certificates of academic degrees, official titles, and appointment to offices. The sale of degrees and titles increased the number of gentry in the districts and thereby strengthened the group. The gentry's contribution was obtained in a form that increased the gentry's local influence and thus further contributed to the new role of leadership the gentry were taking.

Another major source of income for Tseng Kuo-fan's army and for the other regional armies that soon were formed was a new internal customs tax, the likin, introduced first in 1853.[67] Though the government permitted this tax, it had no control or supervision over it. When Tseng and the commanders of other regional armies organized after the Hunan model were later appointed to provincial positions, they also gained control of the regular provincial taxes and used them as contributions to the upkeep of their armies.[68] This combined income made the new regional military leaders as autonomous in their financial support as they were in their organization and leadership. The forces organized by Tseng Kuo-fan and by other gentry leaders were not government troops, although they were fighting on the government side, and accepted the government's final authority for appointments, approval of strategic plans, settlement of jurisdictional conflicts (for instance, over income tax), and a rather perfunctory checking of their sweeping financial statements. Their purpose in defending their social order and the high fighting spirit of these gentry commanders were based on their Confucian beliefs. Men like Lo Tse-nan and other unit commanders in Tseng Kuo-fan's army had studied, written about, and debated the various schools of Confucian thought, and Tseng himself was accompanied during his campaign by a group of scholars who discussed the questions of Confucian scholarship as well as those of strategy and political decisions.

It has been said that the Taipings failed because they could not gain the support of the scholar gentry, and that they could have had that support if they had been more Confucian. This is a totally unrealistic

---

[67] See Edwin George Beal, Jr. *The Origin of Likin* (*1853-1864*) (Cambridge: Harvard University Press, 1958).

[68] For the financing of the Hsiang-chün, see Lo Erh-kang, *Hsiang-chün hsin-chih*, chap. 6, sec. 2.

argument. The Taiping Rebellion was based on its revolutionary system, and any such revolutionary attempt had to lead to a battle with the leading stratum in Chinese society, the scholar gentry. The Taipings were not and could not be Confucians, but in this attack against the Confucian system in China, the incoherent and absurd aspects of the Taiping doctrine made the intellectual battle very uneven and enabled the scholar gentry to organize the resistance that eventually destroyed the Taiping movement.

Tseng Kuo-fan began the organization of his forces in 1853. He began with an army of a thousand men composed of three battalions. Later the size of the battalions was increased to five hundred men each and their number augmented. Naval units and cavalry were later added to the original land forces. When it took on the Taipings, the total Hunan army was less than 20,000 men strong. Later it was at the most not over 120,000 men, and in the campaigns the individual units were rarely above 10,000 men. Since the Taiping armies were often larger, the Hunan army and the other provincial armies formed after the Hunan model had to make up for this disadvantage in number by careful training, good equipment, and the constant use of local strongholds and fortifications in a carefully planned strategic campaign.

Tseng Kuo-fan prepared for a long-drawn-out and well-planned campaign. In spite of the pressure from the court at Peking, Tseng refused to engage his troops in major battles until they had gained some experience in small encounters with local bandits and secret-society groups.

The first engagements between the Hsiang-chün and the Taipings in early 1854 ended in Taiping victories. But on May 1, 1854, Tseng's troops triumphed over the Taipings at Hsiang-t'an, forcing them to retreat. And in the battle at Yüeh-chou in Hunan in July of that year, Tseng Kuo-fan's troops and water forces gained a major victory. This victory proved to be a turning point in the military campaign. It not only greatly increased the prestige of Tseng Kuo-fan's armies and demonstrated the soundness of his plan of organization and campaign; it also deprived the Taipings of their major strategic advantage. The battle cost the Taipings more than half their fleeet of boats and thus the control of the central Yangtze River. It was the first serious setback in a series of military actions that more and more reduced the Taiping perimeter of military operations. Following up their victory, Tseng Kuo-fan's forces entered Hupeh and recovered Wu-ch'ang and Han-yang in October, 1854.

To cope with the new military development, the Taiping leader, Yang Hsiu-ch'ing, sent one of the chief Taiping military commanders, Ch'in Jih-kang, to support the Taiping forces involved.[69] But Ch'in came too late to save the Taipings from defeat. His attempt to stem the advance of Tseng's troops at T'ien-chia-chen at the border of Hupeh and Kiangsi provinces on the Yangtze failed. Tseng's troops overcame the strong defense in the battle of December, 1854, the battle that marked the failure of the Taipings' western expedition. It was with good reason that the accounts in Tseng's camp described the battles of Yüeh-chou and T'ien-chia-chen as the most important victories.[70] The Taipings attempted once more to move westward up the Yangtze River. Shih Ta-k'ai was sent to command another expedition and succeeded in recapturing Wu-ch'ang on April 3, 1855, in order to harass Tseng Kuo-fan's forces in Kiangsi and threaten Tseng's plan of campaign. But the Taiping position was greatly weakened by the internecine fighting among the leaders in Nanking. Wu-ch'ang was recovered for the last time by Tseng's forces in December, 1856. From this time on the Taipings at Nanking were by and large on the defensive.

While the Taipings at Nanking began to lose the political and military initiative to their new gentry opponents, they also lost their standing in the regard of the representatives of the Western countries in China. Western support could not have brought the Taipings success, and Western opposition did not determine their defeat. The fight between the Taiping system and the traditional Chinese order was fought in Chinese terms. But Western policy played its part in the history of the rebellion, and the shift of Western attitudes from pro-Taiping to pro-government sympathy which occurred at this time facilitated the victory of Tseng's pro-government forces.

The first Western information on the Taipings, obtained while they were on their march from Kwangsi and Nanking and when they first settled in Nanking, was favorable. The Taiping army, which according to the reports of their progress appeared well-disciplined, and the Christian character of their beliefs raised hopes for the emergence in China of a new type of government that might be willing to take a different attitude than the Manchu dynasty toward Western missionary and eco-

[69] Some of Ch'in's reports and actions of his mission are found in documents 93, 94, 95, 96, 100, 101, 103, and 104.
[70] See Chang, *Tse-ch'ing, chüan* 11; Hsiang, *Tzu-liao,* III, 203, 296.

nomic activities in China. Western dissatisfaction with the Manchu government's unwillingness to carry out the stipulations of the treaties of 1842-44 was coupled with an interest in finding out the Taipings' attitude toward relations with the West. A number of official missions and private visitors traveled, therefore, to Nanking to evaluate the situation and to attempt to interview the Taiping leaders.

The first official mission that went to Nanking was sent by the British. Sir George Bonham, an official representative of the British government, accompanied by Captain Fishbourne and T. T. Meadows, sailed to Nanking on the British steamer "Hermes." On their way they encountered the Taiping leader Lo Ta-kang at Chen-chiang in April, 1853, and learned from him that the Taipings would be friendly to the foreigners and would not interfere with commercial relations.[71] But on arrival in Nanking, the mission learned that the Taiping government, like that of the Manchus, regarded foreign governments as subordinate to the Taiping ruler.[72] The belief of the dynastic government in the mandate of Heaven for mankind was replaced by the assumption that the Heavenly King, as God's son and younger brother of Jesus Christ, held an equally exalted position among the peoples of the globe. A personal visit by an American missionary, Dr. Charles Taylor, went as far as Chen-chiang, where in June, 1853, the Taiping leader Lo Ta-kang repeated his views on the Taipings' willingness to favor commercial relations with the foreigners once the war was over.[73] In December, 1853, the French minister A. de Bourboulon made an official visit to Nanking on the steamship "Cassini," and was again perturbed by the Taiping attitude. In May, 1854, a United States mission under Commissioner Robert McLane, Captain Buchanan, and E. C. Bridgman went to Nanking on the "Susquehanna,"[74] and in June, 1854, the British representative, Sir John Bowring, went to Nanking on the "Rattler."[75]

[71] See documents 111, 114.
[72] See documents 112, 113.
[73] See document 115.
[74] See documents 116-21.
[75] For an account of the British visit to Nanking by Sir George Bonham, see *Parliamentary Papers*, 1853; see also Fishbourne. Dr. Charles Taylor's visit is reported in *NCH*, No. 151, June 18, 1853, p. 182; *ibid.*, No. 157, July 30, 1853, p. 206. The French visit is reported in R. P. Mercier, *Campagne du "Cassini" dans les Mers de Chine, 1851-1854* (Paris, 1889). The account of the American visit is contained in "Commissioners in China" (35 Congress, 2 session, Senate Executive Document no. 22, pt. 1, vol. 8, serial 982, Washington, 1858-59), pp. 47-92. The British visit by Sir John Bowring is reported in *NCH*, No. 206, July 8, 1854, p. 194.

After these visits the British paper, the *North China Herald*, commented on the question of major interest to the Westerners in stating that the attitude of the Taipings toward the foreigners and the treaties would be the traditional Chinese one, "that whatever mingling of Christianity there might be among the leaders of the great insurrectionary movement and their followers—they would be found veritably Chinese in their relations with foreigners; and that whenever the time came for seriously engaging in negotiations, we should encounter precisely the same difficulties we have always before experienced with the government and officials of the Tartar dynasty." [76] Answering the question whether the Taipings would recognize the existing treaties, the paper said: "Most assuredly they will not, except on compulsion, or unless they willingly descend from their high position. They, the 'second Son' of the Most High God, and his royal associates, they and they alone, are to be the dispensers of all authority and all instruction. . . ." [77] Meadows, the missionary who had been sympathetic to the Taipings from the beginning wrote in 1856: "Their claims of supremacy for their sovereign are in no wise more exaggerated than those of the Manchoos, whom they are endeavouring to oust. The present dynasty continues, notwithstanding the British war and in opposition to the spirit of the treaties, pertinaciously to act on the old national policy of 'making a distinction between natives and barbarians,' of 'avoiding friendly relations' with the latter, and of 'keeping them off.' The Tae pings on the other hand, apart from the claim to supremacy, have, by the testimony of all who have visited them, manifested a decidedly friendly feeling. . . . they called us 'barbarian brethren,' a conjunction in which the first word is necessarily much modified by the second. And, what is of most importance, they are themselves, in certain of their fundamental religious doctrines, sedulously diffusing principles by which that very claim to supremacy, which they now urge, will be overthrown in the minds of their own people, with their future certain increase in geographical and historical knowledge. Hence, with the establishment of the Tae pings, foreigners will be in no respect worse placed as to all legitimate international objects than they were before, while a broad and firm basis will be laid for the assimilation of national fundamental beliefs and for a consequent peaceable extension of free intercourse and commercial privileges." [78]

[76] *NCH*, No. 203, June 17, 1854, p. 182.
[77] *Ibid.*, No. 208, July 22, 1854, p. 204.
[78] Meadows, pp. 324-25.

The foreign powers still maintained their neutrality. But the contact which a more rational Taiping leadership could have established was lost, and the Taipings remained isolated under the irrational leadership of their prophet.

The years from 1854 to 1856 marked thus the decisive turn in the fate of the Taiping Rebellion. From their great drive that had carried them from the south in Kwangsi province to the Yangtze area and to the establishment of their capital at Nanking, the Taipings had turned to a positional warfare centered on their new base at Nanking. Their offensives north against Peking and westward up the Yangtze valley had been turned back, and they had been forced on the defensive. A new military force had been organized against them by Tseng Kuo-fan and other gentry leaders, a force that not only defended the dynasty but took up the Taipings' challenge to the Confucian order. The chance of a contact with the west and of outside support had been missed; indeed there was hardly any possibility of foreign support for a regime that was so irrational, so fantastic in its goals. The inherent weakness of the Taiping Rebellion now revealed itself. The Taipings' main political and military leader, Yang Hsiu-ch'ing, the Tung Wang, had been a brilliant organizer and strategist. He had attempted to assume the role of ideological leader as well by ascribing to himself the revelations which the Heavenly King had brought to the Taipings. And he had tried to inspire the followers by some of the odes in which he reminded them of their companionship and the glory that awaited them. But his farcical impersonation of God the Father and of the Holy Ghost did not take the place of real ideological leadership, and his obvious striving for all the power, his humiliation of the Heavenly King himself, and the degrading treatment that his fellow kings received at his hand aroused a fear and hostility that eventually erupted into a violent power struggle.

The tenseness of the situation and the inability of the leadership to deal with the problems of translating their teachings into an effective program can be seen from the absence of any new major publications by the Taipings during the years 1855 and 1856. The original Taiping doctrinal statements, the revelations of the Heavenly King, and the Taiping land law, fantastic as they may have been, were certainly revolutionary documents of great importance, well suited to inspire the followers, especially the hard core, to fanatical efforts in a campaign that was to establish the promised kingdom. But now at Nanking very little was forthcoming in organized fulfillment of the dream. The Heavenly King remained silent. He may have been intimidated by the growing ruthlessness of the Tung Wang or may have simply abandoned himself to the pleasures of life in his rapidly growing harem. And as his later poems show, he may have already lost at this time what capability of rational thinking and expression he still possessed at the outset of the rebellion. What is more revealing, the East King, Yang Hsiu-ch'ing himself, added no major pronouncement to his former official statements on the organization of the conceptual framework of the Taiping system. The only new official publication sponsored by Yang Hsiu-ch'ing was a work on military tactics made public in 1855.[79]

This growing problem of organization and leadership was temporarily superseded by the immediate danger the Taipings faced at Nanking. Although the regular government forces had been unable to stop the Taiping march and prevent the original success of the movement in establishing itself at Nanking, they had not let up on their concentrated efforts to contain and reduce the Taiping Rebellion. The two great camps that had been established by government forces near Nanking, the Chiang-nan ta-ying, and the Chiang-pei ta-ying, the northern and southern camps,[80] had become a grave threat to the Taipings at Nanking. When the rich stores that the Taipings had found in the southern capital were used up, the supply problem began to be serious, and scarcity of food and resources affected the morale of the Taiping forces. In September, 1854, to relieve the food shortage, the Taipings let a large number of their noncombatant followers, of women and children, leave Nanking. And in March, 1855, to deal with growing discontent and the threat of large-scale desertions, the East King reversed the policy of separating men and women and permitted marriages among the Taiping followers. This change in policy affected a major part of the Taiping doctrinal system, the brother-sister relationship of men and women in the large Taiping family, originally meant to be upheld until final victory had been accomplished.[81]

The pressure of the blockade of Nanking by the northern and southern camps of government troops forced Yang Hsiu-ch'ing to withdraw some of his units from the battle with Tseng's forces and to throw them into an attack against the blockading armies. The Taiping commander

[79] See document 52.
[80] See maps.
[81] For the release of women from Nanking and for the approval of marriages see Kuo, *Jih-chih*, I, 340 and 376-77.

Ch'in Jih-kang was ordered to turn back from his battles with the new Hunan army and to attack the government camp on the north bank of the Yangtze River. In the battle of Yang-chou, Ch'in defeated the government forces under the Manchu T'o-ming-a. Then Ch'in's forces and the army under Shih Ta-k'ai, who had been called back from Kiangsi, combined to attack the southern camp of the government troops to the south and east of Nanking in June, 1856. The battle resulted in a complete Taiping victory. The southern camp was routed, and its commander, Hsiang Yung, died shortly after the battle. The blockade was broken. With the immediate danger to Nanking removed, the pressure that had forced the Taipings to keep together was off, and the internal rivalry exploded in an open battle of assassination and counterassassination that deprived the Taiping movement of its top political and military leadership.

Assassination and Power Struggle

The leadership system of the Taipings had been complex from the outset, and the undefined and loose structure of what today would be called "collective leadership" left the way open for a power struggle which could not be resolved in any agreed-upon constitutional way. There were two major principles in the leadership system. Leadership was sanctioned by divine mandate. Hung Hsiu-ch'üan himself had received his mission when, as he claimed, he had ascended to heaven and had been ordered by God the Father to fight the demons and establish the Heavenly Kingdom on earth. Yang Hsiu-ch'ing claimed to derive his authority from the fact that he had suffered for mankind and that through him God the Father in the form of the Holy Ghost expressed his will. After the death of Hsiao Ch'ao-kuei, who had claimed to represent the voice of Jesus Christ, only the Heavenly King and the East King had maintained a claim of direct divine authority. There was no clearly defined relationship between the authorities of each of the two. The Heavenly King was himself the son of God, the younger brother of Jesus Christ, and therefore a person with direct divine authority. Yang Hsiu-ch'ing was nothing of the kind, though there are indications that he too planned to establish some direct and personal claim of being God's son. From the outset his claim had been to speak for God himself. In this role, which he could maintain, however, only during his trances, he possessed an authority higher than that of the Heavenly King, and used it against him.

This conflicting system of divine sanction of the key leaders was combined with the concept of brotherhood of the whole group of leaders. The concept of the Taiping system in which all men were brothers and sisters and formed the family of God made a distinction between the brotherhood of all followers and the special brotherhood of the leadership, the original kings of the movement, the old comrades who had organized the movement at the beginning, who shared the dangers and adventures of the rebellion and expected to share the rewards. How strong this original idea of the fellowship of leaders had been is still apparent when, after the power struggle, the original unity is recalled in sadness in the note by Shih Ta-k'ai.[82] The principles of divine sanction for some of the leaders and of the brotherhood of all could and did come into conflict. At first, Hung Hsiu-ch'üan, the Heavenly King himself, had held a special and exalted position but—we may assume under the pressure from Yang Hsiu-ch'ing and perhaps the others—he had had to give up his claim to holiness, draw a distinction between God the Father and Jesus Christ, who alone were holy, and himself, who was only the sovereign head of the movement and one of the brothers. Each of the brothers had his own staff; and even though Hung Hsiu-ch'üan, the Heavenly King, as sovereign had a staff that in theory handled all things at the highest level, in practice Yang Hsiu-ch'ing's staff became the central bureaucracy through which all decisions were channeled and prepared for the Heavenly King and his staff. This administrative structure, however, did not eliminate the idea of brotherhood and equality among the top leaders. At Nanking this system was more and more undermined by the Tung Wang, Yang Hsiu-ch'ing, who assumed in practice sole and full authority for all decisions, using his impersonations of the Heavenly Father's voice to back his authority and humiliate the others. The claim of representing the omniscient God, which permitted him to interfere even in the personal life of the Heavenly King, was only possible on the basis of an effective intelligence service. It was this organizational tool that permitted him to assume the role of prophet, which was the basis of his power.

In his reach for personal power and for the leadership of the Taiping movement, the Tung Wang, Yang Hsiu-ch'ing, disregarded both the principle of collective leadership implicit in the brotherhood idea, which he himself had once stressed against the Heavenly King's claim, and what remained of the Heavenly King's own position as prophet of the

[82] See document 184.

movement by assuming the role of a leader with superior divine sanction, that of the Heavenly Father himself. The opposition to his attempt, therefore, came both from the Heavenly King, who must have been frightened by this challenge to his role, and by the other two remaining kings, the North King, Wei Ch'ang-hui, and the Assistant King, Shih Ta-k'ai. Forced to submit to the directions of Yang Hsiu-ch'ing, which came from Yang's staff, they no longer had any real part in policy-making. They still participated in meetings with the Heavenly King, where they knelt while Yang was standing, but military commands and orders were issued by Yang alone; and their complete acceptance of Yang's impersonations becomes apparent from the scene in which Yang Hsiu-ch'ing as the Heavenly Father reproached the Heavenly King himself for his treatment of his concubines, for the license he gave to his young son, and for the arbitrary way in which he had people executed in fits of temper.[83] This remarkable performance by Yang resulted not only in the humiliation of the Heavenly King but, in the follow-up, in Yang's sole assumption of power over life and death in the position of prime political authority that reduced the Heavenly King to the status of a figurehead. The problem for the two other kings was that neither of them had himself any ideological authority to fall back on. The only two of Yang's colleagues who might have been able to put a brake on Yang's ambition had been killed earlier in the campaign. Hsiao Ch'ao-kuei, the West King, had, as assumed spokesman for Jesus, a doctrinal authority of his own. He had supported Yang Hsiu-ch'ing at an earlier stage but even if he had continued to do so would at least have remained as an intermediate figure between Yang and the others had he not been killed. Feng Yün-shan, the South King, had not claimed any divine inspiration but, as original organizer of the worshipper group and as their teacher, might have, had he survived, represented a moderating influence in the movement and a check on Yang Hsiu-ch'ing. As it was, there was no middle ground between the new prophet and his non-prophetic colleagues, who could not match the ideological source of power that Yang used except by challenging it through assassination. A conspiracy against the Tung Wang's life was therefore carried out, which suggests that the schemers at least did not believe in the Tung Wang's divine role.

The organizers and abettors of the assassination plan could make use of the discontent that the Tung Wang's ruthlessness in command as well as his highhanded behavior and dissolute personal life had created.

[83] See document 39.

By 1856 his position with the Taiping followers must have been undermined to such a degree that he had become very unpopular with
the Taiping forces. His ruthless treatment of officers of other kings or
of anyone who showed him disrespect [84] must have created general fear
and opposition. His harem was, according to government accounts, the
largest of any of the Taiping leaders.[85] And the government sources
indicate that his reputation in Nanking was seriously undermined. In
the words of the government's informant: "People laugh behind his
back." [86] In fact, in 1855, a year before the actual assassination and
slaughter in Nanking, the government reports predicted the impending
battle for power in the Taiping camp.[87] The Tung Wang's growing
unpopularity must have extended to the army. He gave the troops and
their commanders no rest. The bitter feelings of a field commander who
did not forget this treatment still showed years later when, after his
capture, Li Hsiu-ch'eng related in his confession that the troops returning from victorious battle were not permitted by the Tung Wang to
enter Nanking until they had again attacked the government forces,
who were in a seemingly unconquerable position, and had given them
a crushing defeat.[88]

The only person who might have prevented this growing discontent
from erupting into violence would have been the T'ien Wang himself,
as far as he was capable of rational thought. And it is therefore indicative of the T'ien Wang's own role that the final crisis occurred after the
T'ien Wang had been forced by Yang Hsiu-ch'ing to bestow upon him
the title of "Ten Thousand Years," which so far had been used only for
the T'ien Wang himself. This attempt by Yang to make himself the
T'ien Wang's equal also in the ritualistic order of rank, so important in
movements of this kind, must have frightened the T'ien Wang and
embittered the other Wangs, and may well have been the final move
that precipitated the violent action by the Tung Wang's main rival.

What had held the Taiping leaders together was the immediate
threat posed by the government forces blockading their capital of Nanking. When this threat was removed by the Taiping victory over the

[84] See documents 78 and 79.
[85] See Yang Hsiu-ch'ing's biography in the government's intelligence report
Chang, *Tse-ch'ing, chüan* 1.
[86] *Ibid.*
[87] See the concluding sentences of the biographies of Yang Hsiu-ch'ing and Wei
Ch'ang-hui in Chang, *Tse-ch'ing, chüan* 1.
[88] See document 382.

government forces, the Tung Wang's main opponent must have thought the time opportune for action. On September 2, 1856, Wei Ch'ang-hui, the North King, assassinated Yang Hsiu-ch'ing and killed all of Yang's family and followers in Nanking. Over twenty thousand men and women are believed to have perished in the slaughter.[89]

That Yang Hsiu-ch'ing and all his followers could be caught by surprise and slain is proof of the decline of his authority over the movement outside his own following. But the background of the conspiracy for the assassination of Yang Hsiu-ch'ing has remained unclear, and the stories on it are conflicting. According to one version, it was the T'ien Wang himself who gave the order of assassination to the Pei Wang, Wei Ch'ang-hui, and the plan was known and agreed to by the I Wang, Shih Ta-k'ai. Another possibility is that the Pei Wang acted on his own or perhaps in cooperation with Shih Ta-k'ai and with Ch'in Jih-kang. According to one version the three conspired to kill only the Tung Wang and his two brothers. Still another version has it that the Pei Wang had been ordered by the T'ien Wang to assassinate the Tung Wang alone; when the Pei Wang killed all of the Tung Wang's family and followers, the T'ien Wang and the others were shocked by the terrible slaughter.[90] Whoever was involved in the conspiracy, the blame was later placed on the Pei Wang, Wei Ch'ang-hui, alone. Yang Hsiu-ch'ing, the Tung Wang, had been too important a prophetic figure in the movement to be de-Tung-Wangized after his death. Instead, he had ascended to heaven, and his role as one of the prophets of the movement was thus retained for future use. Only the Pei Wang, who himself soon fell victim to the inner fight, was purged not only physically but also from the doctrinal pantheon of the movement. For after Yang Hsiu-ch'ing's assassination the bitter conflict for power continued among the

[89] Lo, *K'ao-cheng-chi*, pp. 48-49; Lo, *Shih-kang*, p. 71. The actual date of the assassination of the Tung Wang and his whole following can be ascertained from the Taiping documents. In document 204, in which a new Taiping calendar for the eleventh year is issued under edict of the T'ien Wang, the twenty-seventh day of the seventh month of the Taiping calendar is proclaimed as the day on which the Tung Wang's ascent to heaven is to be commemorated. That day, in the Taiping's sixth year, corresponds to September 2, 1856.

[90] For the various versions see Kuo T'ing-i, *Jih-chih*, pp. 485-86. Kuo believes that the T'ien Wang had given the Pei Wang the more limited instructions. See also the versions of this assassination in the confessions of the Chung Wang and the I Wang. It seems plausible that the Pei Wang acted on his own initiative, but that both the T'ien Wang and the I Wang knew of the Pei Wang's plan beforehand but had not anticipated such wholesale slaughter.

surviving leaders. Whether the Pei Wang, who had, if not instigated, certainly led the slaughter, was after the elimination of the Tung Wang ever actually assigned the position of chief of staff and head of the administration can no longer be determined. He did, however, as we know, attempt to destroy his only remaining rival, the I Wang, Shih Ta-k'ai.

At the time of the assassination of the Tung Wang's group in Nanking, Shih Ta-k'ai had been fighting in Hupeh. When he heard the news he returned immediately to Nanking and is said to have strongly reproached Wei Ch'ang-hui for his wanton slaughter. Wei, determined to make a clean sweep of it, and being stronger than Shih—whose main troops were in the field—attempted to assassinate Shih Ta-k'ai as well. The latter, learning of the threat and unable to fight it out, escaped from Nanking by being lowered over the city wall in a basket, and joined the troops under his command. But the Pei Wang murdered all the members of the I Wang's family and court in the capital.[91] When the I Wang marched with his troops against Nanking to take revenge, the T'ien Wang had his own men assassinate the Pei Wang together with his whole family and following, including the Pei Wang's ally, Ch'in Jih-kang.

The slaughter in the capital had thus removed two, or with Ch'in Jih-kang, three, of the Taiping leaders and a large number of their followers. Only the T'ien Wang with his immediate family, and the I Wang, Shih Ta-k'ai, remained of the original leaders of the movement. The most influential in the T'ien Wang's group were his two older brothers, Hung Jen-fa and Hung Jen-ta, who in their actions did not demonstrate any major ability of leadership, but from all accounts had great influence on their brother, the Heavenly King. They and the leaders of the T'ien Wang's personal guard must have organized the purge of the Pei Wang's group, which may perhaps have been supported by survivors among the followers of Yang Hsiu-ch'ing and Shih Ta-k'ai seeking revenge.[92]

After the elimination of the Pei Wang, the T'ien Wang is said to have sent the head of the slain leader to the I Wang, Shih Ta-k'ai, as a sign that his family had been revenged and to have asked him to return

[91] See document 183.
[92] The successful elimination of the Pei Wang, Wei Ch'ang-hui, and of Ch'in Jih-kang and their group is the least explained action of this internal power struggle that was later covered up by the Taipings' official stories.

to Nanking to take over as the T'ien Wang's chief of staff. The I Wang came in November of 1856 and for a few months attempted to fill the role of chief of staff and administrative head of the government. But soon, so it is said, he felt threatened by the T'ien Wang's brothers and left the capital to separate from the Taiping movement and to continue a campaign on his own.

Thus the Taiping fortune had turned dramatically. The period of their swift campaigns and sweeping victories had ended, and they had not been able to exploit their early great successes before the new resistance of the provincial armies became organized and began to wrest from them the control of the vital strategic area of the upper Yangtze valley. And now their inherent inner weakness of plan and leadership had led to an internal breakdown and fight, the outcome of which left their prophet, Hung Hsiu-ch'üan, the Heavenly King, alone in Nanking with none of the original founders and organizers to supply that theoretical and organizational direction that the Taiping movement needed if it were still to succeed. With all his cruelties and limitations, Yang Hsiu-ch'ing, the East King, was a revolutionary innovator, an able organizer and strategist, to whom must be ascribed the major credit for the Taipings' earlier successes. The battle was still to go on for many years, but after Yang Hsiu-ch'ing's death no other leader was capable of reorganizing the movement and giving it that central direction and plan that alone—if that were at all possible—could have carried it to victory.

Part IV

The Period of Military Campaigns under New Leaders

If the Tung Wang's strategy had been faulty, and if his impersonations of the Heavenly Father and the Holy Ghost had been crude, he had at least succeeded in creating a central political organization under his leadership, in drafting a revolutionary plan for the rebellion, in directing its military strategy, and in maintaining a central control over the whole Taiping movement. After his death no such central direction existed, and no strategic plan was even devised. In the most critical years the Taipings had no over-all plan to meet the strategy of Tseng Kuo-fan and did not even have any central coordination of the moves and actions of the various armies. The only man who could have provided the needed leadership was Shih Ta-k'ai, the I Wang. But Shih Ta-k'ai did not have the qualifications to assert himself at this chaotic moment.

Shih Ta-k'ai has been glorified in later Chinese accounts and political writings as a national hero of the period. He has been celebrated as a highly educated figure, presumably the most literate of the Taiping leaders. A number of poems and letters ascribed to him were used by pamphleteers at the time of the Chinese revolution to express the spirit of a Chinese nationalist who attacked the Manchus, not as the demons that had to be exterminated as unbelievers, but now clearly and with a racist undertone as the foreign barbarians who had conquered and despoiled the Han race. In this nationalist and ethnocentric thinking of the revolution, Shih Ta-k'ai assumed a new role as a predecessor of Chinese nationalist rebellion against foreign rule. In view of this later interpretation and glorification of Shih Ta-k'ai, it is not easy to reconstruct his original role.

From the few documents which we know to be authentic, a somewhat different and more limited personality emerges. Shih did not have the education and the elegant style later ascribed to him, and though he was obviously an able military leader, he did not have or express a political program which would have given his military ventures a purpose. The most crucial reason for his failure to assume a leading role in the critical stage of the Taiping Rebellion appears to be his complete silence in regard to the Taipings' religious doctrine or, at the very least, the absence of any documented statement of his that would show an attempt at doctrinal leadership. At the time of the movement's gravest political and moral crisis, anyone who wanted to renew its original drive would have had to take up an ideological as well as a military and administrative role. There is no indication that the I Wang attempted this during the short months that he was the chief of staff at Nanking. The only hint of such a role can perhaps be found in the title he assumed. Following the example of the Tung Wang, who had called himself the Wind of the Holy Ghost, his successor, the I Wang, now assumed the title of the Lightning of the Holy Ghost. But he made no use of this new title to preach any doctrine or to assume any doctrinal authority in support of his new role of leadership. He tried nothing more than to be a chief military commander, and even in this position he could not maintain himself. The Heavenly King was still under the impressions of the events in which his life and leadership had been threatened, first by the Tung Wang and later perhaps by the Pei Wang. Surrounded by his brothers, who were jealous of anyone who curtailed their influence over the Heavenly King, and doubly suspicious because of his illness he was distrustful of any new potential leader. When he was left alone at Nanking, Hung Hsiu-ch'üan had implored Shih Ta-k'ai to come back and take over. "I am without assistants," he wrote, "only you are both talented and virtuous. . . . and reorganization is urgent." [1] But Shih Ta-k'ai's great popularity with the troops and the Taiping rank and file was enough reason for Hung's suspicion and uneasiness. According to the testimony of one of the younger and rising military leaders of the time, the two brothers, Hung Jen-fa and Hung

[1] See document 183.

Jen-ta, played on this suspicion. Both men "were deficient in talent and military tactics. They were obstinately bent on carrying out their own views, and were obsessed with the notion that Heaven would support them in everything."[2]

Shih Ta-k'ai stayed at Nanking from the end of November, 1856, to the end of May, 1857, but was unable to accomplish anything and believed his life to be threatened by the T'ien Wang's brothers. He therefore left Nanking and proclaimed his determination to lead an independent campaign.[3] With him he took a substantial part of the Taiping forces that followed him when in his proclamation he asked the troops to decide for themselves whether to go with him or to remain with the main movement. With him went some of the best military commanders, and his departure was thus another grave setback to the Taiping movement.[4] When the Ch'ing government learned of the break and of Shih Ta-k'ai's departure, it instructed Tseng Kuo-fan to invite Shih Ta-k'ai to surrender to the government.[5] But Shih refused to surrender[6] and led his army in combat through Kiangsi, Chekiang, Fukien, and westward into Hunan and eventually into the southwestern provinces, from where he tried to gain Szechwan. Though he assumed new titles for himself and his army commanders, he did not promulgate any new political program or even major purpose for his campaign, and became thus a military adventurer rather than a revolutionary leader.

Shih's military forces remained, though, a threat to the government and more directly to Tseng Kuo-fan's Hunan army. In his independent campaign Shih permitted some of his men to leave for home, and the Taipings that returned home to Kwangsi province and survived the end of the rebellion and the great slaughter came in the main from Shih Ta-k'ai's army. But Shih also was able to maintain large armies through

[2] See document 382. For the judgment of Tseng Kuo-fan on the character and lack of ability of the Hung brothers, in particular Hung Jen-ta, see Tseng Kuo-fan's report to the government after the capture of Hung's brother at the time of the fall of Nanking in, Tseng, *Tsou-kao*, 20:84.

[3] See document 184. A discussion of Shih's reasons can be found in Chien, *Ch'üan-shih*, II, 1397.

[4] Li Hsiu-ch'eng listed Shih Ta-k'ai's defection and the departure of a substantial part of the army as one of the ten serious setbacks that caused the fall of the Taiping movement. See document 382. A list of those who left with Shih appears in Chien, *Ch'üan-shih*, II, 1399-40.

[5] See *Ch'ing-shih-lu*, Wen-tsung, 210:11a-b.

[6] See document 187.

continuous new recruitment along his campaign route.[7] In 1858 Shih's forces were still several hundred thousand strong according to government accounts, until they were decimated in battles with commanders of Tseng Kuo-fan's armies, Liu Ch'ang-yu and Li Hsü-i, at Pao-ch'ing, in Hunan, in the middle of 1859.[8]

Though Shih Ta-k'ai's diversionary campaign forced Tseng Kuo-fan to dispatch some of his commanders to deal with him, he was not distracted from his main purpose and concentration of his forces against the Taipings at Nanking. Tseng fully realized that in his new role as military adventurer Shih Ta-k'ai had ceased to be a major danger and that the real threat still came from the seat of the movement in Nanking. When the Ch'ing court attempted to order Tseng Kuo-fan to move his forces into Szechwan to guard the province against the impending danger of invasion by Shih's troops, Tseng refused to follow the government's strategic plan. In his answer to the court's order, he lectured the government on the difference between the rebels who occupied and developed strategic areas for economic bases, meaning the main force of the Taipings in the lower Yangtze area, and what he called "roaming bandits," who did not settle down to establish themselves and defend occupied areas. Shih Ta-k'ai and the Nien belonged to the latter category. The real threat, he maintained, were the Taipings in Anhwei and at Nanking, and with them he was to deal first. The government had no choice but to let him follow his plan.[9]

At Nanking the Taiping situation after the blood bath and the departure of Shih Ta-k'ai remained chaotic. The atmosphere of distrust and depression was expressed in one of the poems entitled "Our Court Suffers from Internal Misfortune":

> In the cities few men will venture out, and
> Fowls and hounds have no peaceful retreat.
> Throughout the streets is blood,
> The forbidden palace has lost its shining glory.[10]

If this poem still shows an understanding of the disaster that had befallen the Taipings, the T'ien Wang's writings indicate that he had lost

[7] See document 185.
[8] See Kuo, *Jih-chih*, II, Appendix, 93. In August, 1859, Shih's forces, which then attacked Kuei-lin in Kwangsi province, were still reported to be a hundred thousand strong. See *Ch'ing-shih-lu*, Wen-tsung, 294:3a.
[9] See Tseng, *Tsou-kao*, 11:26 ff.; Lo, *Shih-kang*, pp. 73-74.
[10] See document 200.

more and more the ability for rational thinking, let alone action. In 1857, a year after the catastrophe of assassination, Hung Hsiu-ch'üan issued what was the only official publication of the time. These were the "Poems by the Heavenly Father," [11] in which Hung concerns himself with maintaining order and harmony among his hundreds of concubines and maids in his large harem. To them he expounded his "heavenly principles," admonishing them to please their master and to follow his rules. The mixture of fantastic ideas and fanatical beliefs in these writings to his women are a measure of the decline of Hung. Hung also concerned himself with having the story of his own religious experience and his ascent to heaven, the story on which the whole Taiping venture was based, retold in more fantastic form by his two brothers.[12] The situation in Nanking can be no better characterized than by these writings of the T'ien Wang.

Hung also played with the ceremonial regulations so important for maintaining a front of government and issued a revision of an earlier publication on that subject.[13] A new Taiping calendar for the Eighth Year was also published.[14] These official publications, which did not contribute anything to the Taiping organization or political decision-making of the time, do contain, however, the official interpretation of the power struggle that had taken place. In all these publications and those that followed, Yang Hsiu-ch'ing, the Tung Wang, is obviously absolved of all blame for the situation. He has ascended to heaven and is treated as the spiritual leader of the movement, so his name and title still appear on the list of Taiping leaders. And, indeed, his role as the spokesman of the Heavenly Father and the organizer of the movement must have been too important for him to be de-Tung-Wangized without fatal consequences for the whole fiction of the Taipings' religious mission. But the name of the North King, Wei Ch'ang-hui, who had started the actual slaughter, is omitted from the lists of the living and deceased Taiping leaders.

Whatever government structure existed at this confused time in Nanking was handled by Hung Hsiu-ch'üan's own family. To create a semblance of a central administrative structure, Hung appointed in 1857 his two elder brothers, Hung Jen-ta and Hung Jen-fa, as adminis-

[11] See document 179.
[12] See document 2.
[13] See document 180.
[14] See document 181.

trative advisers at the court, giving them the titles of Fu Wang and An Wang. These appointments were the first creation of additional titles of kings and opened the way to many more such appointments. It was the creation of new titles and appointments with which the T'ien Wang hoped to re-establish some working organization. The proliferation of titles, however, contributed in turn to further disorganization and chaos in the Taiping government. At the time of the appointment of his older brothers as new kings, Hung Hsiu-ch'üan gave Meng Te-en the position of chief of staff. Meng Te-en had been a member of the administrative staff and was mentioned in Taiping documents as an official who had provided women for the T'ien Wang's harem but who had not played an outstanding role of military leadership. In spite of his nominal position of central administrative and military authority he obviously had no real influence either over the court or over the armies in the field. At the court the T'ien Wang remained under the influence of his brothers, who were using their positions to amass treasures and lead a life of luxury, and in the field the commanders made their own military decisions.

The attitude of these commanders to the newly appointed officials at Nanking can be seen from the remarks made in retrospect by the leading Taiping commander, Li Hsiu-ch'eng, when he was a prisoner of Tseng Kuo-fan. He wrote: "There was no one at court to carry on the government," and "the morale of the soldiers and people was broken and troubled." The military leaders, who in his view were to aid the government, were greatly displeased with Hung's brothers, as both men "were deficient in talent and had no plans." They were distrustful of Meng Te-en, who was "a great favorite of the T'ien Wang and had not been outside the capital." He and his second in command, Li K'ai-fang, were "both men without ability, who were, moreover, kept in hand by the An Wang and the Fu Wang." That Meng was made commander in chief, with control inside and outside the capital, did not please these commanders, since "even" they "were under his command." [15]

The Taiping camp was obviously in a major crisis. And how far the disillusionment had gone, and how close the Taiping movement was to a breakup can be seen from Li's reminiscences of this critical time. Li wrote: "The feeling of the people had undergone a great change. Government affairs were in disorder, and each man was pursuing his own

[15] See document 382.

course. The Sovereign had become mistrustful of others. The affairs between the Tung, Pei, and I Wangs had so alarmed him that he was distrustful of ministers of other surnames and put his confidence in his own family and relations. There was a unanimous desire at this time to separate. However, they did not dare to separate on their own, since they had heard that whenever the Ch'ing generals and soldiers captured Kwangsi men they decapitated them, not sparing a one. Hence they banded closely together instead of dispersing. Had the Ch'ing dynasty been willing at this early date to spare Kwangsi men, a breakup would have taken place long ago." [16] If the lack of commitment to the Taiping ideas and their revolutionary purpose expressed in this confession by the man who was then regarded as the chief Taiping commander can be explained perhaps by the time and place this confession was made, Li Hsiu-ch'eng's statement still remains indicative of the lack of leadership at the time. Obviously this commander was not a man who then or later would have assumed the role of political leadership of the movement that was vacated with the death and disappearance of the first group of leaders.

The inability of Hung Hsiu-ch'üan's older brothers and of the new chief of staff, Meng Te-en, to manage the military campaigns, forced the T'ien Wang, however, to give the military leaders a free hand and even to create for them new titles and positions in the Taiping hierarchy. The two most important of the new military campaign leaders who were appointed in October, 1856, to such positions were Ch'en Yü-ch'eng and Li Hsiu-ch'eng, who were given the titles of second chief commandant and deputy commandant, respectively.[17] Left on their own by the inability of the court to direct the political, let alone military, affairs, the military commanders were forced to make their own strategic decisions and indeed to coordinate their moves if they were to survive. The military situation was extremely critical for the Taipings. Control over the use of the Yangtze had been lost to Tseng Kuo-fan's forces, and with this loss the transportation of military supplies and provisions to the Taiping armies had been seriously impeded. In December, 1856, the Wuhan cities had been recovered for the government by Hu Lin-i's forces. That this recovery of Wuhan was the basic move toward the eventual recovery of the whole lower Yangtze area was clearly seen and stated by Hu

---

[16] For this quotation and the previous one, see document 382.

[17] Before they had been "T'ien-chang," or heavenly general, and "Chiang-shuai," or executive general.

himself.[18] To salvage the situation, the two leading Taiping commanders came together in January of 1857 at a conference at Ts'ung-yang in the prefecture of Anking, to confer on a coordination of their military moves. This and other such consultations were arranged by the commanders on their own initiative. The conference at Ts'ung-yang led to a joint strategy and to a temporary strengthening of the Taipings' military position in the Yangtze area.

Of the two commanders who thus rose to eminence in the Taiping camp during this period of utter helplessness and confusion at Nanking, Li Hsiu-ch'eng and Ch'en Yü-ch'eng, neither had played much of a part in Taiping military affairs before the Nanking time. Ch'en Yü-ch'eng did not take an active part in the fighting on the march from Kwangsi to Nanking because he was too young. At Nanking he was appointed to the rank of Corps Superintendent in Charge of Provisions for the Taiping Left Fourth Army, a desk job. In 1854 he petitioned to be transferred to combat duty and had his wish fulfilled. At the occupation of Wu-ch'ang in June, 1854, he distinguished himself and was appointed Thirty-eighth Commander, and later Thirtieth Senior Secretary in command of the Taiping Rear Thirteenth Army and Front Fourth Army of the water troops.[19] His military accomplishments and personal bravery made him well known to the Ch'ing government as one of the most important Taiping commanders.[20] Ch'en was therefore an important Taiping leader before the crisis occurred in Nanking.

Li Hsiu-ch'eng was a fellow villager of Ch'en Yü-ch'eng.[21] Although he had fought in the ranks during the Taipings' campaign from Kwangsi to Nanking, Li was not promoted to important military positions till later. At Nanking he became an assistant to another Taiping leader, Hu I-kuang, and was on Yang Hsiu-ch'ing's orders appointed to the position of one of the new corps generals and later corps superintendents to lead troops in 1853. According to his own story, he held only lesser positions

[18] See Hu Lin-i, *Hu Wen-chung-kung i-chi,* 14:3a.
[19] See document 94.
[20] He was rated a biography in the government's intelligence report on the Taipings. See Chang, *Tse-ch'ing, chüan* 2, biography of Ch'en Yü-ch'eng. He was labeled in this report the Taiping leader most hated by the government forces. See also Hsiang, *Tzu-liao,* III, 66. In 1856 Ch'en took part in the battle of Chen-chiang, then with the title of chief chancellor of the Winter Department. At the time of the power struggle at Nanking, he was commanding an army at Ning-kuo in southern Anhwei with the title of *ch'eng-t'ien-yü.*
[21] Both were from T'eng-hsien, Kwangsi.

in the campaigns of 1853 and 1854.[22] Before the power struggle, Li had been sent with other Taiping officers to Chen-chiang in Kiangsu to participate in the fighting there.[23] Immediately after the power struggle Li was in command at T'ung-ch'eng in Anhwei in a difficult military position. With a small force of less than three thousand men in a city isolated by government forces, he was surrounded, according to his story, by over ten thousand government troops entrenched in over a hundred camps. To break out of this critical military position, Li not only arranged a cooperation with his fellow Taiping commander, Ch'en Yü-ch'eng, but also took up contact and military collaboration with another rebellious force to the north, the Nien.

At that time the Nien controlled the area of northern Anhwei along the borders of the provinces of Honan, Shantung, and Kiangsu. They had started as groups of local corps formed during the times of general distress and disorder to defend their villages against local bandits and also against raids of neighboring forces. By the mid-1850's these corps had banded together into a regional force held together by a secret-society affiliation and by local clan-gentry leadership. They had formed a formidable military cavalry force and used as their home base their villages, which had been fortified into a system of defense in depth from which they could sally forth on campaigns into neighboring areas.[24] They had become clearly anti-government and a rebellious force with which the Taipings could make common cause.

That no earlier contact had been made can be explained by the difference in the goals of the two rebellious movements. The Nien were a local rebellious group that had little program and major political purpose beyond the control and exploitation of the area their forces domi-

[22] According to his confession, document 382, he accompanied the I Wang to Anking in the position of messenger or aide-de-camp. Later he was transferred to Lu-chou. Li was not one of the seventy-four prominent Taiping military leaders and ninety-seven court officials listed in the government intelligence report of 1855.

[23] See Chang, *Tse-ch'ing, chüan* 1 and 2. At that time he was holding the position of deputy chancellor of the Earth Department. But there is some inconsistency in Li's own narration as to when he held this title. For this see Lo Erh-kang's comment in *Chung Wang Li Hsiu-ch'eng tzu-chuan yüan-kao chien-cheng* (Peking, 1951), pp. 61-62; Kuo, *Jih-chih*, I, 435.

[24] For a study of the Nien Rebellion, its beginnings, organization, and tactics, and its history in the battle with the government forces, see Chiang Siang-tseh, *The Nien Rebellion*.

nated. They had no ambition to establish a new dynasty, let alone the kind of revolution at which the Taipings aimed. The Taipings, in their revolutionary purpose, had at the outset little interest in local bandits and rebels that were not willing to submit to the Taiping faith and the Taiping discipline. Already at the start of the rebellion in Kwangsi, the Taiping leaders had alienated some of the secret-society and bandit chieftains who had at first been interested in the Taiping cause. The same policy had been followed by Yang Hsiu-ch'ing in the Nanking area. But now, with Yang's death and with the disregard for the ideological purpose of the Taipings by men such as Li Hsiu-ch'eng, the purely military interest in mutual support and joint action prevailed. The first collaboration between the Taipings and the Nien seems to have occurred in early 1856 when Li Chao-shou, a Nien leader from the southern Huai area, joined forces with Li Hsiu-ch'eng and participated in the Chen-chiang campaign of the Taipings.[25]

When the crisis had endangered Li's position at T'ung-ch'eng, he attempted to expand his cooperation with the Nien forces and through the southern Nien leader, Li Chao-shou, established contact with the northern and chief Nien leader, Chang Lo-hsing. Chang pledged collaboration with the Taipings under Li Hsiu-ch'eng; and the size of his Nien forces, which were claimed to be a million in number, placed the regular Ch'ing government forces in northern Anhwei on the defensive, easing the pressure on Li Hsiu-ch'eng. The military alliance with the Nien leaders raised Li Hsiu-ch'eng's status also with the Taiping government and brought him a promotion in rank.[26] The cooperation between Li's Taiping forces and the Nien led to the joint occupation of a number of cities in the Huai area in the years 1857 to 1859. But the cooperation, which remained on a purely military basis, did not last. It never extended beyond the Huai area, and even there remained a loose

[25] See Kuo, *Jih-chih*, I, 425, 437, 467-70, 472, 477, and 479. For further detail on Li Chao-shou, see the comment on document 188. See also Chiang, *The Nien Rebellion*, pp. 92-93; Hsieh, *Lun-ts'ung*, pp. 212-37; Lo, *Yüan-kao chien-cheng*, pp. 83-85. As pointed out by Chiang, the Nien in the southern Huai area under Li Chao-shou must be distinguished from the Nien of the northern Huai area under the leadership of Chang Lo-hsing. The northern Nien under Chang formed the main Nien group, which cooperated only loosely with the southern Nien.

[26] See document 382. Li seems to have been promoted at this time to the rank of chief chancellor of the Earth Department. See Lo, *Yüan-kao chien-cheng*, pp. 62.

form of related military moves, because the political structure of the Nien rebels, which was only a federation of autonomous communal units, did not lend itself to any further integration of the two forces, quite aside from their ideological incompatibility.[27] The southern Nien leaders, Li Chao-shou and Hsüeh Chih-yüan, who had been the chief Nien collaborators of Li Hsiu-ch'eng, could not be trusted for long. Opportunists as they were and not prevented from surrendering by government policy as was the Kwangsi man, Li Hsiu-ch'eng, they eventually surrendered to the Ch'ing side together with the cities which they were entrusted to defend.[28] Li Hsiu-ch'eng later ascribed their surrender to their fear to face the results of the undisciplined behavior of their troops. And he tried his best to disparage them: "Li Chao-shou's troops were a disorderly lot; they were constantly troubling the people and plundering any city that was taken, and when this could not be effected they vented their rage on the people themselves. Li chastised the assistant generals of the districts until he was ashamed to meet me and finally sent in his submission to the Ch'ing." [29] But Li's own willingness to contemplate surrender and the indications that Li himself and his troops lived on the land weakened Li's argument. Li was equally dissatisfied with the northern Nien leader, Chang Lo-hsing. According to Li, "These men were only interested in promotions but not in serving when called." In retrospect Li regarded the lack of a more efficient cooperation with the Nien, who disobeyed Taiping directions, as one of the reasons for the Taipings' failure. But Li's argument only indicates that in this period of Taiping campaigns by autonomous local commanders military considerations were primary and the Taiping political and ideological revolutionary purpose was all but lost, at least as far as a commander like Li Hsiu-ch'eng was concerned.

The cooperation with the Nien, however, as well as the joint strategy of the Taiping commanders resulting from the conference at Ts'ung-yang in January, 1857, enabled the Taiping commanders to maintain themselves and gain local victories in the central Yangtze area. The strategic plan agreed upon at Ts'ung-yang provided for an immediate flank attack by Ch'en Yü-ch'eng's forces against the supply lines of the Ch'ing troops. This attack was successful, and as a result, the forces of Li and Ch'en and other Taiping commanders united and completely defeated

[27] For the problem, see Chiang, *The Nien Rebellion,* especially p. 133.
[28] See documents 186 and 188.
[29] See document 382.

the government forces at T'ung-ch'eng on February 24, 1857.[30] After their victory, the Taiping leaders pursued the retreating government forces northward and began one phase of the joint operations with the Nien.[31] This success resulted in Li Hsiu-ch'eng's promotion to *Ho-t'ien-hou*.

Ch'en Yü-ch'eng attempted now to enlarge his own economic base through a new western campaign in which he tried to regain lost ground in Hupeh. He made two thrusts into the province, one between April and September of 1857 and the other in April and May of 1858, but on both occasions he was frustrated by the Hunan army under Hu Lin-i and other government troops. Thus Ch'en had to retreat and to content himself with northern Anhwei as his economic base.[32] Of the two main commanders, Li had thus gained control over a larger area of his own and was with his forces also based closer to the Taiping capital at Nanking. He was therefore in control of the supply lines to Nanking and also the commander on whom the protection of the capital largely depended. This enabled him to assume a dominating role in the Taiping camp, and the record that he left in his confession clearly indicates that he regarded himself as the main defender of the Taiping kingdom.

Though Li Hsiu-ch'eng's and Ch'en Yü-ch'eng's operations and the alignment with the Nien had slowed down the advance by the Hunan army and provided a respite for the Taipings at Nanking, Tseng Kuo-fan's strategic plan proved itself, and his forces slowly advanced in the Yangtze area. In May, 1858, contingents of the Hunan army under Li Hsü-pin, recovered the city of Kiukiang, which had been the Taipings' last remaining strategic base in the middle Yangtze area, a base which they had used to draw on the resources of the provinces of Kiangsi and Hunan and recruit their additional manpower. From Kiukiang, Tseng Kuo-fan's army could prepare for its march into the province of Anhwei.

At the same time that Tseng Kuo-fan advanced his long-range plan to deny the Taipings the upper Yangtze area and to bottle them up in Nanking for eventual destruction, the regular government forces continued their campaign around Nanking and rebuilt their camps which had been destroyed in 1856. Their blockading forces in the north and south camps were rebuilt in 1857 under the command of such Manchu

[30] For a description of the losing battles fought by the government forces in northern Anhwei during this period, see Hu Ch'ien-fu, *Feng-hao shih-lu*, in Hsiang, *Tzu-liao*, V, 3-22; Hu, *Feng-hao Hsiao-ts'ao*, in *ibid.*, pp. 23-40.

[31] See Map 8.

[32] See Map 8.

and Chinese generals as Ho-ch'un and Chang Kuo-liang at the southern camp and Te-hsing-a at the northern camp. At the end of the year 1857 they were advancing to take the city of Chen-chiang, which the Taipings had held since 1853, and threatened to attack Nanking.

To face this immediate attack the Taiping commanders again gathered for another conference at Ts'ung-yang to map out their joint strategy. In addition to Li Hsiu-ch'eng and Ch'en Yü-ch'eng, a number of other Taiping generals had gained prominence. The two most important among them were Yang Fu-ch'ing and Li Shih-hsien. Yang Fu-ch'ing was a cousin of the Tung Wang, Yang Hsiu-ch'ing, but escaped the fate of the Tung Wang's family and followers in Nanking, since he had been sent to Kiangsi to participate in the military campaigns. There he had distinguished himself and became the commander of a Taiping unit that occupied and held part of the province as well as a few cities in neighboring Fukien.[33] Li Shih-hsien was a cousin of Li Hsiu-ch'eng and had fought under him. Early in 1858 he assumed his own command and moved into southern Anhwei, where he occupied with his troops the region between Wuhu and Ningkuo and the neighboring region of Kiangsu as an economic base for his forces.[34]

The Taiping government depended on the loyalty of these generals, who paid no attention to Meng Te-en and the other administrative leaders at Nanking. In August of 1858 when the concentration of government forces in the camps near Nanking posed a growing threat, Hung Hsiu-ch'üan gave the army commanders new titles and assignments. As at the outset of the campaign at Yung-an, the government forces were nominally divided into a forward army, a rear army, a central army, and a left army. Ch'en Yü-ch'eng was appointed as chief general of the forward army, the title which had formerly been held by Feng Yün-shan;

---

[33] See Tso Tsung-t'ang, *Tso Wen-hsiang-kung ch'üan-chi* (1890), section on "Lo Wen-chung-kung tsou-kao," 5:56, in a memorial written by Tso for Lo Ping-chang. See also Lo, *Shih-kao*, pp. 242-43. Tso Tsung-t'ang in his memorial states that Yang Fu-ch'ing was sent in July, 1856, with a group of Taiping reinforcements to Kiangsi and had been given then the title of Royal Kinsman. Lo describes Yang Fu-ch'ing's military ventures in Kiangsi and recounts how Yang Fu-ch'ing had joined for a time Shih Ta-k'ai when the latter began his independent campaign into Kiangsi; but when Shih Ta-k'ai decided to march westward in 1858, Yang refused to follow. Instead he retreated into southern Anhwei and sent a memorial to Hung Hsiu-ch'üan in which he pledged his support for the Heavenly King and declared his willingness to participate in the defense of the Taiping capital.

[34] See Map 9.

Li Hsiu-ch'eng became chief general of the rear army, the title formerly held by Hsiao Ch'ao-kuei; the title of chief general of the central army, which had formerly been held by Yang Hsiu-ch'ing, was given to Yang Fu-ch'ing, who, however, had to share this position with Meng Te-en, who supposedly was the chief commander at Nanking; Li Shih-ch'eng became the chief general of the left army, the title formerly held by Shih Ta-k'ai.[35] These were the generals whom Li Hsiu-ch'eng called for the second conference at Ts'ung-yang. In Li's words: "I then wrote to the garrison generals of the different places, calling on all officers of the Heavenly Dynasty to hold a council of war on an appointed day at Ts'ung-yang near Anking. The generals and officers of the various places responded to my call. . . . we each took an oath that we would support each other and agreed to join forces in the conflict before us."[36] As a result of the plans made at the conference, Li Hsiu-ch'eng joined forces with Ch'en Yü-ch'eng, whose troops had returned from Hupeh and were at Ch'ien-shan in Anhwei and who, though not invited, had been present at the conference. Ch'en was to march through the cities of Shu-ch'eng, Lu-chou, and Ch'u-chou, to link up with Li Hsiu-ch'eng's forces, which were at the time at Ch'üan-chiao at the Anhwei-Kiangsu border. Their armies were to meet at Wu-i. These Taiping armies clashed with the government troops between Wu-i and P'u-k'ou and inflicted a complete defeat on the northern camp under Te-hsing-a in December, 1858.[37] This Taiping victory broke the northern half of the government siege at Nanking and ended the immediate threat to the city.

Fresh from their victory over the regular government forces of the northern camp, the Taiping armies had to face the advance of a large force of the Hunan army that had meanwhile marched into Anhwei. It was under the command of Li Hsü-pin, who was accompanied by Tseng Kuo-fan's brother, Tseng Kuo-hua.[38] This attack was threatening the Tai-pings in their position in the province of Anhwei itself. To face it Ch'en Yü-ch'eng's army rushed to the defense of the threatened position, and Li Hsiu-ch'eng's forces followed. A major battle on November 15, 1858, ended with the complete annihilation of the Hunan army and the death

---

[35] See Kuo, *Jih-chih,* II, Appendix, pp. 48-49.
[36] See document 382.
[37] See the strategic development on Map 9.
[38] This army recovered a number of cities: Su-sung, T'ai-hu, Ch'ien-shan, T'ung-ch'eng, and Shu-ch'eng, and was attacking the city of San-ho-chen, which was a major supply point between Lu-chou, Anking, and Nanking.

of its leader and of Tseng Kuo-fan's brother. Once more the Taiping position in Anhwei had been saved. Tseng Kuo-fan had suffered a major setback, and the Taipings had gained a new breathing spell, which did not, however, affect the over-all strategic situation. Li Hsiu-ch'eng and Ch'en Yü-ch'eng reoccupied the territories in Anhwei that had been lost, and then parted. Ch'en remained with his forces in the northern and western sections of Anhwei around the city of Anking, while Li Hsiu-ch'eng went back to the eastern section of Anhwei to the neighborhood of Nanking, where he continued to play the dominant role.

In this special position, Li Hsiu-ch'eng attempted to introduce some order into the confused situation. According to his own account, he remonstrated with the T'ien Wang, requesting him "to select men according to talent, enact laws for the relief of the people, promulgate strict decrees, renovate court discipline, enforce rewards and punishments. . . . treat people with compassion. . . . and reduce the taxes in grain and money. . . ." and "advised him to re-employ the I Wang and discard the An Wang and the Fu Wang." [39] The only result of this memorial was that Li was temporarily demoted, though soon restored to his previous rank. A demotion could not affect his actual power. And when in 1858 a new siege of Nanking was established, Li was entrusted with the general direction of affairs. He was then himself at Nanking, where, so he claimed, he succeeded in re-establishing order and control. Then he convinced the T'ien Wang that to save the capital Li had to leave to collect forces outside for its relief. Each of the leaders continued thus to hold his own area of supply, until the pressure of a new government advance on Nanking forced them to join their armies again for a defensive campaign near the cities of Chiang-p'u and P'u-k'ou in April of 1859.[40]

During this whole period from 1856 after the death of the Tung Wang to 1859 when a new attempt at leadership was made, the Taipings were thus on the defensive. Their military moves were worked out in conferences by the commanders of the main Taiping units themselves without regard to the government of the Heavenly King in Nanking. These commanders thought in military terms and were no longer truly concerned with the ideological campaign and the revolutionary purpose of the Taipings. This may be one of the reasons for their defensive strategy and their shortsighted policy, under which each devel-

[39] See document 382.
[40] See Map 9 for these military developments.

oped his own area of supply and support and joined forces with the others only at the time of immediate threat. They did succeed though not only in staving off and destroying regular government forces but also in holding off Tseng Kuo-fan's campaign, inflicting a serious defeat on his advancing armies.

But none of these victories affected the over-all situation. No attempt was made by the Taiping leaders to regain the initiative, and the disintegration of central control led obviously to a continuing deterioration at the capital itself. Where formerly the Tung Wang had had central control over military moves and supply, now the capital depended on the good will of the army commanders, who developed their own areas of financial control and sent to Nanking only what they found necessary. The Heavenly King's edict to a commander: "Gather and train local troops to help in defense. Collect food and revenue and let an endless stream be sent to Nanking," [41] sounded more like a plea than a command. And Li Hsiu-ch'eng's later recollection of his own importance in providing the supply for Nanking[42] clearly shows how much the capital had come to be at the mercy of the commanders. Li Hsiu-ch'eng even boasted of his frequent distribution of funds out of his own pocket among the officers and followers at the capital, with whom he claims to have become very popular as a result of his largesse.

Transport to the capital had become far more complicated with the loss of the control of the river to the forces of Tseng Kuo-fan. In the early period under the Tung Wang, the Taipings had not only a centralized control of supplies but also completely dominated the Yangtze River from "Chin keang [Chen-chiang] on the east to Yo chow [Yüeh-chou] on the west, together with the country on each bank, extending from 50 to 100 miles inland, and further inclusive of the two large lakes, Tung ting and Po yang, with their shores and navigable feeders." [43] This control of the Yangtze and lake communication system was already being lost before 1856 as a result of Tseng Kuo-fan's victory at Yüeh-chou. Now the river was in Tseng Kuo-fan's hands, and even though the Taipings still held the important cities on the banks of the river, the use of the waterway itself was denied them.[44]

[41] See document 186.
[42] See document 382.
[43] See Meadows, p. 182.
[44] See the report after the British visit up the Yangtze River in November and December, 1858, in Brine, p. 219: "When Lord Elgin's mission proceeded up the Yangtze they found that the Taepings were in possession of all important

In what form the Taipings ruled and taxed the areas their troops occupied seems to have depended much on the individual commander. In
the area of Anking, at least, the population seems to have been grouped
into units and under officials as provided in the land system of the Heavenly Dynasty.[45] The general decline of the Taipings' position became
also apparent to foreign observers. The only foreign contact during the
period from 1857 to 1859 was made by the journey up the Yangtze
River of the British mission under Lord Elgin. The purpose of the mission was to investigate, after the signing of the treaties of Tientsin in the
middle of 1858, the possibilities of the navigation of the Yangtze River
and the commercial prospects of the region and to report on the political
situation.[46] The ships under Lord Elgin passed Nanking on November
20, 1858, and exchanged shots with the Taipings. They proceeded as
far as Wu-ch'ang and Hankow, which was then held by Tseng Kuo-
fan's forces. On its return trip the mission arrived at Nanking again on
December 29 and this time had a cordial exchange of messages with the
Taipings. From the letters exchanged between the Taipings and the
mission at different points along the river, it is evident that the Taipings
apologized for the exchange of shots,[47] inquired about the nature of the
British journey,[48] and attempted to use the contact to appeal for foreign
help.[49] The British refused this request, stating their position of neutrality.[50] But they also received in "The T'ien Wang's Manifesto to the
Foreign Brothers," [51] a new indication of the Taiping leader's assumption of authority and of what to the Westerners were the distorted and
fantastic religious views of Hung Hsiu-ch'üan and his claim to divine
origin. Hung's religious fantasies and his demand that the foreigners

---

places on the banks of that river, from the provincial capital of Ngan-hwui
[Anking] to Nankin. The river itself was entirely in the hands of the imperialist
fleets that appeared to be employed more as a force of observation than of action."
The Taipings thus had to transport their supplies by land routes, which made the
supply of Nanking more costly and problematical.

[45] See document 191, which contains a rescript concerning the operation of a
commercial oil press. The administrative official concerned was in charge of oil
and salt affairs in Anhwei and was obviously trying to encourage the commercial
production of oil in order to gain more taxes from that source.

[46] See Oliphant, p. 466.

[47] See document 197.

[48] See document 193.

[49] See documents 192, 198, and 199.

[50] See comment on document 198.

[51] See documents 194 and 195.

pay their respect to him as God's son, together with the personal impression that the foreign visitors gained from the Taipings and the situation in the areas under their control, helped to eliminate whatever sympathies with the Taiping cause had been held in the foreign communities. The T'ien Wang's manifesto led Alexander Wylie, who accompanied the Elgin mission as interpreter to the "opinion that the religious eccentricities which began to appear soon after its [the rebellion's] commencement, are now assuming such prominence as to threaten the extinction of the vital truths of Christianity." [52] The secretary to Lord Elgin, Oliphant, himself says of the Taipings at Wuhu: "The leaders were Canton men of the worst description. Drunkenness and opium-smoking were prevalent vices, as one of their number, who spoke Canton English, and was evidently a blackguard of the first water, unhesitatingly admitted." [53] Wylie, who covered some of the countryside, further reported "the absence of all sympathy with the rebels on the part of the peasantry. Not only do they [rebels] harry and squeeze these unfortunate people, but press the men into their service by violence, retaining for themselves all the best-looking of their women." [54]

The growing Western disregard for the Taipings, which eliminated any chance of foreign support for their movement and contributed to the willingness of the foreign powers to provide auxiliary forces to the government side in the last stage of the campaign, was not entirely due to the settlement of the Western demands in the treaties with the Ch'ing government. When the Westerners learned more of the fantastic claims of the Taiping leader and of the decline of Taiping discipline and organization, they realized that this movement had no chance of success in establishing a new order in China. It was the disintegration of the Taiping movement itself that affected the Western view and stand. Whether it was still possible to turn the tide and to give new meaning to the Taiping revolution and to reorganize its political structure and re-map its strategy is very questionable. The attempt was made by a new leader who arrived at Nanking in April, 1859.

[52] See Oliphant, pp. 462-63.
[53] *Ibid.*, p. 330.
[54] *Ibid.*, p. 347.

Part V

Hung Jen-kan's Attempt at Government Reorganization and Centralization

THE chaotic state of affairs of the Taiping government caused the T'ien Wang to look for any able man who could take over the central direction of his government. From the start of the rebellion the T'ien Wang himself had never undertaken the task of organizing the movement or administering the government. At first, Hung Hsiu-ch'üan's faithful lieutenant, Feng Yün-shan, had established the God Worshipper society and had prepared the meeting at Chin-t'ien. In the beginning of the uprising Yang Hsiu-ch'ing had come to the fore, and at Yung-an he had taken over as the chief commander and organizer. It was Yang Hsiu-ch'ing, the East King, who had created the Taiping government at Nanking and had prescribed its laws. But Yang's ruthlessness and ambition had led to the power struggle, to Yang's assassination, and to the leaderless situation at Nanking. None of those who might have succeeded as chief leaders of the movement had the qualifications called for.

But political leadership was desperately needed. Hung Hsiu-ch'üan, the Heavenly King, was now utterly incapable of directing the government himself. His state of mind, affected by his illness, had from the beginning led him to entrust others with the organizational and practical aspect of the rebellion. By now it was apparent from all the references to his behavior and from his own writings of the time that he had declined much further. For long periods of time he withdrew from all

134

government affairs, as his commanders and high officials complained.[1] Hung's older brothers, who for a time managed affairs for him at Nanking, had no grasp at all of the strategic or administrative problems and no authority over the military leaders. Meng Te-en, who was then appointed commander in chief at Nanking, had been in charge of the women's camp and was obviously a confidant of the Heavenly King and in reality not much more than a chief secretary. The commanders, as Li Hsiu-ch'eng indicated, had contempt for him, and he was certainly in no position to direct policy and to unify the government.

It is therefore easy to understand with what relief the Heavenly King welcomed a new arrival at Nanking who seemed to him to be ideally suited to take over the vacant leadership position in the government. In April, 1859, Hung Jen-kan, a cousin of the Heavenly King, arrived at Nanking. Hung Jen-kan had been one of the earliest followers of Hung Hsiu-ch'üan and had shared with his older cousin some of the adventures of his earlier life as a preacher of the new faith. Like Hung Hsiuch'üan himself, Hung Jen-kan had been a student who had attempted to pass the government examination but had failed. He had thus the same reasons to be dissatisfied with the ruling system and to turn to new ideas and beliefs. During the first stage of the organization and growth of the God Worshipper Society, Hung Jen-kan had been close enough to events to give later a detailed description of them to a Protestant missionary in Hong Kong, whose account of the early Taiping movement is still one of the most important primary sources for its history.[2] When the uprising started at Chin-t'ien, Hung Jen-kan was regarded by his family as too young to join. In 1853 he had gone to Hong Kong to study under a Protestant missionary, the Reverend Issachar Roberts. In 1854 when the Taiping government had been established at Nanking, Hung Jenkan went to Shanghai in an attempt to get through to Nanking, but he failed and returned to Hong Kong, where he lived for the next year and worked as a catechist of the China Inland Mission.[3] In addition to his Chinese education, Hung Jen-kan had thus received in those years a rather thorough missionary training and knew a great deal about the world outside China, more than any of the other Taiping leaders.

The Western education he had received did not destroy Hung Jen-

---

[1] See document 382 and the interview between Hung Hsiu-ch'üan and a Western visitor as reported in *NCH,* No. 524, August 11, 1860, p. 127.

[2] See Hamberg.

[3] See Hung Jen-kan's confession, document 385; Kuo, *Jih-chih,* I, 615-17.

kan's belief in the Taiping movement and in the possibilities it represented of realizing a Chinese form of Christian development. This was demonstrated by his continuing efforts to get through to Nanking and join the movement. Finally, on April 22, 1859, he arrived in Nanking after a lengthy and adventurous journey overland from Canton.

According to his confession, Hung Jen-kan had no great political expectations when he arrived at Nanking. His welcome and immediate success surprised him. In his words, "On the thirteenth of the third month, I arrived at T'ien-ching and was blessed by my Sovereign, who conferred upon me the noble rank of *fu*. On the twenty-ninth day I was made a noble of the rank of *i* and a chief general. On the first day of the fourth month, I was promoted to founder of the dynasty, loyal chief of staff, upholder of Heaven, adjudicator of court discipline, and the Kan Wang. I tried to decline these honors on the ground that I had but just arrived and that such rapid promotion would tend to create a great amount of resentment among the generals. However, this did not meet the Sovereign's approval. My original desire was merely to go to the capital, represent to the T'ien Wang the distressed state of my home, and rely on his gracious protection in order to enable me to live out my normal span of life. To my great surprise the T'ien Wang showered great favors on me, and out of consideration for my industry and aspiration to seek fame he did not shrink from the odium of creating a spirit of jealousy among his ministers but elevated me to this extraordinary appointment. Since my appointment I have felt it my duty to exert myself strenuously to carry out the work before me as a return for favors received." [4]

After his elevation to the position of Kan Wang and chief of staff, Hung Jen-kan tried his best to serve the cause of the Taiping movement, in which, from all evidence, he strongly and sincerely believed. What has survived of his writings as leading administrator of the Taipings and, at the end, as a prisoner of Tseng Kuo-fan awaiting execution shows him to be a man of strong religious faith, of character, and of great political and strategic vision. The program that Hung Jen-kan proposed showed that he was the first of the Taiping leaders who understood enough of the modern world of his time to see the Taiping movement within the setting of the world of modern national states and who regarded its Christian beliefs as a basis for a new Chinese national or-

[4] See document 385

der. In fact, Hung Jen-kan's combination of Western and Chinese ideas may qualify him as one of the earliest Chinese modern nationalists.

It has been said that when he arrived at Nanking, Hung Jen-kan had hoped to accomplish two tasks for the Taipings. First, he wanted to bring them the right religion, the Protestant Christianity which he had been taught by his missionary teachers; and second, and connected with the first purpose, he wanted to bring about an improvement of relations between the Taipings and the foreigners, especially the foreign missionaries. And indeed Hung Jen-kan attempted to accomplish both these purposes when he had been established at Nanking.[5] But the new position as political leader conferred upon him by his cousin, the Heavenly King, forced him to draw up a whole program of political reorganization, of doctrinal revitalization of the movement, and of a military campaign strategy—a program that in its scope and many-sidedness shows the unusual qualities of the man. Even though he failed, Hung Jen-kan must be credited with a broad and singlehanded attempt to reverse the trend of defeat and to provide a reorganization of the beliefs and institutions of the Taiping movement that would lead the rebellion to the success in which Hung Jen-kan still believed.

The first treatises and proclamations which Hung Jen-kan issued after he had been made the Kan Wang and given authority to direct the government show his grasp of the whole problem of organization and planning involved in bringing a new life to the movement. He dealt with the problems of government, ideas on the development of the economy, on reforms of the whole official system, of re-establishment of law and order, but most of all with the religious faith of the Taipings. The revival, reform, and reinterpretation of the Taipings' religious beliefs were for Hung Jen-kan not only an important factor in rebuilding the Taiping government and program but also a matter of personal belief. He ascribed the Taipings' earlier successes to their religious faith, and his endeavors to restore this faith were therefore as much an effort to rebuild the ideology of the movement on which its success had to be based as they were a matter of his own conviction. He admitted the decline of religious beliefs among the Taipings, even in an interview with a Western visitor who asked him about the state religion in the movement among the Taipings and received Hung Jen-kan's answer: "It has deteriorated considerably. The Kan Wang observed this on arriving at Nanking. Even

[5] See documents 203, *et al.*

among the Kwangsi men there is less religious warmth than there was at the beginning of the movement. The Kan Wang has printed a prayer for distribution among them." [6] How seriously Hung Jen-kan took this problem is apparent from the great number of religious exhortations, interpretations, and prayers that he produced shortly after his arrival and in the years that followed. His first important treatises already give a great deal of space to religious discussions, and in all his later publications he never neglected this aspect of his leadership.

The interpretation of Christian religion revealed in these treatises is very different from that expressed by the T'ien Wang and by the Tung Wang in the past. In his Treatise on Aids to Administration,[7] Hung Jen-kan deals with the definition of the Trinity and a description of God which differs completely from that of the T'ien Wang, who indeed went to much trouble in his annotations and in his own statements to show his disagreement with Hung Jen-kan. To Hung Jen-kan: "God is the Father and embodies myriads of phenomena; Christ is the Son, who was manifest in the body. . . . The Wind of the Holy Spirit, God, is also a Son. . . . God is one who gives shape to things, molds things into forms, who created heaven and created earth, who begins and ends all things, yet has no beginning or end himself. . . ." and "God and the Saviour are one." More explicit still are the religious issues taken up in the second of Hung Jen-kan's treatises,[8] written at almost the same time. This treatise, which consists of a number of essays, gives even more clearly the idea of a Protestant Christian belief. In the second essay of this treatise, which deals with the overcoming of temptations and delusions, Hung Jen-kan reveals a faith concerned with the individual and his salvation, an aspect not stressed before by the Taiping leaders. Hung Jen-kan emphasizes the inner self and mentions the conscience, and had clearly the Christian concept of original sin, which had not been understood by any of the previous Taiping leaders. The fourth essay deals with sin, repentance, and forgiveness. Christ is the Saviour through whom one's sins can be forgiven. Though previously Christ had been called the Redeemer, there had been no indication that the idea of redemption had been accepted or even understood. There had been a rather vulgarized use of the concept in the claim of the Tung Wang that through his own illness he had become the "redeemer of sickness." Hung Jen-kan,

---

[6] See *NCH*, No. 524, August 11, 1860, p. 127.
[7] See document 203.
[8] See document 202.

educated as a catechist of the London Missionary Society, understood the concepts and tried to propagate them. While the religion of the T'ien Wang and the Tung Wang had mainly been concerned with concepts of a wrathful God, and of punishment, and as far as their religious understanding had gone had stressed the Old Testament, Hung Jen-kan based his religious ideas on the New Testament and on the Sermon on the Mount. He ends his essay with a complete listing of the Beatitudes, and his emphasis on the meek sounds very different indeed from the teachings of the T'ien Wang and the Tung Wang, which had been the basis of the ideology at the outset of the movement. The fifth essay of the Kan Wang's treatise is a lengthy prayer which contains the whole catechism of his Protestant faith. What he had learned in his four years as catechist with the London Missionary Society in Hong Kong, Hung Jen-kan now expressed in this prayer, as he continued to do in his later prayers and statements in the years to come. He believed, however, also that the guidance of the Heavenly Father had led the Taipings to the capital of Nanking; and he introduced into his prayer the story of the T'ien Wang and his experience in 1837 in his ascent to heaven.

This story Hung Jen-kan believed. He himself had experienced these early years and makes the most of his knowledge. After all, the story had been taken seriously by his missionary friend and had been the basis of the first Western enthusiastic description of the early Taiping movement. Now this early story, while maintained, had to be fitted by Hung Jen-kan into his fuller understanding of Christian teachings. The T'ien Wang's story of his ascent to heaven is interpreted now as a religious experience. The T'ien Wang's soul, not his body, had been to heaven. What in the T'ien Wang's account had become more and more a fantastic magic tale on which his authority was based, became in Hung Jen-kan's interpretation a religious conversion, which is given as proof not of temporal authority but of God's spiritual guidance of the movement.

Hung Jen-kan obviously believed in the power of prayer, and this prayer had a purpose. He prayed for success in unifying China and in propagating the gospel, and he wanted all the followers of the Taiping movement to pray in the same way in order to accomplish this purpose. The prayer was written and was to be distributed, and each person had to keep a copy and use it for prayer in the morning and in the evening. When in the early days the God Worshippers had been given their samples of simple prayers by Feng Yün-shan, they had still followed the Buddhist practice of saying prayers written on a paper, which was then burned so that the smoke would ascend, transmitting the prayer to God. This more simple and naïve practice was now replaced, and a deeper, more meaningful concept of prayer was to be adopted.

There is no indication that Hung Jen-kan had much success with his singlehanded effort to introduce into the Taiping movement a different concept of religion and a revival of what had been—in whatever form— a strong faith. The early faith of the Taipings had been a belief in miracles and in charismatic leadership by men who had been to heaven or who spoke in trances with heavenly voices. For these leaders—the T'ien Wang, the Tung Wang, and the Hsi Wang—ideological leadership was the basis of political power, and their ideological leadership was based on the naïve acceptance of their magical authority by their followers. The Kan Wang, however, attempted to introduce the principles of a rational system and a religious faith, which he preached without claiming any supernatural role himself. Had he succeeded he would have been the leader of what might have become a truly Christian movement. As it was, he failed. And in his effort to maintain his political leadership of the Taiping government, he even compromised his own faith when in later descriptions of the Taipings' religious experience he again has the T'ien Wang ascend to heaven in person as well as in spirit and reintroduces the Tung Wang, who was omitted in Hung Jen-kan's first accounts. But even then these concessions to politics did not basically affect Hung Jen-kan's Christian beliefs and his continued faith in the power of prayer and in the religious basis as the foundation of the whole movement.

Hung Jen-kan's whole concept of the state and government that the Taipings were to establish was linked with his ideas on religion. All the reforms that he wanted to introduce were based on his missionary educational background and his view of the West that he had gained in the treaty ports. In Hung Jen-kan's program the whole emphasis of the movement had shifted from that of an agricultural group to a westernized urban life. His "New Treatise on Aids to Administration" gave a whole list of Western innovations which to him seemed most important for the Taiping state. New means of communication, railroads, highways, postal services, shipping lines, were obviously meant to serve a Western economy with an expanding commercial development and private enterprise. His proposals for the establishment of modern banks show that he wanted to introduce private enterprise and initiative on the Western model, and his suggestions on the development of mining seem to indicate that he favored some form of state-private enterprise cooperation. He propagated the idea of an insurance system for life and property, of hospitals supported by voluntary contributions. Behind all these Western ideas that he had taken from his life in the treaty ports was the moral influence that he obviously derived from his experiences with the missionary organization. Hung Jen-kan's idea that inventions and modern developments were "beneficial" to the people was in line with nineteenth-century Protestantism. He considered these developments morally good, and although in his treatise he names the Holy Trinity as the "most precious" thing in the spiritual realm, he lists as "secondarily precious" such "useful" objects as steamships, trains, clocks, modern guns, and other practical Western inventions. These are not, like jewelry, mere embellishments for women and children but are "eternally useful." Hung Jen-kan's views on charitable foundations for a "worthy cause," his idea that recipients of charity should be made to work for what they receive, indicating his belief in the moral quality of work, all these concepts show the influence of his missionary education. He was against the vices of wine, tobacco, and opium, which of course the earlier Taiping leaders had condemned but later tolerated in practice. But Hung Jen-kan was also against dramatic performances, not simply because the Heavenly Father had forbidden them, as the Taiping leaders had stated earlier, but because they "deluded" the people. Such Chinese customs as the scholars' long fingernails, women's bound feet, the rituals and formalities at the traditional offerings of sacrifices, at funerals, at the meeting of guests and other occasions were inferior habits and should be abolished, not by law but by social condemnation. The moralizing of his missionary teachers is reflected in Hung Jen-kan's list of bad habits, which include bird-raising and cricket fights and the use of cosmetics by women and the wearing of jewelry. Instead, people should engage in commendable undertakings, such as the establishment of hospitals, churches, and schools, or of helping the poor and unfortunate and carrying on other charitable activities. He was against all forms of laziness, which to him was morally wrong, and his list of improvements contained many of the Western criticisms of Chinese society of the time. He held that families should not be held responsible for the criminal acts of their relatives, that all forms of slavery should be abolished, and that measures should be taken to prevent infanticide. This catalogue of reforms, which includes with equal emphasis important social problems as well as the minor matters that found missionary disapproval, showed the naïveté of the new convert, eager to preach among his Taiping compatriots in his new role everything he had learned of the advantages of the Western world as seen through the eyes of his Protestant missionary friends.

There can be little question of Hung Jen-kan's sincerity, but while his list of reforms interested and pleased the T'ien Wang, they were hardly suited to make him the new religious leader of the Taiping movement, made up in the main of followers from rural areas with little education and interest in the things Hung Jen-kan propagated. But at first they got Hung Jen-kan his position as chief administrator. In an interview in the fall of 1860, Hung Jen-kan described this reform program to a Westerner in the following exchange: "Question: Do the other kings, and especially the T'ien Wang, accept your views of social and political improvements? Answer: They are at one on this point. The proposition to introduce European improvements, railroads, steam power, and the like is looked on with great favor by the T'ien Wang in particular. He was highly pleased with the memorials on these and similar subjects, presented by his cousin on his arrival at Nanking in 1859, and insisted in consequence on his accepting the duties of chief in the administration, the post formerly filled by the eastern king." [9] Even though his ideas on Western reforms linked with his Protestant faith helped him at first to impress the T'ien Wang, one wonders whether they did not stand in the way of his success as a religious teacher with a large number of the Taiping followers and their officers.

The Kan Wang's attempt to introduce a new ideological basis into the Taiping system was to him essential not only for the success of the Taiping movement but also for his own success in his new position of leadership as chief of staff of the Taiping movement. Since he could not base his authority on supernatural connections, he had to base it on a system in which he was the teacher rather than the prophet, and the system which he tried to establish was based on this role of his as the propagator of a rational faith. On this basis the Kan Wang tried to reestablish a system of central government and of central control, which the Tung Wang had maintained but which had fallen to pieces after the Tung Wang's assassination. He was obviously well aware of the decline of the central control and of the disorganization that had resulted. Already in his first treatise, on Aids to Administration, he dealt with the problem of a centralized organization when speaking of the handling of

[9] See *NCH*, No. 524, August 11, 1860, p. 127.

appointments and impeachments. He stated that there must be no "cliques" and warned of the dangers of cliques in the military as well as in the administrative organization. With the former he must have had in mind the autonomous organizations of the generals in the field, and with the latter the groups around the T'ien Wang at the court. One of the main tasks of the central government was to eliminate such cliques. To get things in hand he established a new central administrative staff under his own direction. For a time at least he attempted through this staff to manage general administrative and military policy and bring order into the state of affairs at Nanking and in the whole Taiping movement. The administrative organization that the Kan Wang established was still in operation as late as the spring of 1861 when the Kan Wang's central authority had already been undermined. At that time he issued an official publication serving the avowed purpose of educating a Manchu deserter. It was prefaced by a list[10] of the Kan Wang's administrative organization and its staff, and one may wonder whether the listing of an organization that had already existed for some time was not a measure to strengthen its authority against the generals in the field and the relatives of the T'ien Wang in Nanking at the time when this authority had been challenged. According to this list, which, we believe, represented the original organization created by the Kan Wang at the time of his takeover, his staff consisted of a chief director of civil affairs, a deputy director of civil affairs, and the presidents of six boards. This seems to have been the only government organization existing at the time. The generals no doubt had their own military staffs, and the T'ien Wang had his attendants and relatives upon whom a bevy of titles had been bestowed, but no mention is made and no trace seems left of the old multiplicity of administrative organizations established originally at Yung-an. At that time the T'ien Wang and each of the kings had their own complete administrative staffs, and the Tung Wang's staff was the central controlling agency for them all. Now this structure had disappeared and the Kan Wang's recreated administrative organization was apparently without organizational competition. However, there seem to have been dignitaries appointed to administrative positions over which the Kan Wang had no control. We learn from the Kan Wang's confession that the most crucial post controlling funds and supplies at Nanking was—at least at a later time—in the hands of the Chang Wang, Lin Shao-chang, a friend of Li Hsiu-ch'eng, who refused to accept the Kan

[10] See document 205.

Wang's orders. Whether this post duplicated the Kan Wang's own Board of Revenue or came to replace it later, its existence illuminates his problem of bringing military and administrative matters under the effective control of his own organization.

To gain central authority he had obviously taken great pains to include in his administration all the most able men available in Nanking. The staff lists show that many of the men had scholarly qualifications and that they came from different provinces. Many were from the Yangtze area and cannot have been known to the Kan Wang before he came to Nanking. He obviously made an attempt not to build a personal following but to establish a real central organization.

That the Kan Wang was aware of the problem of re-establishing central control is very obvious not only from his organizational measures but also from his statements. In a proclamation on government reorganization[11] he referred expressly to the problem. He stated that formerly under the Tung Wang great progress had been made while at the present time there was more retreat than progress. The reason for this was that: "Today, however, the power of life and death is in the hands of individual armies, and the control of power is not in one hand." To regain central authority he emphasized that all decisions on promotions had to come from the central government alone. And altogether there must not be so many promotions since, as he points out, an inflation of titles will not help if all perish together in the end.

To carry out this administrative reorganization, the Kan Wang needed support from some of the men then in power. His appointment had of course come from the T'ien Wang himself, but this was an uncertain support because of the instability of the T'ien Wang's personality caused by his illness. As much as he had welcomed the Kan Wang, he could not overcome his fears and suspicions, and soon the Kan Wang's attempts to introduce a rational administration and bring order into the government at Nanking met with the distrust and opposition of the T'ien Wang and the relatives and men around him. The absence of any reliable support and backing by the T'ien Wang and the court made it all the more difficult for the Kan Wang to establish his authority over the generals in the field, most of whom had no inclination to give up their autonomy and control of resources of the areas they occupied. To establish some central administrative, financial, and military authority, the Kan Wang needed some backing from the military commanders

[11] See document 210.

themselves. He could hardly receive such support from Li Hsiu-ch'eng, who until the Kan Wang's arrival had been the dominant military figure and had not recognized any authority in Nanking save that of the irrational T'ien Wang himself. So the Kan Wang secured the support of the other leading military commander, Ch'en Yü-ch'eng, whom he included in his staff and who seems to have been willing to accept the new system which the Kan Wang tried to establish.

Shortly after Hung Jen-kan was made the Kan Wang the two major commanders, Ch'en Yü-ch'eng and Li Hsiu-ch'eng, were also given the titles of Wang. Ch'en became the Ying Wang, and Li the Chung Wang. These appointments were obviously meant to placate the feelings of the two generals, who until Hung Jen-kan's arrival had been on their own and who would not easily accept subordination under the newcomer who had been immediately given the title of king, heretofore reserved for the original leadership. It was then in the relationship of these three men, now all appointed to the highest rank, that Taiping politics and military strategy were fought out in these decisive years.

Li Hsiu-ch'eng, the Chung Wang, emerges from his own accounts, and from the general history of the time as the most ambitious and self-glorifying of the military commanders. His area of command—by his own decision—was closest to the capital, and he made every effort to be the chief protector and adviser of the Heavenly King. He might have succeeded in becoming the successor to the Tung Wang had he combined with his military ability the qualities of religious leadership and a grasp of administrative organization and the necessities of government. But these he obviously lacked, and thus his ambition based on his military merits only served to bring about his opposition to anyone else's efforts at central organization.

Ch'en Yü-ch'eng, on the other hand, seems to have been more willing to accept a new political leadership and in fact became the main supporter of the Kan Wang. Aside from his role as commander in the field, he accepted a position as member of the Kan Wang's staff. It appears that he actually helped to formulate for the Kan Wang some of the regulations on government reorganization,[12] and he was also a member of the Kan Wang's board for the newly organized state examinations. Though the documents are silent on any conflict between Ch'en Yü-ch'eng and Li Hsiu-ch'eng over their relationship to the new central administration of the Kan Wang, this difference has to be kept in mind in

[12] See document 210.

evaluating the military actions of both men during the critical campaign of 1860.

Although the Kan Wang had to seek support from at least one of the leading military men, his whole concept of government did not presuppose a rule by personal power based on his own group of followers—a clique of his own—but rather the establishment of what he hoped would be an organized system of administration. The orderly administration which he had in mind was to be based on what he called "rule by law." This rule by law was to take the place of what under the Tung Wang had been "rule by revelation" and also of the arbitrary decision of the generals based on their military power. In this way, Hung Jen-kan tried to overcome both the irrational actions of the T'ien Wang and the insubordination of the military commanders. If he could succeed in establishing a firm system of rules, of laws, he would be able to base his authority on it and bring order into the Taiping government. It was the only rational way in which a central government could have been established, and it was also the only possible move for a man who could not use revelations himself and did not possess his own military force. As he said: "Be it known that for a state, rule by law is a prerequisite, and for rule by law enforcement is of paramount importance. If enforcement is possible, then there can be laws; and if there are laws, then there can be a state. This is the great principle that has undergone no change for a thousand years, and it is an especially urgent matter that must not be delayed today." [13] That he had some genuine understanding of the role of law can be seen from Hung Jen-kan's essay in which he describes the function of law and states: ". . . when law is supreme, [the people] will be appreciative of the government. Thus, the people will exert a restraining force among themselves, talent and virtue will daily increase, and customs will daily improve. If laws are introduced with good intent and are universally enforced, then after a long period of strict enforcement and preservation . . . , the people will be so firmly bound together as to be indissoluble, and the empire will last eternally without degeneration." [14]

For the important task of organizing and heading a government based on law, Hung Jen-kan could profess to be the right man. In his words, "the framers of law must first of all be experienced and possess a thorough understanding of the nature of Heaven and man." And he added

[13] See document 210.
[14] For this and the following quotations see document 203.

that they must also know foreign countries and have a clear understanding of all things. Since his whole treatise was meant to indicate how well he understood the world and how well he could apply his knowledge to the problems of the Taiping government, he was obviously the man to make these laws and to head the government. This was then his claim to authority. And, possibly in order to allay fears of too rigid a rule, he added that the letter of the law could be subject to alteration, though its spirit must be unchangeable.

How naïve this plan was is a matter of argument. That the uneducated group of rebels under their irrational leader and his small-minded relatives, and under the command of ambitious but limited military men, could ever be made to accept such an orderly system of abstract rules must have seemed rather implausible to say the least. But Hung Jen-kan had strong faith in his newly-learned principles and he went about applying them in a logical way. A government based on law, in his view, could only function if the people had an understanding of the law. He stressed therefore the need of education for the people: "To lead them to the right way it is necessary to introduce education and law at the same time." Measures were included in his program that would bring the people the needed education. And with the new enthusiasm of his Western learning, Hung Jen-kan proposed that newspapers were to be established to win popular allegiance and form public opinion and to provide information on such things as commodity prices and the discussion of public affairs so that "the scholar readers will understand the trends of the time, and the merchant and farmer readers will be helped in their trade." Education and public opinion formed therefore an important part of the Kan Wang's plan.

If these plans seemed rather farfetched and perhaps not very practical, his approach to the government organization itself and to the creation of a staff for it was much more realistic. He did select the best available men in Nanking to staff the new offices that he established. But to create a more permanent and orderly official staff, he had to have a trained group of people and a way of testing their knowledge and ability, a group of candidates for office on whom he could draw to fill the positions. It is therefore quite understandable that one of the first measures taken by Hung Jen-kan was the revival and reorganization of the examination system for the selection of officials.[15] Such an examination system had already been established under the Tung Wang, and even

[15] See documents 201 and 208.

after the Tung Wang's assassination and in the chaotic time at the capital before the arrival of Hung Jen-kan it must have been continued throughout, because there still exists a list of names of the candidate who finished first in these examinations each year. But the earlier examination system under the Tung Wang and in the years after his death had been crude and not a real test of knowledge, and practically every candidate seems to have passed. The intelligence report of Tseng Kuo-fan's army had ridiculed this system as nothing more than a farce. In the Kan Wang's plans and program, the examination system now regained new importance. He attempted obviously to make it the real basis for a career in government service, as it had been in the imperial tradition. This traditional attitude enabled him also to make a special appeal to the educated upper group, the gentry, to serve the Taiping government.

This special appeal to the Chinese gentry has sometimes been interpreted as a compromise with the traditional system, which in fact meant the abandonment of the Taipings' revolutionary goal. This was by no means the Kan Wang's purpose. He wanted to create a bureaucracy staffed by an educated group, but the beliefs and ideas of this educated group were not to be the Confucian concepts of the past but the Christian beliefs that the Kan Wang tried so much to propagate. And it was the content rather than the form of the examination that would be decisive for the type of government which he tried to realize.

One of the first proclamations issued by the Kan Wang as chief of staff after his arrival and appointment in Nanking dealt therefore with the theme of the metropolitan examination in the ninth year of the Taipings.[16] He took the examination seriously enough not only to take charge of it himself but also to write an essay for this examination.[17] In this essay he deals with the Christian doctrine and gives his interpretation of the Christian belief in words that show his sincerity.

The examination papers, of which a whole series has survived, stress, aside from military and geographical factors—such as the theme of the location of the capital at Nanking—the religious doctrines as interpreted by the Kan Wang. Their generally not very high standards show that the Kan Wang's attempt to appeal to the educated to serve the Taiping government was not very successful, at least as far the quality of the

---

[16] See document 201. For a discussion of the Kan Wang's examination system, see Chien Yu-wen, *T'ai-p'ing T'ien-kuo tien-chih t'ung-k'ao*, I, 285-93.

[17] See document 202

candidates was concerned. Their number seems to have left nothing to be desired.

It is of course important to remember that the Kan Wang expressly stated that the Confucian classics—the Four Books and the Five Classics —should be a part of the educational material for the candidates to be used together with the Bible and the religious texts of the Taipings themselves. But the Confucian classics were only to be used in the re- vised form issued by the Taipings. Though these revised texts have un- fortunately not survived, we can assume that their general principles were cloaked in Taiping Christian teachings. The Kan Wang wanted to use an educated elite selected through examination for managing the government, and to that degree he was carrying on the imperial tradi- tion; this elite should be characterized not only by ranks and titles but should also be exempt from labor service. But while the form of the examinations and the privileges of those selected were similar to the imperial system, the substance of the Kan Wang's system was different. The imperial gentry was a stratum that had a uniform outlook based on the study of the Confucian classics and on the belief in the Confucian ethical principles. The Kan Wang wanted to create a Christian gentry whose common outlook would be based on the Christian teachings of the Taipings. And his examination system was truly a selection of quali- fied candidates for official service. There was not to be any autonomous educated group that was to manage affairs on its own. The principles of the Taiping organization that combined religious control and manage- ment of the administration and military affairs all in the hands of the same appointed officials were not to be changed by the Kan Wang.

Hung Jen-kan obviously regarded it as his responsibility to make sense of the Taiping system within and without, to propagate it with the Chi- nese as well as with the foreigners. He tried to rectify some of the errors and fantasies of the Taiping claims and to elevate the conflict with the Confucian system to a higher level. He corrected the Taiping calendar system,[18] and he tried to explain away some of the fantasies of Hung Hsiu-ch'üan, for instance, the Heavenly King's claim that he was the Son of God. Hung Jen-kan quoted from the Chinese classics, and he recognized the sages as great men but thought it incorrect to worship them.[19] He attempted to have the Taiping system and religion recog-

---

[18] See document 204.
[19] See document 205.

nized by the foreigners, especially the foreign missionaries. In his early years he had laid the foundation for a favorable interpretation of the Taiping movement, as given in Hamberg's book, and had come to Nanking to correct the Taiping errors from the point of view of his missionary teachers. After his arrival in Nanking he cultivated the contact with foreign missionaries and also in his treatises tried to advise the T'ien Wang on how to deal with foreign governments. His attempts fall in the crucial period of 1859 to 1860, the time when the missionary attitude and policy of the foreign governments toward the Taipings underwent a critical test. In his treatises on government, Hung Jen-kan suggested that missionaries and technical advisers be permitted to come to Nanking and to the area under Taiping control. Obviously he thought that his proposals for westernization could only be carried out with Western support. He boasted of his own acquaintance and friendship with foreigners, and named a number of them including James Legge, Joseph Edkins, and Alexander Wylie. There were other foreign missionaries who visited Nanking, such men as T. P. Crawford, J. L. Holmes, and Hartwell of the American Baptists,[20] Josiah Cox of the English Wesleyans,[21] and others. Issachar J. Roberts, also an American Baptist, from whom Hung Hsiu-ch'üan had received some instruction in Christianity in 1847, joined the Taipings at Nanking in October, 1860. He was offered the title of Foreign Secretary of State, with the duties of examining foreign criminals and directing mercantile affairs,[22] but repeatedly refused to accept the position.

To educate the Taiping leaders and the Heavenly King, Hung Jen-kan described and characterized the different Western countries he knew of. Of special interest is his indicated preference for "the Flowery Flag Country, or America . . . , the most righteous and wealthy country of all," whose system of electing a President and of voting by "officials and people of virtue and wisdom" had greatly impressed him. He knew of the problem of equality between nations and the importance of recog-

[20] See L. S. Foster, *Fifty Years in China* (Nashville, Tenn.: Bayless-Pullen Co., 1909), pp. 109 ff.

[21] See Kenneth S. Latourette, *A History of Christian Missions in China* (New York: Macmillan, 1929), p. 293.

[22] See document 285. Roberts, whom Latourette describes as eccentric (p. 219), and Lindley, who is described as "irritable, peevish, inconsistent, and vacillating" (see p. 566), left Nanking in January, 1862, denouncing the Taipings, thus ending the last phase of favorable missionary attitude toward the Taipings. By that time the Taiping government's relations with Westerners, except for some adventurers, had already deteriorated.

nizing this equality before any official relations could be established. He stressed that in the relationship with England, for instance, the Taipings should use the concept of "equal status" and should not use such insulting expressions as "the payment of homage from ten thousand directions," and other similar terms indicating foreign submission to a Chinese rule of the world.[23]

The program that the Kan Wang developed when he was so suddenly appointed to the highest administrative position in the Taiping system was thus far-reaching and coherent. He realized the major problems and tried to find an answer. If some of his ideas seemed impractical and naïve, the whole program appears impressive, especially when one remembers with how little experience and preparation Hung Jen-kan suddenly faced such a crucial test of all his abilities. And if he failed, his plans were at least a rational answer to the problems of the Taiping Rebellion. His attempts to revive the movement, or rather to give it a new form, to reorganize the government under his direction, and to develop a new military strategy deserve far more attention than they have heretofore received.

In his attempts to open relations with foreign governments and with foreign missionaries, Hung Jen-kan could not bring the mentally ill Heavenly King to understand, let alone accept and put into practice, Hung Jen-kan's ideas and proposals. The concept of equality in the relations of modern nation-states was never even understood by the T'ien Wang, who continued to live with the idea of his special mission. And the impression which the foreign envoys who came to Nanking received there did not give them any confidence in the Taipings as a government with which one could establish foreign relations. In the meantime, the ratification of the treaties with the imperial government in Peking in 1860 marked a political decision of the foreign governments to continue to deal with the Ch'ing dynasty. Any possibility that the foreign governments would cooperate more closely with the Taipings, as Hung Jen-kan had obviously hoped, would have ended then. But this was also the time of general disillusionment with the Taipings and their religion among the foreign missionaries. At the beginning of August, 1860, Hung Jen-kan met in Soochow with two foreign missionaries, Joseph Edkins and Griffith John. He had given them his "New Treatise on Aids to Administration," and had told them about the T'ien Wang's religious studies, his reading of the Bible and of *Pilgrim's Progress,* all of which im-

[23] See document 203.

pressed the visitors very favorably. When another missionary, Holmes, came to Nanking later in the month, he had been prepared to gain a favorable impression. But when he met the Taiping leaders there he was shocked by the "revolting idolatry" of the T'ien Wang and his court. The T'ien Wang gave Holmes one of his edicts,[24] which showed again the T'ien Wang's fantastic notions and gave new proof that he still regarded himself as the divine ruler of the world. In the long run it would have been impossible for Hung Jen-kan to keep from foreign observers the facts about the T'ien Wang and his beliefs and about the situation at the Taiping court. His own beliefs and ideas were of no avail as long as he could not impose them on the leader of the movement. As it was, he failed not only to impress the Heavenly King but also the Taiping commanders and followers, who by this time showed little concern or interest in problems of the Taiping religion.

Hung Jen-kan well realized that the ideas he tried to present and the government he tried to establish needed the backing of men with actual power. Since Li Hsiu-ch'eng was his natural opponent, he had turned to Ch'en Yü-ch'eng and had made him a key man on his staff; but in the absence of a true backing by the Heavenly King, the support of one of the military men was not enough to overcome the resistance of the others, especially since the challenge to his autonomous power seems to have turned Li Hsiu-ch'eng against the new chief of staff. And yet the Kan Wang attempted to assume a leading role in planning the military campaigns; and the strategy agreed upon under his guidance was initially successful in reversing the critical military situation of the Taipings. In May, 1860, the Taiping armies succeeded for the second time in breaking the siege of their capital at Nanking and gaining a major victory over the government forces. This victory was accomplished through a combined strategy of the military commanders, Li Hsiu-ch'eng, Li Shih-hsien, Ch'en Yü-ch'eng, and Yang Fu-ch'ing, which could only have been the result of joint planning. According to Hung Jen-kan, he had proposed the strategic plan of this battle and discussed it with the others beforehand.[25] And though Li Hsiu-ch'eng in his confession gives no credit to Hung Jen-kan at all, it is hardly possible to see how the different moves could have been made without such previous consultation. A major part of the plan was the diversionary move of Li Hsiu-ch'eng's army by an attack on Hangchow. This move enticed the imperialist gen-

---

[24] See document 238.
[25] See his confession, document 385.

erals to divert troops for Hangchow's defense, whereupon Li Hsiu-ch'eng's army rushed back to attack the government camp from the south. At the same instant, Ch'en Yü-ch'eng, who had fought at Anking, hurried back and attacked the government camp from the north. This coordinated strategy, which led to victory, could not have been worked out by any of the Taiping generals on his own, and it is only logical to believe that Hung Jen-kan was the moving spirit behind it.

Right after this victory Hung Jen-kan and the generals held a council of war, and a major strategic plan was adopted which, if successful, might have greatly changed the Taipings' position.[26] Two proposals were made by two of the generals. Ch'en spoke for a campaign to relieve Anking, a proposal which is understandable for him since it concerned a major city in Ch'en's area of control. Li Shih-hsien proposed operations in Fukien and Chekiang, provinces in which he had an interest as areas of supply. But Hung Jen-kan combined these proposals with his own ideas into a major strategic plan for which he got the consent of Li Hsiu-ch'eng and the others. The Kan Wang's plan envisaged a first move to the southeast to occupy Soochow and Hangchow with the obvious intention of securing the rear for the main drive. This main drive was to be a vast pincers movement on both sides of the Yangtze to regain the control of the upper river from the Hunan army, to safeguard the capital, and to re-establish Taiping control over the Yangtze area. This plan was to counter Tseng Kuo-fan's strategy and was to reopen the Yangtze valley to the Taiping forces. To carry out this strategy, one army was to move north of the river beyond Anking into Hupeh province, and then cut through to the river at Huang-chou below Wu-ch'ang. This was to be Ch'en Yü-ch'eng's army. This part of the campaign was a further development of Ch'en's idea of moving upriver on the north shore to relieve the siege of Anking. The second arm of the pincer was to be formed by the army of Li Hsiu-ch'eng. After occupying Soochow and Hangchow he was to move along the south side of the Yangtze into Kiangsi and Hupeh provinces to reach the river from the south at the same point that Ch'en's army was to reach it from the north. After the two armies had met they were to fight their way on into Hupeh province and to clear the area on both sides of the upper Yangtze of the Hunan army. To facilitate this move it was hoped that some twenty steamships could be gotten from Shanghai and employed on the river to open it for the Taipings' communications and supply.

[20] See document 385.

This strategic plan was to serve several purposes. One was to secure Anking. Another was to regain the lower Yangtze area in Kiangsu and Chekiang, which was important to the Taipings as a source of tax income and as an access to Western supplies. It also offered an opportunity of obtaining Western ships for this campaign. But these parts of the campaign were preparatory and of secondary importance. The main assumption of the strategic plan was that the fate of Nanking depended on the control by the Taipings of the upper Yangtze area. And the main part of the plan was the two-pronged attack on both shores of the Yangtze that was to encircle this area and clear it of the enemy.[27]

After initial successes, the plan failed. The reason for the failure was that halfway through the campaign Li Hsiu-ch'eng decided on his own not to carry it through. Chen Yü-ch'eng had reached the Yangtze on the north side—as agreed—in March of 1861. Since Li Hsiu-ch'eng had not yet arrived on the south shore, Ch'en left his subordinate, Lai Wen-kuang, in command and moved downstream along the river to attack the Hunan army besieging Anking. He thus carried out his part of the plan. Li Hsiu-ch'eng marched, as planned, through Chekiang, where he took Soochow and Hangchow, and from there through Kiangsi into Hupeh. He arrived at the Yangtze between Wu-ch'ang and Hsing-kuo in June of 1861. But from then on he disregarded his part of the over-all strategic plan. Instead of connecting with the Taiping forces to the north of the river, he turned back to Kiangsi and there collected some of the remnants of the army of Shih Ta-k'ai and incorporated them in his own force. Then he moved back to Chekiang to build up there his own regional control. Ch'en Yü-ch'eng on the north shore was thus left to his own resources in his continued fight to relieve Anking and to maintain the Taiping position on the upper Yangtze.

The reasons Li Hsiu-ch'eng gave for turning back and abandoning the plan was that he found the Yangtze River too high and had difficulties in communicating with Ch'en Yü-ch'eng and his subordinate on the north side of the river. He therefore did not know what was going on on their side. That he sought information is apparent from the letter that he sent to Lai Wen-kuang.[28] And that the Yangtze carried high water at the time is confirmed by the account given by Hung Jen-kan, who

---

[27] See document 385. For a discussion see Chien, *Ch'üan-shih,* III, 1743-45.

[28] See document 254.

was certainly not willing to cover up for Li Hsiu-ch'eng's action.[29] But this was hardly enough reason to disobey the plan of campaign that had been agreed upon and to act independently without consulting or informing either Ch'en Yü-ch'eng or the government at Nanking. Li's decision to turn back and give up the plan of campaign was, in Hung Jen-kan's view, the decisive mistake that led to the loss of Anking and to the military defeat of the Taiping movement.[30]

The Kan Wang's view was shared by Tseng Kuo-fan, who himself regarded the control of the upper Yangtze area as crucial in the battle with the Taipings. To him, Li Hsiu-ch'eng's retreat must have come as a surprise, and later, when he had captured Li he was obviously interested to learn from him why he had made this move, which must have seemed to Tseng a major strategic blunder. The answer Li gave to that specific question in his interrogation was as weak as the argument given in his written confession. Li confessed orally to having been afraid of the opposing forces of the Hunan general Pao Ch'ao, Tseng Kuo-fan's commander. This regard for the strength of the Hunan forces may have been an implied flattery for Tseng Kuo-fan by his prisoner, who at this time still tried to save his life by accommodating his captor, but it was hardly convincing, and the interrogator confronted Li with the fact that his own forces at the time were larger than those of General Pao Ch'ao, who had not yet even come close to Li when Li turned away. To this argument Li simply answered that he felt insecure because his army's rear might be threatened.

[29] See document 385.

[30] See document 385. The question of the responsibility for the failure of the Taipings' strategic plan has been discussed by a number of historians. Chien Yu-wen, in his outstanding, most recent work, *T'ai-p'ing T'ien-kuo ch'üan-shih,* has divided the share of responsibility between Ch'en Yü-ch'eng and Li Hsiu-ch'eng. See Chien, *Ch'üan-shih,* III, 1853 and 1875-76. Following Lindley, Chien criticizes Ch'en for not carrying the attack westward to Wu-han on his own when Li Hsiu-ch'eng had not yet arrived, and believes that part of the reason for Ch'en's hesitation was that he was cautioned against an attack on Wu-han by three Britishers, H. S. Parkes and two others. Ch'en's return to the relief of Anking is interpreted as a partial abandonment of the original plan. It seems to us that, though naturally concerned with the critical situation at Anking, Ch'en had not given up the plan, had left his subordinate at the river, and was waiting for Li's support, which never came. Chien Yu-wen shares our view of Li's major responsibility for the failure of the plan, which Li himself admitted at the time. And Chien holds with us that Li's unwillingness to come to the rescue of Ch'en Yü-ch'eng and the city of Anking not only spoiled the plan of attack but led to disaster.

It is obvious from Li's moves that he actually was more concerned with strengthening his own position than carrying through the planned strategy, short-sighted as his policy may have been. The augmentation of his own forces through the recruitment of Shih Ta-k'ai's men and the retreat to his base in Chekiang indicate that Li was more interested in building up his own military strength and regional base than in participating in the over-all battle. The tone and content of his letters to his subordinates support this view. He thought and spoke of himself as if he were the only leader of the Taipings' military forces. He claimed for himself the whole credit for the strategic plan which liberated Nanking from siege in 1860 and for the execution of this plan. He spoke of his own strategy for the Yangtze campaign, never mentioning that there was a joint plan.

Nor was this the first time that Li had acted on his own. In May, 1860, he had already sent his emissaries north of the Yangtze to establish contact and cooperate with the Nien leader Chang Lo-hsing without, as far as we know, bothering to consult his colleague Ch'en Yü-ch'eng, whose army operated north of the river. Ch'en had himself a few months before established cooperation with the Nien forces, a fact which is ignored in Li's letter to the Nien leader. In all these statements of the time and in his later confession Li spoke as an independent regional commander rather than as a Taiping general responsible to his government and carrying out a joint plan of strategy. The result of Li's move was that the Taiping strategy failed, that Anking fell to Tseng Kuo-fan, that Ch'en himself was defeated and killed, and that Li's own redoubt could save neither the Taiping capital and government nor himself from final destruction.

Li Hsiu-ch'eng, the Chung Wang, has been regarded by many contemporaries and historians as the most brilliant of the Taiping military leaders during this time and as the hero of the Taiping movement. Li was a very able commander, whose rapid marches and repeated victories proved his great ability as a tactical leader. But it was Li who through this disobedience to the over-all strategy in the upper Yangtze campaign spoiled the Taipings' last chance for a military victory. The importance of the upper Yangtze was understood by the Kan Wang, who planned this campaign. It was also understood by Tseng Kuo-fan, who concentrated on this area in his strategic planning. And it was even brought up again in 1862 when Li Hsiu-ch'eng attacked Shanghai and when he received a letter from one Huang Wan (or Wang T'ao), who urged the Taipings not to attack Shanghai but the Hunan army on the upper Yangtze.[31] It is by accident that this letter has become more widely known and discussed than the original strategic plan of the Kan Wang, devised two years earlier when there still might have been a possibility of success through such military action.

The reasons for Li's actions are not far to seek. He was obviously jealous of the Kan Wang's authority, and wanted himself to be the first man in the service of the T'ien Wang, as his self-appraisal in his confession clearly indicates. The Kan Wang is almost entirely ignored in Li's account of the Taiping story. When Li was directly questioned about him, however, he showed how much he despised the Kan Wang. Li disposed of him in one sentence: "None of the books compiled by the false Kan Wang were worthy of reading for Chief Li." [32]

Since in his administration and even in the examination system the Kan Wang had used the support of Ch'en Yü-ch'eng, the only commander who could compete with Li Hsiu-ch'eng's ability, Li was not anxious to cooperate with Ch'en in the joint campaign. After Li had taken Soochow and Chia-hsing in Chekiang, he made no move to carry out the second part of the strategic plan to move up the Yangtze. He then received a "stern decree from the T'ien Wang," sending him upstream "to sweep the north." [33] This order, which must have originated from the Kan Wang, forced the Chung Wang to proceed to Hupeh as planned. But then he turned back, and the campaign collapsed. Ch'en was left without support and, as his letters indicate, was frustrated and bitter about the bad treatment he received. Anking was lost to the Hunan army in September, 1861. Ch'en Yü-ch'eng was killed, and his Taiping army destroyed in May of 1862. And one must agree with the Kan Wang's judgment that it was as a result of Li Hsiu-ch'eng's retreat that "the whole plan to be carried out was thus frustrated." [34]

The Kan Wang's attempt at military leadership was thus condemned to failure because of his inability to establish control and authority over this most powerful, vain, and self-willed of the Taiping commanders. And as the Kan Wang's position was undermined in the field of military strategy, so he also lost out in the battle at Nanking for the control of a reorganized central government. In the spring of 1861 the

---

[31] See document 259.
[32] See document 383.
[33] See document 382.
[34] See document 385.

Kan Wang seems to have lost his position at the court. He was no longer the "chief of staff," but had become the "assistant chief of staff," and in some of the documents[35] we find his name listed after a number of brothers and nephews of the T'ien Wang, who thus outranked the Kan Wang.

The order of the listing of names was in this system an important indication of the authority held by each person. After Hung Jen-kan's arrival in Nanking and his appointment as Kan Wang, he had been listed in the hierarchy as following the Tung Wang and the Hsi Wang. Both these men were dead, and while at a later time their positions seem to have been taken up by their younger sons, these boys did not play more than a symbolic role. But in 1861 the proclamations of the T'ien Wang listed Hung's close relatives before the Kan Wang and showed that these men had by that time gained a closer influence over the T'ien Wang than the Kan Wang had; and they used it to turn the T'ien Wang's already suspicious mind against the Kan Wang, who with his plans of an orderly government may have interfered with their free access to the resources of the Taiping treasury, which they used for a luxurious life at the court.

The clearest indication of the Kan Wang's demotion was his loss of the control of the seal for official proclamations. After the Kan Wang became chief of staff, all memorials had to bear his seal; but in February, 1861, an edict issued in the name of the son of the T'ien Wang, the Young Monarch, proclaimed that "henceforth all memorials from within and without shall not be affixed with Uncle Kan's golden seal," and it was expressly stated that the reason for this restriction was that it was "feared that among the people rumors may arise that he is following in the footsteps of the Tung Wang." [36] The fear of a repetition of the Tung Wang's usurpation of all power was thus exploited by the T'ien Wang's brothers and other relatives to undermine the Kan Wang's position. Hemmed in by his rivals at the court, the Kan Wang was therefore greatly handicapped in carrying through any rational measures for the government.

The T'ien Wang withdrew at this time more and more into his harem, and his mind was, as is indicated by his writings, rapidly declining. No statement on government matters appeared during this period under his name. His proclamations were fantastic religious state-

[35] E.g., document 225.
[36] Proclamation 15, document 226.

ments, repeating the dogma of his kinship with God and Jesus.[37] He had dreams and visions, and on one occasion ordered that the Taiping Heavenly Kingdom should be renamed the Lord's Heavenly Kingdom (*Shang-ti T'ien-kuo*), a command observed by no one. The Kan Wang himself admitted this situation in an interview with a Western visitor who asked: "Does the T'ien Wang determine all state matters?" and received the answer: "Yes, but on most affairs not connected with religion he looks with contempt, remarking that they are 'affairs of this world,' and not heavenly affairs (*t'ien ts'ing*). He often approves of memorials and propositions of a 'worldly' kind at a glance, and without careful examination." It was finally proclaimed in Nanking that God had told the T'ien Wang's wife in a dream that the T'ien Wang was no longer to attend to worldly matters.[38] Deprived of the authority to act as the head of the government and handicapped by his dependence on a monarch who could no longer be induced to rational action, the Kan Wang was in an extremely difficult position and could hardly have carried through any measure that would have restored a reasonably well functioning government.

One figure at the court who now gained some importance was the Young Monarch, who, because of the incapacitation of his father, could be used as a front by anyone trying to assume authority. He had been used in this way by the T'ien Wang's relatives to reduce the Kan Wang's power. But he could also be used by the Kan Wang for issuing urgent government edicts and proclamations, which the T'ien Wang refused to handle. The Young Monarch, a boy in his early teens, who had only known the palace life at Nanking and the uncles surrounding him, was a pliant tool in whose name a number of proclamations were now issued.[39] These documents seem to have been drafted for him by the Kan Wang, who overcame the T'ien Wang's suspicion of this procedure with the argument that the Young Monarch had to be educated in government affairs. But some of the edicts issued in the Young Monarch's name were dictated by others and also by the T'ien Wang himself, who had his son sign some of his irrational edicts.

Confusion at the court combined with the autonomy of the military commanders prevented any coordinated program or plan which could have saved the Taiping movement. The Kan Wang's courageous at-

[37] See document 225.
[38] See Forrest, p. 191.
[39] See document 224, *et al.*

tempts to restore the faith, to provide order in government, and to im-
plement a central strategy which might have revived the original élan
of the Taiping movement failed, and in spite of continued successes in
some of the battles the Taipings were doomed. The Kan Wang, who
must have realized this situation, decided to leave the capital himself
and to join the Taiping forces on the south side of the Yangtze in an
obvious attempt to strengthen his position by assuming himself command of troops and gaining military experience.[40] He brought with him
a part of his administrative staff, including his chief director of civil
affairs. How much he actually directed military campaigns of the forces
which he had joined is difficult to determine. The record of this venture
only indicated the use he made of his stay to propagandize the troops
and also the Confucian scholars, whom he still hoped to convert to the
Taiping cause. His "Proclamation to the Soldiers" does not have the
tone of a commander but rather that of a preacher. His appeals to the
scholars are attempts to make the Taiping doctrine acceptable to the educated, whose support the Kan Wang still tried to gain. He played on
feelings of Chinese racial pride and contempt for the "Tartar barbarians."
He conceded that the reading of the classics and of history was useful
because there was a possibility of finding guiding principles in them.
But he stressed at the same time that "heavenly inspiration" was more
important as a source of ideas than these traditional writings. He was
against the empty phrases of the flowery language used in Confucian
writing. He appreciated Chinese history, but his two greatest heroes
were men who came from the common people and established Chinese
dynasties—the Han and the Ming.

The Kan Wang also wrote a poem for the local commanders, following the example of the Tung Wang, who had written poems of inspira-
tional appeal for his followers. The Kan Wang thus reverts to the
appeal of the charismatic leadership of the early days of the Taiping
movement. But he makes no attempt to make himself the object of
worship. It was the Tung Wang whom the soldiers were to venerate.
The Kan Wang quoted the T'ien Wang as saying: "First of all, acknowl-
edge the grace of Heaven, the Sovereign, and the Tung Wang, and
Hsi Wang . . ." The Kan Wang had thus been forced to accept the
use of the traditional Taiping doctrine in propaganda for the army even
though he himself was not attempting to become another Taiping
deity.

[40] See document 206.

After the Taipings' strategic plan of the Yangtze campaign had been abandoned, Li Hsiu-ch'eng remained the strongest and still the most successful and therefore most powerful of the Taiping commanders. His reoccupation of Hangchow at the end of 1861 and of much of the area surrounding the city gave Li the base and the financial support he wanted. He and his commanders tried their best to develop the parts of Kiangsu and Chekiang that they controlled. They urged the people to return to their occupations.[41] They warned their soldiers not to disturb the people.[42] They tried to re-establish local government organizations, compiled family registers, and asked the people to select their local officials from "persons well known to the villagers and neighbors." And of course they collected taxes.[43]

By this time the Taiping government and the forces and followers at Nanking were dependent on the supplies which could be shipped to the city from the commanders of nearby occupied areas, and they became therefore more and more dependent upon Li as their only source of supply.[44] But this was no longer a centrally controlled orderly system of taxation. Li took what he wanted and delivered as much to the capital as he chose. The relationship between Li and the capital was also indicated by an edict that praised Li for the delivery of support and urged him to continue to send funds. The edict was a plea for help rather than an order.[45] How much personal wealth Li accumulated is also shown by the fact that when he returned to the capital he was forced to disgorge some of his wealth for the support of the group in Nanking, a far cry from the sacred treasury or any orderly system of financial control.

To gain the financial support from the areas occupied, Li as well as other Taiping commanders relied mainly on collecting land tax in kind and money. But there was also income from likin and other commercial taxes.[46] In order to get this income, the Taipings had to try to restore peace and confidence in the rural areas and permit trade. It is quite clear that during this period the Taiping commanders no longer attempted

[41] See documents 214, 215, 216, 219, 237, 238.
[42] See document 223.
[43] See documents 213, 221, 232, 233, 234, 241, 244, 246, 344, 345, 351-56, 366, 368, and 371.
[44] See document 382.
[45] See document 217.
[46] See documents 343, 346, 347, and 348. For a discussion of the Taiping tax system, see Chien Yu-wen, *T'ai-p'ing T'ien-kuo tien-chih t'ung-k'ao*, II, 665-84.

to carry through any changes in the rural situation. They had never put into practice their land law, which prescribed an equal distribution of land for use and the collection by the government of all products beyond the immediate needs for food and seed. But they had at first driven away the landlords, so that in those areas where tenancy was widespread the rent payment was discontinued. Now they even gave up this part of their policy, and not only permitted landlords to collect rent from their tenants but used the landlords as the main source of tax income. As a notification stated: "The tenant farmers should pay their rent as usual, in order that this rent income may be used for paying taxes in money and grain." [47] Some of the Taiping documents indicate that the Taiping leaders were specially concerned with protecting wealthy families.[48] "Rural administrators" and local officers were warned not to disturb these families or to extort money from them. These families were encouraged to maintain friendly relations with the Taiping leaders in the cities. The Taipings obviously tried to prevent looting by local officers in order to gain a sustained financial support from these families. The amount of tax levied by the Taipings may have varied from place to place. An English visitor reported that the Taiping land taxes were three times as high as those imposed by the imperial government.[49] But other data, including Taiping material, support the claim that the Taipings were collecting a much lighter tax from the land-owners than the imperial government had.[50]

It is difficult, therefore, to generalize on conditions within the Taiping area. Not only do the reports conflict according to the outlook and partisanship of the writer, but the conditions themselves must have varied greatly during different years and under different commanders. Li Hsiu-ch'eng himself, who maintains in his confession that he tried to do everything in his power to spare the people from suffering and maintain an orderly system, admits that some of his commanders—and they happen to be those with whom he later fell out—were corrupt exploiters. Foreigners who traveled up the Yangtze through the Taiping territory described the Taiping movement as a destructive one which "annihilates trade, alike native and foreign; it scatters large and flourishing com-

[47] See documents 233 and 234.
[48] See document 245.
[49] *Parliamentary Papers,* April 8, 1862, No. 4, enclosure.
[50] See, for instance, document 234.

munities, and blasts the peace and prospects of the empire."[51] Michie reports on his trip up the Yangtze and on his stay in Nanking with Taiping leaders: "I tried to prove to them the folly of burning and destroying towns and villages, and stopping trade at its fountainhead, as without trade they could never prosper. They assented, but said it was difficult. . . . The fact is they lived on loot."[52]

On the other hand, visitors to areas under the control of Li Hsiu-ch'eng gave an entirely different picture. Forrest, for instance, made the following statement concerning trade near Soochow, Li Hsiu-ch'eng's stronghold from June, 1860, to November, 1863: "Observing a large number of vessels evidently trading between Shanghae and Soochow, I made inquiry and found that there exists a constituted society, having friends among the contending parties; for heavy consideration the boats are allowed to trade unmolested to the large number of nearly 5,000."[53] Lindley, an admirer of Li Hsiu-ch'eng, gives a more favorable picture of Taiping policy as follows: "In striking contrast to the excessively corrupt Imperialist customs the Ti-ping revenue organization was just, regular, and simple. Throughout every part of Ti-ping-tien-kwoh but one custom-house was established at each town or village where trade was carried on. The rate of tariff has always been moderate, and the great advantage of the system consisted in being able to clear goods by one payment, upon which a pass would be given to take them free of further charge or hindrance to their destination. The Ti-ping government deserved no little credit for the simplicity and effectiveness of their Board of Revenue, and it is mainly due to that branch of the administration that the valuable silk trade *increased* and continued progressing so favorably during their possession of the producing districts [in Kiangsu and Chekiang]. . . . Every customs established in the late Ti-ping territory was composed of a superintendent, several deputies, and a very efficient staff of surveyors, clerks, and weighers, and at places frequented by Europeans, one or more interpreters were always found. Rice and other grain were quite free of duty, and that upon dried and preserved provisions was very low. All other produce and general merchandise were moderately taxed, either by tariff or *ad valorem*."[54] But these

[51] "Memorandum by the Rev. W. Muirhead," *Parliamentary Papers,* April 8, 1862, No. 7, enclosure 2, p. 19.
[52] *Ibid.,* No. 4, enclosure.
[53] *Parliamentary Papers,* 1861, No. 6, enclosure 7, p. 27.
[54] Lindley, pp. 485-86.

favorable and unfavorable foreign remarks mainly concerned the opportunities for trade in the areas under the Taipings. As far as land tax
is concerned, the Taipings seem, at least in the Yangtze River area, to
have taken what they could get. The lot of the population depended
on the attitude and the needs of the local commander and the closeness
to whatever battles occurred. Especially in the Yangtze area the Taipings
seem to have lost by this time whatever appeal their promise of a new
order had held for the discontented.

In contrast to the Taipings, who had lost their last chance at a
centrally directed program and strategy, their opponents planned and
carried through a co-ordinated plan of military action backed by a program of tax relief that was aimed at gaining the support of the population in crucial areas. The leader of this campaign against the Taipings,
Tseng Kuo-fan, was in 1860 appointed by the imperial government as
governor-general of the central Yangtze provinces with whose defense
he was entrusted. By this appointment the Ch'ing government had
broken its own long-established rule that no official should be sent to
serve in his home province. It was the last step taken by the government
in giving up its whole system of checks and balances, meant to maintain
secure control over the administrative staff. Tseng Kuo-fan, who had
been permitted to recruit his own troops from his fellow provincials,
select his own staff, and collect his own funds, was now given the official
administrative position which, combined with his own organization,
gave him in fact autonomous regional power. The taxes he collected
and the likin he raised went now directly to the support of his armies.
While imperial confirmation of the appointments he proposed was still
necessary, there would be little chance that his proposals would be re-
jected. Officially, he was still responsible for an accounting of his funds,
but the records indicate that his accounting was a mere formality. For
the likin he collected, the government had no records to evaluate his
take, let alone his expenses.

But Tseng Kuo-fan had from the beginning realized that his own
organization could not be large enough for a campaign that was to
encompass the whole area of central China. On his initiative and with
his support, a second regional force was established in the lower Yangtze
area by Li Hung-chang and his Huai army, and Li too was appointed
governor-general of the area he controlled with his troops. A third such
regional organization was established south of the Yangtze in Chekiang
by Tso Tsung-t'ang, a former member of Tseng Kuo-fan's staff. The

central control of the Ch'ing government over the administration in the critical area had thus ended. But under Tseng Kuo-fan's direction there was a close coordination of the anti-Taiping forces and their policy, their planning, and their execution of military strategy. In spite of their regional decentralization, the anti-Taiping side had therefore the military and political coordination that the Taipings lacked.

In this strategy Tseng Kuo-fan had the same concept of the importance of the upper Yangtze area that the Kan Wang had shown in his plan. And it is from Tseng Kuo-fan that we receive the clearest indication of the disposition of the Taiping armies with which he had to deal. In a letter written in the spring of 1861 to his brother Tseng Kuo-ch'üan, his subordinate commander in the battle against the Taipings, Tseng Kuo-fan described the position of the Taiping armies as follows: north of the Yangtze: Ch'en Yü-ch'eng; south of the Yangtze: Li Hsiu-ch'eng in charge of Soochow, Ch'ang-chou, and Chen-chiang and at that time penetrating into Kiangsi; Li Shih-hsien in charge of Hui-chou in Anhwei, Chia-hsing in Chekiang, etc.; Yang Fu-ch'ing in charge of Ning-kuo in Anhwei; Huang Wen-chin in charge of Wuhu in Anhwei; and Liu Kuan-fang in charge of Ch'ih-chou, etc. The latter three were Li Hsiu-ch'eng's associates. Each of these armies had a strength of from 80,000 to over 100,000 men. It was this situation with which Tseng had to deal, and he seems to have counted firmly on the Taiping armies carrying through their two-pronged attack toward the upper Yangtze region. When Li Hsiu-ch'eng retreated, however, Tseng could follow his own strategy of first gaining control of the upper Yangtze region and from there pushing the attack downriver against Nanking. When Li Hsiu-ch'eng's successes at Soochow and in the province of Kiangsu alarmed the local gentry and officials, who clamored for military help by Tseng's forces to reconquer these cities, and when pressure in that regard was brought upon him by the court, Tseng stood firm by his strategy. He justified his plan in the following way: "When Soochow and Ch'ang-chou were not yet lost, soldiers should have been sent for relief in the hope that these territories might be kept unmolested. But after Soochow and Ch'ang-chou were lost, then an over-all strategy should have been devised in order to select strategic points for initial attacks and to seek the building of a foundation for a foothold. Since ancient times, in order to suppress rebels in Kiangnan, one must first control the upper stream [of the Yangtze]; then, like water pouring from tiles, success can be achieved. Since Hsien-feng third year [1853], when Chin-ling was lost, Hsiang Yung, Ho-ch'un, and others have all directed their troops to attack from the east. Their original purpose was to protect Kiangsu and Chekiang, and at the proper times they made their appropriate moves. Yet their numerous advances have been met with numerous defeats, and they have so far been unable to recover Chin-ling but in turn have lost Soochow and Ch'ang-chou. It was not that their military strength was weak but that they did not enjoy topographical advantages. Now that the southeast is split, the rebels' courage has been strengthened. In order to recover Soochow and Ch'ang-chou, a southern force has to advance from Chekiang and a northern force from Chin-ling. To recover Chin-ling, we must first recover Anking and Ho-chou on the northern bank [of the Yangtze] and Ch'ih-chou and Wuhu on the southern bank. Through this measure, then, the situation will be that of controlling the bottom from the top. If we continue to try to attack from the east, the advantageous position of staying inside rather than outside, and being host rather than guest, will be lost. It will necessarily lead to our following a beaten track without an end in sight. This official's forces, numbering over 10,000 men, have advanced to the foot of the city wall of Anking. They have dug deep trenches, built strong fortresses, and have dredged a long moat. If they should be removed, then To-lung-a's forces of Ying-shan and Hou-shan would all have to retreat. When these forces retreat, their morale will be shattered and the morale of the rebels strengthened. Not only will the Hupeh border be hard to protect, but the forces of the northern route of Yüan Chia-san and Weng T'ung-shu will also suffer by isolation. Thus the forces at Anking are at present related with the entire picture of the southern Huai and will in the future be the basis for the recovery of Chin-ling. This is the actual situation which, after repeated consideration, leads this official to say that the siege of Anking should not suddenly be removed."[55]

Tseng Kuo-fan adhered firmly to this plan of strategy, and to him Li Hsiu-ch'eng's retreat was an unexpected aid to his plan. It is therefore no wonder that when he captured this general he was interested in finding out the reason for this blunder by the enemy.

After Anking was taken, Tseng carried out his plan of attack on three fronts against the Taiping positions. The major force of the Hunan army moved down the river from Anking toward Nanking. This force

[55] Tseng, *Tsou-kao*, 11:44a-b.

was led by Tseng Kuo-ch'üan. Li Hung-chang and his Huai army were based on Shanghai and from there moved westward to recover Soochow. Tso Tsung-t'ang's forces campaigned in the south in Chekiang to reconquer this important supply area from the Taipings. The importance of Li Hung-chang's position was that he controlled the custom and likin income from the growing foreign and inland trade. This income, denied to the Taipings, not only financed Li Hung-chang's armies but also provided support for the armies of Tseng Kuo-fan. The roles of the armies of Li Hung-chang and Tso Tsung-t'ang were as important in the battle for funds and supplies as for strategic position. And since the Taipings had lost the upper Yangtze they were now entirely on the defensive. As the records·show, it was the economic blockade as well as military defeat that eventually led to the fall of Nanking and the collapse of the movement. Their internal dissension, the lack of centralized leadership, the vast number of newly created and autonomous kings, the economic starvation, the breakdown of morale and of all faith in the movement, all these contributed to the end of the revolution.

This end came as much as a result of internal disintegration as through the clearly conceived and well executed plan of Tseng Kuo-fan. Early in 1863 Tseng Kuo-fan was willing to predict in his report the imminent defeat of the Taipings. His account of the situation indicates that he understood the breakdown of the Taiping plan and program and was therefore certain of the outcome: "In the early days of the Kwangsi rebels, they generally had regulations and principles. They were capable of prohibiting rape, and they pacified the people, who were forced to stay with them. They let the people enjoy the tilling of the soil so as to maintain peace in the occupied districts. The proceeds of the people's harvest were equally divided with the rebels. Thus they could have the grain of several prefectures of Chiang-nan, sent out of Chin-chu-kuan, which, together with the grain of several prefectures of Chiang-pei, sent out of Yü-ch'i-k'ou, was transported to Chin-ling. Ho-ch'un and others had succeeded in the siege of Nanking. Yet the rebels still enjoyed the profit of using the Yangtze and made use of an endless stream of supplies. People along the river had also become accustomed to living under the rebels.

"Now when the people hear of the arrival of the rebels, pain and regret pierce their hearts. Men as well as women flee, and kitchen fires no longer burn. The tillers do not have harvests of a single grain, and one after another they abandon their occupations. When the rebels travel through a territory without people, it is like fish trying to swim in a place without water. When the rebels live in a region with the soil uncultivated, it is like birds staying in a mountain without trees. This is obviously the road to certain poverty and there is no reason to believe that this can last long. As for the strategic forts of the southeast, such as Anking, Wuhu, Lu-chou, Ning-kuo, East and West Liang-shan, Chin-chu-kuan, Yü-ch'i-k'ou, and Chin-hua and Shao-hsing in Chekiang, these are places with mountains and streams, sinews and pulse, which one must struggle to hold. If these places are not lost again, we will eventually cause the death of the rebels.

"In former years, wherever the Kwangsi rebels penetrated, they built fortresses like city walls and dug trenches like rivers. These were defense projects of incomparable durability. Recently they have day by day become careless in such works. On the other hand, the government forces have far surpassed former days in their construction of fortresses and trenches. Among the rebels the multitude of leaders with the rank of Wang number more than ninety. They strive against each other for power. Disappointments and enjoyments are not equal for all. When one suffers defeat, the others do not go to his rescue. As for the government forces who have received the sacred instructions, all the water and land forces of San-Chiang and Liang-Hu can harmoniously assist each other and respond to one another. . . ."[56]

The disintegration of the Taiping forces was clearly seen by the man who brought them their defeat.

[56] *Ibid.*, 18:24a-b.

Part VI

The End of the Taipings

As Tseng Kuo-fan had predicted early in 1863, the Taiping Rebellion had by then become a lost cause, and the end was only a matter of time. Strategically Nanking's position had become untenable with the loss of the city of Anking and the area on the upper stream of the Yangtze in late 1861. In mid-year 1862 the Hunan army began to build up its final siege of the Taiping capital city, which without the control of safe access to areas of supply and defense was doomed.

Not only Tseng Kuo-fan but the Taiping leaders themselves seem to have been aware that the Taiping position at Nanking could not be redeemed. We do not know what plans, if any, Hung Jen-kan, now no longer in full charge of the Taiping government, may have had in mind. Li Hsiu-ch'eng, the Chung Wang, recounts that the T'ien Wang "had been inwardly conscious for some time past of an impending crisis with regard to provisions and the insecurity of the capital." [1] But the T'ien Wang was unwilling to accept Li Hsiu-ch'eng's proposal that Nanking should be abandoned and that the Taipings go on the march again. He must have felt that the Taipings could not survive if they abandoned their capital and with it the base of their government. As long as Nanking remained the seat of the T'ien Wang's government and of the Taiping power, the system could at least be maintained from day to day; and there could always be that miracle of delivery that the T'ien Wang in his deranged mind seems to have hoped for. Outwardly the T'ien

---

[1] Document 382.

Wang continued to maintain and express his faith in the success of his heaven-ordained mission and was determined to stay until the end. And so the battles dragged on around Nanking and in the lower Yangtze area, where Li Hsiu-ch'eng had established his own base of power.

The Ever Victorious Army and Its Role in the Taiping Defeat

It was in this area around Shanghai and at Soochow that the armies of Li Hung-chang received the support of foreign troops under the leadership first of the American F. T. Ward and later of the British Captain Gordon.[2] The role that these foreign units played in the defeat of the Taipings has been greatly overrated by a number of writers who have ascribed the Taiping defeat to foreign intervention. Since it was in the defense of Shanghai against the Taipings that foreign forces were first used, it is often believed that the Taipings brought this intervention on themselves by committing the blunder of attacking the Chinese city of Shanghai and thus causing the foreigners to intervene in the civil war.[3]

Indeed, in May, 1860, the British diplomatic representative, the Honorable Frederick Bruce (later Sir Frederick), and the French Consul General, M. de Bourboulon, announced that the naval and military forces of England and France would be used to defend Shanghai against any attack by the rebels.[4] The willingness of the British and French to take an active part in the defense of Shanghai and the lower Yangtze against the Taipings resulted from their new evaluation of the Chinese situation. They were at the point of gaining a treaty from the imperial government in Peking—eventually concluded in October, 1860—and as a result of their impressions of the hopelessness of the Taiping system

---

[2] For the lives and roles played by these two men see R. S. Rantoul, *Frederick Townsend Ward* (Salem, Mass., 1908) and Holger Cahill, *A Yankee Adventurer* (New York, 1930), and D. C. Boulger, *Life of Gordon* (London, 1896), Archibald Forbes, *Chinese Gordon* (London and New York, 1884), and A. E. Hake, *The Story of Chinese Gordon* (London, 1883). For a short time, August-October, 1862, a unit of the "Ever Victorious Army" under Major Morton fought in eastern Chekiang in cooperation with other units led by foreign officers under the over-all command of Tso Tsung-t'ang. There were two such foreign-led units, one under British and one under French officers, both made up of Chinese soldiers. These units played a role somewhat similar to that of the "Ever Victorious Army" in Kiangsu and carried similar names. The British-led force was known as the *Ch'ang an chün* or the *Ting sheng chün* or the *Lü yung*. The French-led force was the *Ch'ang chieh chün* or the *Hsin yi chün* or the *Huang yung*.

[3] See Teng, p. 74; Forrest, p. 188.

[4] Cahill, *A Yankee Adventurer*, p. 123.

and its policies, were less inclined to maintain a strict neutrality.[5] They "were getting impatient of the unsettled state of affairs. A few foreign adventurists joined the imperialists, and aided them in drilling their soldiers. The best foreign weapons were furnished them by foreign merchants."[6] In June, F. T. Ward, with the assistance of a prominent Chinese merchant in Shanghai, Yang Fang, and the intendant of Soochow and neighboring prefectures, Wu Hsü, began to recruit a foreign contingent, the original force of foreign mercenaries that was to participate under Li Hung-chang in the defeat of the Taipings. This foreign unit, later led by Captain Gordon, became the "Ever Victorious Army," which has since in many foreign and some Chinese accounts been given the decisive role in the defeat of the Taipings.

Yet the Ever Victorious Army played only a supporting part in the last stage of military affairs, and its theater of operation was limited to the area around Shanghai.[7] And although in these battles the Ever Victorious Army played a decisive role, the fighting in this area, though it may have speeded up the end for the Taipings, no longer affected the outcome of the war, which had been determined in the battles for the upper Yangtze area and was brought to an end in the attack against Nanking itself, in which the Ever Victorious Army did not participate.

One of the most misleading images of the Ever Victorious Army was created by its name. It was by no means "ever victorious." At several occasions, both under Ward and later under Gordon, it was dealt major defeats by Taiping armies, and a high percentage of its unit and its officers was killed in battle. Some others deserted to the Taipings and fought with them, and substantial desertions took place on a number of occasions. Several times the unit was reformed through new recruitment.[8]

[5] See L. S. Foster, *Fifty Years in China*, pp. 112-13.
[6] *Ibid.*, pp. 117-18.
[7] It participated in the battles for such towns as Sung-chiang, Chia-ting, Ch'ing-p'u, and other small towns in the neighborhood of Shanghai. Parts of the unit were also used at Ningpo in Chekiang, and later from Sung-chiang attacked places like Fu-shan, K'un-shan, Wu-chiang, and finally the city of Soochow in December, 1863. After the fall of Soochow the "Ever Victorious Army" participated in the capture of I-hsing, Li-yang, and Ch'ang-chou. For a full account of the actions fought by the "Ever Victorious Army" see Kuo, *Jih-chih*, and Andrew Wilson, *The Ever Victorious Army: A History of the Chinese Campaign under Lt. Col. C. G. Gordon, C. B. R. E. and of the Suppression of the Tai-ping Rebellion* (Edinburgh and London, 1868).
[8] Originally, when it was organized by Ward in June, 1860, for the protection of Shanghai and the capture of towns nearby, it consisted of "100 Manila men"

During the last months of 1862 difficulties with the Ever Victorious Army increased, partly as a result of the conflicting ambitions of its commanders but mainly because the pay was constantly in arrears, and Li Hung-chang, under whose command the Ever Victorious Army was, defaulted on his promises a number of times. When Ward had been wounded, other officers in turn took over temporary command.[9] In March, Major Gordon was appointed to command the army and began to lead its operations. He too had his difficulties with Li Hung-chang on the payment for his men. Some of his officers and men went over to the Taipings, but when the Taiping cause declined, most of them left the Taipings again. In December, 1863, Major Gordon had a violent personal clash with Li Hung-chang. Gordon had negotiated the surrender of the Taiping leaders at Soochow, with some of whom he had had personal connections,[10] and had guaranteed their safety. Li Hung-chang's action in executing the leaders who had surrendered, embarrassed and infuriated Gordon. But with the intervention of Robert Hart, the Commissioner of Chinese Customs, Major Gordon joined the war again. In March, 1864, the Ever Victorious Army suffered two more major defeats at the hands of Taiping forces and lost a substantial number of men and weapons. Gordon himself was wounded. But on the whole the Ever Victorious Army participated successfully in the defeat

---

under the command of Ward and his lieutenants, Edward Forrester and Henry Andrea Burgevine. It grew a month later to a unit of about "200 Manila men and 100 Europeans" and, together with Li Hung-chang's forces, suffered a major defeat in August at the hands of the troops of Li Hsiu-ch'eng, losing about one-third of its strength and a good deal of its equipment. Ward himself was wounded five times in that battle. Li Hsiu-ch'eng's claim in his confession (document 382) that he killed 600 to 700 foreign soldiers, captured over 2,000 guns, over 10 cannons, over 300 swords, and several hundred boats in this battle is obviously exaggerated. See Kuo, *Jih-chih,* I, 697. This unit was reinforced but suffered another setback in its attack against Ch'ing-p'u on August 9, 1860, when almost 100 Europeans were killed. See Kuo, *Jih-chih,* I, 698. For a while Ward did not receive any support from the British and French, since the foreigners he enlisted were mainly deserters from the British navy. In April, 1861, he reorganized his army on the basis of recruiting Chinese as soldiers and Westerners as officers. See Kuo, *Jih-chih,* II, 766. With the success of the military action by the army in late 1861 and 1862, and the failure of the British Admiral Hope in his efforts to disband the contingent, the Ever Victorious Army grew in size and gained, together with the regular Chinese forces, a number of victories, receiving its reward in the main from the plunder of towns taken and garrisoned.

[9] In the battle for T'ai-ts'ang on February 14, the unit again received a major setback and lost some of its officers.

[10] See documents 317 and 318.

and destruction of the Taiping units in the towns of the lower Yangtze area until it was disbanded at the end of May, 1864.[11]

The Fall of Nanking

The fighting in the lower Yangtze area and in Chekiang province was, however, only secondary to the main battle that mounted around Nanking and brought the final downfall of the Taiping Rebellion and its system. The loss of access to the supply areas in Chekiang and Kiangsu was not even crucial, once the fatal vise around the capital itself had closed. A substantial backing and support through Shanghai would have been out of the question, even if the towns that gave access to the coastal city and foreign settlement had not fallen to Li Hung-chang. The continuing attempts of Taiping leaders, such as Li Hsiu-ch'eng and by now also Hung Jen-kan, to recruit troops and gather supplies outside for the support of the capital no longer formed a part of an over-all strategy and could not turn the tide.

Nanking fell on July 19, 1864, to the besieging forces under the command of Tseng Kuo-fan's brother, Tseng Kuo-ch'üan. The fall of the city was anticipated by the Taipings, as we know from the Kan Wang's confession. But the quick success of Tseng Kuo-ch'üan in breaking down a part of the main wall came as a surprise to the Taiping leaders and foiled their plan of an organized breakthrough.[12] But this plan may have been instrumental in enabling the chief leaders to escape with a small force and with the person of the Young Monarch, the son of the Heavenly King.

The T'ien Wang, Hung Hsiu-ch'üan himself, did not live to see the end of his government. On June 1, 1864, he died at Nanking at the age of 50, after a lingering illness of twenty days, possibly after taking poison.[13] The news of the death of Hung Hsiu-ch'üan was suppressed by the Taiping leaders at Nanking for more than ten days.[14] Hung's son was then placed on the throne as the Young T'ien Wang. As he later stated

[11] For the story of these actions, see Kuo, *Jih-chih*, I, II, 684-1073. On the fighting around Shanghai, see documents 280, 281, 282, and 309; on the fighting at Ningpo, where units of the Ever Victorious Army and regular foreign troops participated, see documents 306, 307, 308, and 310-16.

[12] See documents 382 and 385.

[13] At the age of 52 according to Chinese reckoning. For the question of possible suicide see the comment on document 382 and note 118 of that document; see also Kuo, *Jih-chih*, II, 1074-76.

[14] See Tseng, *Tsou-kao*, 20:84-85a.

in his confession: "Court matters were under the control of the Kan Wang, and military affairs in the hands of the Chung Wang. All decrees which were issued were drawn up by the two persons mentioned above, and I was directed to subscribe my name to them." [15] The Taipings had thus not solved the problem of central authority.

The fall of Nanking led to a terrible slaughter. The bloody process of the occupation of the Taiping capital and the fanatical death of many Taipings in Nanking who refused to surrender can be read in Tseng Kuo-fan's reports to the throne: "On the 17th and the 18th, Tseng Liang-tso . . . and others searched through the city for any rebels they could find, and in three days killed over 100,000 men. The Ch'in-huai creek was filled with bodies. Half of the false *wangs,* chief generals, heavenly generals, and other heads were killed in battle, and the other half either drowned themselves in the dikes and ditches or else burned themselves. The whole of them numbered about 3,000 men. The fire in the city raged for three days and nights. . . . Not one of the 100,000 rebels in Nanking surrendered themselves when the city was taken but in many cases gathered together and burned themselves and passed away without repentance. Such a formidable band of rebels has been rarely known from ancient times to the present." [16]

This slaughter was the combined result of the fanatical Taiping defiance and of the policy of Tseng Kuo-fan, who had determined long before that the surrender of the main Taiping group from Kwangsi was not to be accepted. His goal was the extermination of the whole movement through the death of its core of leaders and followers. A policy of encouraging surrender might well have led to an earlier breakup and prevented such slaughter.[17] But it might also have left a residue of potential successors who might carry on the Taiping ideas and renew the attack against the traditional order, which Tseng Kuo-fan wanted to protect. The ruthless extermination of all the original Taiping force virtually ended this chance, if indeed it ever existed. Yet even if the Taipings knew that they had no choice, their determination to fight to the death and their mass suicide testified to their fanaticism and dedication and indicated how much strength there was still left in the movement even at the end. And the slaughter may have been at least partly re-

[15] See document 386.
[16] See Tseng, *Tsou-kao,* 20:81b-82b.
[17] See Li Hsiu-ch'eng's confession, document 382.

sponsible for the almost complete evaporation of the Taiping movement after its military defeat.

The End of the Taiping Movement

At first, though, the leading figures escaped from Nanking and joined some of the troops still in the field. Whatever hope the surviving Taiping leaders may have had of continuing their rebellion depended on the survival of the son of the Heavenly King, the Young Monarch, who now nominally headed the rebellion. Li Hsiu-ch'eng, who was in Nanking at the time of the fall of the city, helped the Young Monarch in his escape. Li himself, in his later confession, described his actions as motivated by traditional loyalty to the monarch he had served: "Though the T'ien Wang's days had been fulfilled, and the country had fallen, still, as his official and one who had received his favors, I could not do otherwise than evince my faithfulness by endeavoring to save his son." [18] On the flight from Tseng Kuo-fan's pursuing forces, however, Li Hsiu-ch'eng was separated from the Young Monarch and his guard. Shortly afterward Li was captured, and was executed after he had written the important, detailed confession that gives his interpretation of the Taipings' history and the Taipings' failure.[19]

With the fall of Nanking, the death of Hung Hsiu-ch'üan, and the uncertainty among most of the units still in the field regarding the fate of the Young Monarch, many of these remaining contingents of Taiping troops, especially those headed by men not from Kwangtung and Kwangsi, began to disintegrate and surrender. They made use of the government distinction between the hard core of the movement and those who had joined later without, presumably, sharing its religious and revolutionary fanaticism. The petition for surrender by an Anhwei man, Ch'en Ping-wen, the T'ing Wang, for instance, made it a point that he and his men had been forced to join the Taipings and had long attempted to surrender.[20]

What remained of the hard core, those who came originally from Kwangtung and Kwangsi and who had actually no choice, tried to rally around the Young Monarch. Hung Jen-kan, the Kan Wang, seemed to have been away from Nanking at the day of its fall. He had attempted to

[18] See document 382.
[19] See document 382.
[20] See document 384.

recruit and organize new forces to strengthen the defense of the capital. Now he joined, together with Li Ming-ch'eng and others, the Young Monarch's party. They went first to Kuang-te, Anhwei, then to Hu-chou, Chekiang, where another Taiping leader, Huang Wen-chin, the Tu Wang, was in command of the Taiping forces defending this city and its surrounding area.

Huang Wen-chin, a Kwangsi man from Po-pai, had distinguished himself in many battles though he was only thirty-three years old at the time.[21] But while Huang may have been an outstanding military commander, he was obviously incapable of establishing a functioning administration in his area. Instead of building up the rich region into an economic base, he permitted his troops to carry on a military occupation based solely on looting.[22] An account of this occupation of Hu-chou was given by two Englishmen, Conroy and Nellis, who were captured by the Taipings and confined at Hu-chou for some eight months before its fall. According to their story the city was without a shadow of municipal government.[23] Generalizing from this testimony on the Hu-chou situation and combining it with the information about the political system as it had existed at Nanking, the newspaper ascribed the whole failure of the Taiping movement to its leadership: "With such chiefs as it possessed it were a miracle had it ever attained its professed object; with men of a systematic turn of mind it might have accomplished the conquest of the country. Utter ignorance and imbecility were the distinguished peculiarities of the policies adopted, imbecility with respect to the internal working of a government, ignorance of the relations in which the insurgents stood to the power against which they were rebelling, and to those foreign nations whose aid would have been success, and whose opposition was certain destruction." [24]

[21] See document 387. Huang Wen-chin first was among the followers of the Tung Wang, Yang Hsiu-ch'ing, and fought along the Yangtze in 1853 and 1854. See Chang, *Tse-ch'ing, chüan* 2; and Hsiang, *Tzu-liao,* III, 72. In the late Taiping period, Huang Wen-chin had fought under the command of Li Hsiu-ch'eng in the Chekiang campaign. The city of Hu-chou was occupied by the Taipings on May 30, 1862. See Yao Chan, *Hu-pien chi-lüeh,* in Hsiang, *Tzu-liao,* VI, 749 ff. And shortly after its capture by the Taipings, Huang became the defender of Hu-chou.
[22] See Hu Ch'ang-ling, *Chien-te chi sui-pi,* in Hsiang, *Tzu-liao,* VI, 760.
[23] On the basis of their report, the *North China Herald* concluded in an editorial that "the rebel movement was brought to an ignominious end solely through its own inherent weakness." No. 746, Nov. 12, 1864, p. 182.
[24] Ibid.

If the Kan Wang had failed to establish an effective administrative system in Nanking, his presence with the nominal head of what remained of the Taiping government at Hu-chou could hardly, under these conditions, have given him an opportunity for a new start. And even had he tried, there was no time left. The position rapidly became militarily untenable. When the capture of Hu-chou by the joint forces of Li Hung-chang and Tso Tsung-t'ang was imminent, the remaining Taiping leaders, Hung Jen-kan, Hung Jen-cheng, and Huang Wen-ying, the brother of Huang Wen-chin, left the city with the Young Monarch and continued their flight. Huang Wen-chin remained and died shortly after, when the city fell. The others entered Kiangsi in an attempt to join the forces of the K'ang Wang, Wang Hai-yang, and the Shih Wang, Li Shih-hsien.[25] But they were captured one after another by the troops of the Kiangsi governor, Shen Pao-chen. Each of these leaders was given the opportunity to write his story on his role in the rebellion in the traditional confession.[26] They were executed in November, 1864. With the death of the Young Monarch and his remaining paladin, Hung Jen-kan, the Taiping movement came to an end.

Whether an earlier death of the deranged Heavenly King would have enabled Hung Jen-kan to assert himself and, in the name of the Young Monarch, develop a more rational system and a more effective strategy, is a matter of speculation. Even if the irrational leadership had been removed, Hung Jen-kan might have found it impossible to exercise authority over the self-willed military leaders, such as the Chung Wang, Li Hsiu-ch'eng. After the fall of Nanking and the flight of the leaders to the remaining armies in the field, there was neither the time nor obviously the organization to build a political structure around the figurehead of the Young Monarch and recapture something of the original spirit of the movement. The young Monarch died as "a youth with no special talents," in the words of Governor Shen Pao-chen.[27] And from his confession one gets the impression of a sympathetic, rather innocent young person whose hope to continue his education under the guidance of his captors is an indication of his simplicity.[28] Hung Jen-kan wrote an interesting and important record and seems to have died with dignity.[29]

[25] Document 386.
[26] See documents 385-88.
[27] Shen Pao-chen, *Shen Wen-su-kung cheng-chu*, 3:103.
[28] Document 386.
[29] Document 385.

The Destruction of the Taiping Remnants

What still followed was anticlimactic. The remaining Taiping armies in the field fought on even after their government no longer existed. But since they had already been on their own for some time they could continue to battle against the opposing armies of Tseng and his comrades-in-arms. But the loss of the center of their movement deprived them of any future possibility of increasing their support or providing a motivation for their battles, in which they had now become isolated and faced inevitable destruction. Since for the hard core there was no possibility of surrender, they could only fight to the end. These remaining Taiping armies consisted in the main of two groups, one in south China and the other in north China. The southern group was led by the Shih Wang, Li Shih-hsien, and the K'ang Wang, Wang Hai-yang, and had been the force that Hung Jen-kan and the Young Monarch had tried to reach when they were captured.[30] Li and Wang fought against Shen Pao-chen's troops in Kiangsi in the summer of 1864. Cut off from the Yangtze delta area after the fall of Nanking and blocked in their attempts to advance westward, they moved south into Kwangtung and Fukien provinces. Li Shih-hsien occupied Chang-chou in Fukien from October 14, 1864, to May 15, 1865. He attempted to build up this area, located along the seacoast and near the treaty port of Amoy, as a base for his military and political power and tried to stimulate farming and revive trade.[31] He obviously hoped to use the location of his base to gain foreign aid,[32] and actually obtained some Western ammunition and was joined by some European adventurers.[33] Li's companion, Wang Hai-yang, occupied Ting-chou, an inland city in Fukien province at the border of Kiangsi in a location where Li and Wang could mutually support each other. Both were forced from their bases by the superior armies of Tso Tsung-t'ang. Wang Hai-yang retreated to Kwangtung province in June, 1865, and was joined by Li Shih-hsien in August. But once they had to join forces, the two leaders fell out and engaged in a power struggle, inherent in this type of movement. The clash ended in

[30] Wang Hai-yang was actually an Anhwei man who had first joined the forces of the I Wang, Shih Ta-k'ai, but had later fought under Li Hsiu-ch'eng. See Kuo, *Jih-chih*, II, Appendix, p. 26.

[31] See document 389.

[32] See document 390 and also Kuo, *Jih-chih*, II, Appendix, 115.

[33] Western support was, however, also given to the government forces battling Li Shih-hsien.

the assassination of Li Shih-hsien and a number of his close lieutenants by the K'ang Wang, Wang Hai-yang.[34]

Wang was able to establish himself in Chia-ying-chou, Kwangtung province in December, 1865, where he maintained himself until February, 1866. The population of this area was largely made up of Hakka, the group from which the Taipings, in the main, had come; and Wang Hai-yang was able to recruit into his forces former members of disbanded local-corps units.[35] He was thus still able to maintain a strong force, which was, however, finally annihilated on February 7, 1866, when over 10,000 Taipings were killed and over 50,000 surrendered.[36] Before Wang's defeat, the knowledge of his ability to establish a base and maintain himself caused Lindley, a Taiping sympathizer, to declare that "the Taipings may rise from the ashes of their former glory and yet succeed in their great religio-political movement," [37] a statement that disregarded the absence of a political-religious foundation for these purely military ventures of the Taiping aftermath. The destruction of Wang's forces ended all Taiping resistance south of the Yangtze River and marked the formal ending of the Taiping Rebellion in official accounts.[38]

The Taiping armies campaigning to the north of the Yangtze River survived for a somewhat longer time. They were not immediately faced by any large government armies, and they had the further advantage of being able to align with the forces of another rebellion carried on in the Huai area by the Nien. These northern Taiping armies had been units under the command of the Ying Wang, Ch'en Yü-ch'eng, who had been in charge of the Taiping forces north of the river until his death in 1862.[39] They were led by the Fu Wang, Ch'en Te-ts'ai, and the Tsun Wang, Lai Wen-kuang. These leaders had all along maintained contact with the Nien leaders in the Huai area. Lai Wen-kuang especially had advocated close cooperation with the Nien, and when, in the fall of 1861, Anking was lost to the Taipings, he had proposed in a report a concept of strategy based on close alliance with the Nien leaders: "Now that Anking has been lost, we must ally with Chang [Lo-hsing] and Miao [P'ei-lin] to the north, in order to strengthen the defenses to the left of

[34] See Kuo, *Jih-chih*, II, 1138.
[35] *Chiao-p'ing Yüeh-fei fang-lüeh*, 413:30b.
[36] See *ibid.*, 414:17-20.
[37] See Lindley, II, 822.
[38] The above-quoted item in the *Chiao-p'ing Yüeh-fei fang-lüeh* is the last entry in this official history of the suppression of the rebellion.
[39] Document 260.

the capital. Then we shall send out surprise troops to go on and seize the areas of Ching and Hsiang [Hupeh]. . . . Then we may plan to re-cover Anking, so that the gates of the capital will be strengthened." [40] But, as Lai pointed out in his confession after his capture, Ch'en Yü-ch'eng did not follow his advice.

It is of interest that this military plan was disregarded by Ch'en Yü-ch'eng, whose position by this time was weakened as a result of the failure of Li Hsiu-ch'eng, the commander to the south of the river, to carry through his part of the Taipings' last great strategic plan. From a military point of view Lai's suggestion must have made good sense. And such cooperation with the Nien was also, as we know, envisaged by Li Hsiu-ch'eng himself, who attempted to establish his own connections with the Nien rebels. Why then did Ch'en Yü-ch'eng ignore it? We can only speculate that Ch'en, closer to Hung Jen-kan and his political plans, had a more genuine belief in the Taiping religious and political concepts than was at that time held by those military commanders who had come up through their military successes and thought in terms of military advantage without much regard for the fate of the revolutionary political order with which the Taiping Rebellion had started out and which Hung Jen-kan still attempted to restore. Any cooperation with the Nien could only be at the expense of sacrificing the political con-cepts of the rebellion for the sake of military gain. Instead of following Lai's suggestion, Ch'en sent him and Ch'en Te-ts'ai to northwest China and ordered them to build up their forces there by new recruitment into their armies. When these commanders learned of the fall of Anking and the death of Ch'en Yü-ch'eng, they marched eastward but were turned back to Shensi by the order of Li Hsiu-ch'eng to continue their assign-ment of recruiting troops for the defense of Nanking. They had started on their march back eastward when they learned that they were too late to rescue Nanking. In the words of Lai Wen-kuang, when they heard the news of the loss of the capital, "The people's morale was shat-tered." [41] Ch'en Te-ts'ai committed suicide in September, 1864, and his men either dispersed or surrendered to the government forces. But Lai now carried out his previous proposal and merged his smaller force with the larger Nien forces. [42] Lai's description of his action indicates the purely military character of this decision by a rebellious force no longer

[40] Document 391.
[41] Document 391.
[42] See Chiang, *The Nien Rebellion,* p. 85.

concerned with the religio-political purpose of the Taiping movement. In Lai's words: "At that time the troops north of the Yangtze who had no place to return to numbered altogether several tens of thousands. All were natives of Meng-ch'eng and P'o-chou [Anhwei]. Their chieftains, Jen Hua-pang, Niu Hung-sheng, and Chang Tsung-yü, had sworn to live and die together. They did not shirk any sort of hardship and asked me to lead them in order to render service." [43]

The merger of Lai's Taiping troops with the Nien turned the combined forces into a more formidable threat to the government. It thus gave new impetus to the Nien Rebellion.[44]

There has been some question whether the combined forces should be counted as a continuation of the Taiping Rebellion or as an extension of the Nien Rebellion.[45] The combined force was indeed led by Lai Wen-kuang and was thus under the leadership of a Taiping rebel who had been one of the original participants in the Chin-t'ien rising of 1850. But the program and the religion of the Taiping movement had ended after the death of Hung Jen-kan and the Young Monarch, and it seems therefore misleading to regard this remnant force of the Taiping military organization as a continuation of the rebellious movement itself.

But if it had lost its political and religious purpose, this Taiping remnant force gained in military strength through the acceptance of a strategy of mobile warfare borrowed from the Nien. This strategy was based on a combination of mobile campaigns of cavalry forces with fortifications that provided an interlocking defense system in depth of the home base.[46] After initial successes over the government forces under the Mongol prince, Seng-ko-lin-ch'in, who was himself ambushed and killed in May, 1865, Lai's unit was eventually defeated by a strategy separating the mobile forces of Lai from the home base and containing and annihi-

---

[43] Document 391.

[44] See Chiang, The Nien Rebellion, p. 85; Chiang's account of this merger is based on the Anhwei t'ung-chih, 108:26; and Wang K'ai-yün, Hsiang-chün-chih (1886), 14:7.

[45] Kuo T'ing-i declares that from that time on the Taipings and the Nien were two but yet one, and that one could regard this new group as Taiping remnants. See Jih-chih, II, Appendix, 120. Lo Erh-kang goes so far as to call these forces the new army of the Taiping and suggests that 1864 should not be considered the last year of the T'ai-p'ing T'ien-kuo, but 1868, the year when Lai Wen-kuang and his combined group of Taiping and Nien were finally annihilated. See his T'ai-p'ing t'ien-kuo hsin-chün ti yün-tung chan (Shanghai, 1955), and his T'ai-p'ing t'ien-kuo shih-kao (Peking, 1955), chüan 3.

[46] See Chiang, The Nien Rebellion, pp. 32 ff.

lating them.[47] When the strategy of containment conceived by Tseng Kuo-fan and carried out by Li Hung-chang began to show results in 1866, Lai decided to divide the Taiping-Nien coalition group and gain a broader base by an alliance with the Moslem rebellion in Kansu and Shensi. Lai described his policy in his confession: "I was afraid that by standing alone it would be difficult to hang on, and that an isolated stand could hardly last long. Therefore, in the autumn of *ping-yin*, the sixteenth year [1866], I specially ordered the Liang Wang, Chang Tsung-yü, the Young Wu Wang, Chang Yü-chüeh, and the Huai Wang, Ch'iu Yüan-ts'ai, to advance to Kansu and Shensi and make an alliance with the Moslems for the purpose of mutual assistance."[48]

This policy split the Nien forces into two groups. The group led by Chang Tsung-yü, Chang Yü-chüeh, and Ch'iu Yüan-ts'ai was called in government accounts the West Nien. The group that remained with Lai Wen-kuang was called the East Nien, since it operated in the provinces of Shantung, Honan, and Hupeh. In the middle of 1867, Lai was forced by the shortage of supplies to venture from his fortified home area into eastern Shantung. Li Hung-chang's Huai army successfully cut him off from his base and established a blockade around the area of Shantung which Lai's forces had entered. In a series of battles in late 1867 most of Lai's troops were wiped out within this encirclement. He himself was able to break through the blockade with a few hundred men and regain the Huai area, only to be captured there in January, 1868. With his capture and execution ended the military career of the last of the Taiping leaders.

The West Nien, harassed by Tso Tsung-t'ang's forces in Shensi, were unable to make contact with the Moslems, and turned instead eastward into Shansi and Chihli provinces, threatening Peking. But the strong government armies there forced the West Nien into Shantung province, where by August, 1868, they were annihilated by Li Hung-chang's Huai army. With their defeat, the last rebellious force that could claim any connection with the Taipings had been eliminated.

The Chung Wang's and the Kan Wang's Confessions

But the Taiping Rebellion had truly ended four years before with the fall of its capital and the capture and execution of its political leaders. The imperial government's practice of giving captured rebels the oppor-

[47] *Ibid.*, pp. 100 ff.
[48] Document 391.

tunity before their execution of telling their story as a historical record and source of information has resulted in an extraordinary documentation of the Taiping leaders' moves and ideas. Their so-called confessions, properly analyzed, offer much insight into almost all aspects of the Taiping movement, as well as into the character and thinking of the men concerned. Those written by the key leaders give us the most valuable information on major political and strategic concepts, for the problems of leadership under a deranged Heavenly King, and on the internal conflicts and power struggle that beset the movement and contributed to its downfall.

Two confessions in particular are of major importance, those of the Chung Wang, Li Hsiu-ch'eng,[49] and those of the Kan Wang, Hung Jen-kan.[50] The Chung Wang has been for many contemporaries and later historians the main hero of the last years of the Taiping Rebellion. He has been regarded as the ablest Taiping commander of that period, and his lengthy confession, in which he describes himself as the chief commander and supporter of the Heavenly King, became widely known among Chinese and Westerners alike. This confession was written in the week after Li's capture, July 30 to August 7, 1864, when he was held in Tseng Kuo-fan's headquarters before his execution. It was reprinted in part in the English press,[51] and its acceptance at face value was the reason that Li's role was seen by many in the way he himself had characterized it. His confession was taken all the more seriously since he concerned himself not only with his own role in the movement but also with the problems of the movement itself, and especially with what he considered the reasons for the Taiping failure.

The reasons that Li listed dealt with either failures in the military campaigns or with political problems. They were easily understood and widely accepted, but they did not provide a deeper political or even strategic analysis of the weaknesses of the movement, let alone of its ideological purpose. The military failures which Li lists in his confession were: (1) the failure of the northern campaign; (2) the failure of the first reinforcement of the northern campaign; (3) the failure of the second reinforcement of the northern campaign; (4) the decisive defeat of Lin Shao-chang by the Hunan army at Hsiang-t'an; and (5) the mistake

[49] Document 382.
[50] Document 385.
[51] *NCH*, Nos. 743-49, 753-55, and 757-65, October 22, 1864, to March 25, 1865.

in concentrating the Taiping strength on the defense of Nanking. In other words, in four of his five points Li concentrates on battles lost rather than on problems of military strategy, and these four military setbacks all occurred in the early Taiping period under the leadership of the Tung Wang, Yang Hsiu-ch'ing. But while Li criticizes these military setbacks, he does not concern himself with the strategy that led up to them. Whether the failure of the northern campaign and of the supporting reinforcement campaigns were the necessary outcome of the decision to make Nanking the capital and give up the mobile sweep of the first stage of victorious advance, what reasons caused the Hsiang-t'an setback, these are not problems that occur to Li Hsiu-ch'eng. For him these are battles lost on the spot. In mentioning the problem of the defense of Nanking, listed last by him, Li does not include any reference to the strategy of the upriver campaign in which he himself played such a fateful part.

In his discussion of the political disasters that overtook the Taipings, Li mentions the following points: (1) the assassinations of the Tung Wang and the Pei Wang; (2) the T'ien Wang's suspicion of the loyalty of the I Wang, Shih Ta-k'ai, and the latter's withdrawal from Nanking, combined with the T'ien Wang's confidence in his incompetent brothers; (3) the T'ien Wang's neglect of governmental affairs; (4) the appointment of too many Wangs; and (5) the failure to use the virtuous. Nowhere does Li deal with the causes of the power struggle, the reasons for the T'ien Wang's inability to handle problems, and the problems of the government's system itself, or of the revolutionary faith and the program and policy of the Taiping movement. Li's own role as the benefactor of the movement, the support he had, and his fruitless attempts to impress an effective policy on the Heavenly King are stressed. And it is this role that became generally accepted when Li's confession became widely known.

The interest in Li's confession was also increased by the persistent belief that a part of it had been suppressed by Tseng Kuo-fan in his report to the emperor. This part, so some thought, contained an appeal to Tseng Kuo-fan to lead a Chinese rebellion against the alien Manchu dynasty.[52] The texts of the full confession which was seen and, in abbreviated version, reproduced first by the Chinese historian Lo Erh-kang, contained no such proposal. The full handwritten text, which has since been published by Tseng Kuo-fan's descendant on Taiwan in photo-

[52] See comment on the confession.

graphic reproduction, is with minor unimportant additions identical with that published by Lo Erh-kang and does not alter the substance of the document, which was used by Lo Erh-kang himself to build up Li as a heroic figure in the rebellion. There is no indication in it, though, that Li possessed either the strategic concept or the political insight to play the role ascribed to him.

One particularly disturbing aspect of Li's confession is his obvious attempt to save his neck by playing up to the sympathies of his captor, Tseng Kuo-fan, by flattering Tseng and his generals and troops, critically belittling at several occasions his own side, and at the end offering his services to bring about the surrender of the remaining Taiping forces in the field if he is permitted to live. Worse still, Li indicates in his confession that already before the fall of Nanking he had negotiated through his brother-in-law with members of Tseng Kuo-fan's staff about his own surrender, if his life was guaranteed. But since Li was uncertain about the reliability of his guarantor in Tseng's camp, he "could not venture to make a definite answer." When he was found out by other Taiping officials, he bribed his way out of punishment for himself and his accomplices. Li's attempt to save his life is certainly understandable, even if it shows that he misjudged the possibilities, but it does not add to the picture of the hero of the rebellion. Other Taiping leaders, such as Hung Jen-kan, were more consistent in remaining loyal to their cause to the end.

The role of Li Hsiu-ch'eng, who at first had been glamorized also by Communist writers, recently has become a subject of controversy in Communist China. The interpretation by Lo Erh-kang, regarded still as the leading Chinese historian of the period, and his lionizing of Li as the true Taiping hero have been criticized by younger Chinese Communist writers. Lo's interpretation[53] contained a defense of Li against the accusation that he had humiliated himself in trying to save his life. Lo's argument was that Li really used a feint and only pretended to submit in the hope of being able to gain with his release another opportunity to lead the Taiping forces still in the field. This view was strongly attacked by some younger Communist Chinese writers who criticized Lo Erh-kang for eulogizing a traitor who had actually "demeaned himself by seeking submission," had no faith in the Taiping Revolution, had de-

[53] See Lo Erh-kang, *Chung-wang Li Hsiu-ch'eng tzu-chuan yüan-kao chiencheng*, first published by the K'ai-ming Book Company in 1944 and reprinted in Peking in 1951.

serted his social class, the peasants, and betrayed the Taiping movement.[54] Lo Erh-kang, in his rejoinder, maintained his view that Li meant to deceive his captors in order to lead the Taiping forces still in the field in carrying on the Taipings' historic mission.

In our view, Lo's attempt to ascribe to Li the plan of escape to carry on the battle seems unconvincing. We believe, indeed, that Li's surrender was as genuine as the document in which it was expressed. What detracts most from Li's prestige, however, more than his humiliating attempt to save his life and his belittling of the movement of which he was a part, or even his attempted treason at the end at Nanking, is his whole role in this movement in which he shortsightedly sought to build up his own glory and power at the expense of a joint strategy and program which he seems not to have understood. In fact, we believe that Li's independence of action was a major factor in the collapse of the Taiping Rebellion.

In contrast to Li, Hung Jen-kan retained to the end his loyalty to his cause. Hung Jen-kan's confession provides, indeed, what is perhaps the most rational review of the movement and its chances. It is unfortunate that—at least as of this day—we possess only a truncated version of this document.[55] But the document we have reveals a clear and incisive

[54] See the symposium on *Kuan-yü chung wang tzu-chuan yüan-kao chen-wei wen-t'i te shang-ch'üeh* in *Hua-tung shih-ta hsüeh-pao*, 1956, No. 4. The main argument of this symposium was that the confession was actually a forgery, but one of the writers, Nien Tzu-min, attacked Lo's view of Li Hsiu-ch'eng's loyalty and heroism. The argument whether Li was a hero or a coward became thus confused with the question whether Li's confession was genuine or a forgery. The historian Chin Yü-fu came to Lo's defense in reaffirming that the confession was genuine and that Lo's speculations about Li's motives were plausible. See Chin's article in *Li-shih yen-chiu*, 1957, No. 4, pp. 41-46. A later attack against Lo's evaluation of Li Hsiu-ch'eng appeared in an article by Ch'i Pen-yü in *Li-shih yen-chiu*, 1963, No. 4, pp. 27-43. Ch'i pointed to the language of the confession to show that Li Hsiu-ch'eng had denounced the Taiping Revolution and had a high esteem for its opponents. He had disparaged the T'ien Wang for lack of virtue while he had praised Tseng Kuo-fan, Tseng's commanders, and the Hsiang army, even though they had massacred his own family. Li had even made secret overtures to hand over the city of Nanking before its fall and had helped the enemy by releasing prisoners and inducing the Taiping defenders to lay down their arms. Li's surrender was real, Ch'i concluded. He was hoping to save his own life, and this was the reason that he hinted he would be able to help his captors by appealing to Taiping forces still holding out to capitulate.

[55] Document 385. The governor of Kiangsi province, Shen Pao-chen, whose captive Hung Jen-kan was, sent only the first part of the confession in his report to the throne. An additional section is known through an English translation that appeared in the *North China Herald* at the time. Whether the missing section

mind capable of seeing the major issues and presenting them. It also shows a man who remained a faithful believer to the end and was unwilling to placate his enemies. Even in this account written as a prisoner, Hung Jen-kan calls the troops of his enemies the "imps" and does not hesitate to point out the blunders made by Tseng Kuo-ch'üan and other generals in Tseng's camp.

To the end Hung Jen-kan maintained that the movement and its early success would not have been possible without divine guidance, that whatever its outcome, it was therefore a true expression of God's purpose, which it claimed to represent. Hung Jen-kan did not take refuge in blaming the Heavenly King for the failure. In fact he did not discuss with his captors the cause of the Taipings, in which he obviously still believed. He did reassert his loyalty in comparing himself with the Sung statesman who had fallen into the hands of the enemy and chosen death in preference to disloyalty.

What Hung Jen-kan was willing to discuss was military strategy, and here he asserts that he himself had discussed with Li Hsiu-ch'eng the plan of the diversionary maneuver that had broken the siege of Nanking in 1860, which Li Hsiu-ch'eng in his confession had claimed all for himself. The major military setback was seen by Hung Jen-kan in the failure of the campaign for the control of the Yangtze in 1861, caused by Li Hsiu-ch'eng's neglect in carrying out his assigned part. It was the loss of this campaign which, combined with the increasing foreign aid that the government forces received, sealed the fate of the Taipings in Hung Jen-kan's view. Hung Jen-kan may well have felt more strongly about Li's self-willed actions than he indicated in his statement to his enemies, and may eventually have said more to them when shown Li's confession. But this we do not know, and what Hung Jen-kan said is clear enough.[56] If there ever was still a chance to reorganize and revitalize the movement, Li's unwillingness to submit to central strategy planning and central administration would have foiled it. Hung Jen-kan's complaint that Lin Shao-chang, the Chang Wang, who was in charge of funds and supplies at Nanking and a friend of Li Hsiu-ch'eng, refused to take

_____

contained important information we do not know. Of special interest would be a discovery of the document that contained Hung Jen-kan's reaction to Li Hsiu-ch'eng's confession, with which he was confronted by his captor.

[56] Other Taiping leaders expressed in their confessions a critical view of Li Hsiu-ch'eng. Lai Wen-kuang listed the attack on Shanghai by Li as a military and diplomatic blunder. See document 391. Huang Wen-ying spoke of Li's self-interest. See document 387.

central orders but dealt directly with the army commanders, provides a clear enough picture of Hung Jen-kan's inability to overcome the selfish nearsighted interests of Li and other Taiping commanders and to stem the growth of that confusion and disorganization in Nanking that Li Hsiu-ch'eng himself so well describes in his confession. Behind the question of the argument over military strategy appears the issue of central administrative as well as military control. It was the failure to reassert unity of command in all fields which prevented Hung Jen-kan from carrying through the program which he had so well conceived.

An Evaluation

The question remains: Could indeed any new leadership have made sense of the Taiping Rebellion and still have led it to success? We can only speculate. All such speculation, however, will be inseparably connected with our evaluation of the character and meaning of the Taiping movement as expressed in the ideas of its leaders and their professed goals. In attempting such an evaluation we have to realize that the movement itself went through different stages, and success would have meant different things at least to the two most important leaders who had a plan and a program, Yang Hsiu-ch'ing and Hung Jen-kan.

The Taipings started as a fanatical religious group with a strong ethnic cohesion, inspired by an irrational prophetic leader who had the charismatic appeal that remains undefinable. There was enough rational appeal in the Christian concepts professed by the deranged leader to enable his lieutenant, Feng Yün-shan, to organize a disciplined group of believers. The God Worshippers, whose whole existence was threatened by the chaos of the time and the hostility of their neighbors, gained new confidence in joining with their kindred fellow-sufferers in a larger family group that took its solace from the idea of a divine Father to whom they could turn in prayer. Their new religion provided the reassurance that the Heavenly Father could give them help and protection in their day-to-day problems and against the dangers of an increasingly hostile world, and that there was a life after death in which the loyal members of this family were to be compensated for their suffering. The ethnic unity of the threatened group, its inclination to band together in the traditional organization for common defense, was thus reinforced and deepened by the new faith and the new bonds of a religious congregation.

Yang Hsiu-ch'ing, a brilliant organizer and strategist, could build on this religious foundation and establish a military-political structure that claimed complete control over all aspects of the life of its militant followers. There is no reason to doubt that his concepts of organization were in complete accordance with the notions of the prophet himself and of those fellow lieutenants, including Feng Yün-shan, who made up the first leadership of the movement. But it was Yang who at the outset of the rising at Chin-t'ien and through the organizational structure formed at Yung-an established himself as the actual organizer and military and administrative mastermind of the movement.

The movement as he formed it was totalitarian in character. It was based on a complete control by the leaders of all aspects of the life of their followers. In all their actions they were under military discipline and under the command of military-political officers, who themselves were completely subjected to the leaders' orders. Neither the followers nor the officers had—in theory at least—anything they could own or use that was not given to them by those in control. Their food, their clothing, their equipment, all were issued to them from the common property managed by the staff of the leaders. Their most personal life was affected by the separation of the sexes and the prohibition of sexual relations even between married couples. The breakup of the family—though declared temporary—and the military organization of women as well as of men shaped the movement entirely into a military system in which every aspect of life was regulated by the leadership. Most important, the religious faith on which the movement was based was a means to establish the control of the leaders over the belief and the thinking of all the followers. Each member had to direct his life according to the divine will as it was presented and interpreted to him by the leaders themselves. Not only Hung Hsiu-ch'üan's own fantastic interpretations gave this prophet his special role and his complete power to enforce what was described as God's command, but Yang Hsiu-ch'ing, impersonating God the Father's voice, could bring the divine authority at any moment into any given situation. The fear of this authority and the cruel punishment meted out to all violators of Taiping discipline provided the terror necessary to maintain such absolute control. The assertion that the Taiping leaders had the divine truth which had to be unquestioningly obeyed was not only the sanction of their leadership but also the basis of its totalitarian character. The combination of political, economic, social, and intellectual authority which the leaders maintained was exercised through the hierarchy of the official staff, as in any totalitarian movement. The Taiping officers were to be at the same time military commanders, administrators, and preachers, as was clearly indicated by the organizational regulations of the Taiping land law.

The leaders' claim of possessing access to the divine truth led also to the type of power struggle that occurs in all totalitarian movements whenever issues of leadership are unresolved. The original leadership was in the hands of what amounted to a collective group of six who, in the later mournful words of one of them, formed a brotherhood by themselves. The battle for position within this collective leadership group can be traced to the beginnings of the movement. Whether Hung Hsiu-ch'üan was "sacred" or "holy" and above the rest or, as "the Sovereign," human like the rest of them and only distinguished by his experience and the mandate of the mission given to him by God, was of basic importance for determining authority in a movement where authority was based on the claim of access to divine truth. Hsiao Ch'ao-kuei's impersonation of Christ ranked him potentially above the prophet. Yang Hsiu-ch'ing, of course, with his claim of being seized by the Holy Ghost and speaking with the voice of God the Father himself, had usurped the number one position of power and used it, step by step, to build up his own authority and reduce that of the others, including that of Hung Hsiu-ch'üan, until the fear and jealousy of his remaining colleagues led to his assassination and the bloody power struggle that destroyed the leadership and with it the cohesion of the movement.

The disintegration that followed and that could not be reversed is further proof of the limited and totalitarian character of the movement. The kingdom on earth and the promise of happiness after death which the Taiping leaders had held out to their followers as a reward for the sacrifice of their individual lives had had its appeal to the original group of followers in a time of chaos. What they were giving up of their regular life and possessions was already threatened; and any promise of a way out was more effective with people who had little to lose and might well despair. Under the impact of a prophecy in which they believed and of religious concepts which even in the form presented to them must have had their appeal, they were willing to take off as a military band for a nebulous life of power and glory in another, richer part of the Middle

Kingdom. This was the appeal that could be effective with the desperate who joined up originally and those who swelled the movement in its march northward. It was this appeal which Yang Hsiu-ch'ing tried to revive at Nanking when he reminded the Taiping officers and followers of the common heroism of their campaign, of the rivers and mountain ranges they had crossed, the victories they had won, and the sacrifices they had made for the common cause.[1]

But what had worked with the militant and fanatical group of the Taiping followers themselves did not gain the Taipings the support of the settled population in areas which they controlled and where they would have to rebuild the government. As long as their victory was complete and their leadership intact they could dominate the areas occupied by their armies and force acceptance of their authority. They may even have gained a measure of popular acceptance in these areas where they eased the burden of the rural population without attempting—at least as yet—to carry out any of the program revealed in the plan of their new order. But once their leadership was in disarray and the discipline of their armies had disappeared, the lack of any general appeal of their beliefs and of their program would be exposed.

It was not only their inability to carry out their basic economic program but it was the program itself that showed that the Taipings were not a movement concerned with the interests of that social group that made up the vast majority of the Chinese people and had suffered most from the government's decline and the chaos of the preceding decades —the Chinese peasants.

Chinese rebellions have often been described as "peasant rebellions," a term which has been very misleading. For the student of European history, peasant rebellions concerned risings in which peasants, under whatever leadership, fought for their professional interest and against the existing order and status system of their time. Under the slogan: "Wenn Adam grub und Eva spann, wo war da der Edelmann?" the peasants in the Holy Roman Empire fought against hereditary aristocratic rule, against serfdom and for their independence. The men who fought the German peasant wars were peasants who wanted to remain peasants with free ownership of their land. In traditional China, rebellions were directed against oppression but did not aim at a change of the system itself. And though rebellious armies, like all Chinese armies, were in the main drawn from peasants, the goal of the peasants who joined

[1] See Yang's odes to the Taiping followers, document 50.

was not an improvement of their status as peasants but an escape from their plight. They sought their luck in the opportunities provided by military adventure and tried to gain power, wealth, and official status in a career made possible by the turnover produced by the rebellion.

In contrast to earlier rebellions, the Taipings did, of course, attack the social order and sought to replace it by their own. But though the majority of their followers had most likely been peasants, they too did not aim at improving their status as peasants. In fact, in the hierarchy of rank which the Taipings established and in which constant promotion and demotion was to be based on merit and demerit in action, the lowest demotion was to the status of husbandman—the worker in the field and the lowest rung in their hierarchy. No pride of peasant status there! Nor would the Taiping land law, if actually applied, have provided the free ownership of one's own plot—the goal of peasant rebellions—and the enjoyment of the fruit of one's own agricultural labor. The Taiping land law was to apply to agriculture the concept of the common treasury. The land, though allotted according to labor, was to belong to the Heavenly King; and the surplus was to go to the state.

A popular support for the Taiping Rebellion, as far as the peasants in the rural areas occupied by the Taipings were concerned, could therefore not be based on a peasant's hope to have free use of his land and the fruits of his labor. Any appeal the Taipings had would not have been based on their theoretical system, but, in a much more limited way, simply on the question of how well the Taiping armies and officers would treat the peasant population—whether in practice the peasant's lot would be bettered or worsened under the Taipings' rule. When, therefore, the original attraction of an opportunity to escape from local misery by joining a military force out to conquer the empire was past, when the Taipings had to settle down to govern the population of the rich Yangtze delta, they could control by military force but could not draw to their side a population whose loyalty would not be captured by religious promises or by a new form of all-inclusive tax for a "sacred treasury" had it been applied. Finding it difficult to collect taxes without the management experience of local landlords, the Taipings had, however, to protect landlordism as a practical means of getting the tax on which they so desperately depended.[2] The longer the fighting lasted and the more difficult the Taipings' situation became, the harsher their armies behaved in the treatment of the local population. It was, we believe, the

[2] E.g., see documents 234, 365, 366, 368, and 373.

lack of true popular support that deprived the Taipings of any chance for victory. It was their system that was at fault. This system could not have an appeal to the large majority of the population; and the hard core of the Taiping force could in the long run not maintain itself without such support—perhaps even if the Heavenly King had not been deranged, and if the system had not by its nature provoked hostility and power struggle among its leadership.

This problem of the Taiping Rebellion, inherent in its program, already became apparent in its first phase, under the leadership of Yang Hsiu-ch'ing. The very fact that the Taiping land law, which was to apply the concept of the sacred treasury to the rural community, was not applied shows the problematical relationship of this concept to agricultural production, on which the Taipings depended. It was not a distribution of land or the end of landlordism which was at issue; it was this revolutionary concept of the "sacred treasury" which formed the core of the Taiping program and which ran counter to all peasant interests, as the later story of collectivization and communization has demonstrated. This basic weakness of the Taiping program, apparent already under Yang Hsiu-ch'ing, became critical once the power struggle had led to Yang's assassination and the disintegration of the leadership in the second phase of the Taiping Rebellion with its assumption of power by autonomous military commanders.

In fighting the Taiping movement Tseng Kuo-fan was farsighted enough to contest the Taipings not only in the field of military strategy but in the whole area of popular support. In the battle for the loyalty of the population of the Yangtze area, he used not only political measures, such as alleviation of taxes, but propaganda warfare aimed at discrediting the Taiping system as a whole. In his "Proclamation Denouncing the Yüeh Rebels," which he issued in 1854 at the outset of his campaign, he attacked the harshness of the Taipings in their treatment of the population. In Tseng's words:

> They brought calamities to several millions of human lives and devastated *chou* and *hsien* districts over more than five thousand li. . . . whether the people were rich or poor, they looted them all to the bare, leaving behind not even inch-long grass. . . . Men were daily given one *ke* (one-thousandth of a picul) of rice. They were driven to the battle front to be the vanguards. They were driven to build city walls or dig ditches. Women were given daily one *ke* of rice. They were driven to ascend the ramparts and stand guard at night. They were driven to transport rice or carry coal. . . . The Yüeh rebels placed themselves in

comfort, wealth, elevation, and glory, but looked upon us, the oppressed people of the two lakes and three rivers, as inferior to dogs, pigs, cattle, or horses. Such is the nature of their cruelty and atrocity. Any man of vigor, when hearing this, would feel bitter and resentful. . . . The peasants cannot have their own land to toil and to tax, for they say all land belongs to the Heavenly Lord; the merchants cannot trade by themselves and make money, for they say all commodities belong to the Heavenly Lord; the scholars cannot study the classics of Confucius, for they have what is called the teachings of Jesus and the New Testament. They are throwing overboard the principles of *li* (propriety) and *i* (righteousness) which govern human relationships and the orthodox teachings contained in the Book of Poetry and the Book of History— principles which have been in effect in China for thousands of years.[3]

Whether or not Tseng's propaganda made an impact, the Taipings did not gain the loyalty of the Chinese peasants as a social group. It was this lack of support which may have been the basic reason for their failure. And this lack of support seems to us to be related to their totalitarian program. In this totalitarian setting Hung Jen-kan could not have asserted himself, nor could his more rational program have fitted.

What then was Hung Jen-kan's chance? Had he been able to assert his authority, to retain the backing of his monarch, the deranged prophet, and with this authority been able to bring the insubordinate commanders and officials in line, to carry through his strategic plan and establish a centralized functioning administrative system, what would he then have accomplished? What was his program?

Hung Jen-kan was first and basically concerned with the Taiping religion. But to him religion was not the sanction of authority that it had been for Yang Hsiu-ch'ing and for Hung Hsiu-ch'üan himself. He accepted the mission of bringing Christianity to the Chinese people. But his own authority was not to be sanctioned by his possession of divine truth. He attempted to re-establish an administrative staff under his central authority but not to gain complete submission by using the fear of God's ability to penetrate all human thought. Hung Jen-kan was concerned with problems of conscience, with laws and their enforcement, with such questions as that of the right of government to take life—the problem of capital punishment.

While Hung Jen-kan was the new head of the government, the land law was reissued; but in all his declarations and proclamations on government and policy he never mentioned it. The assumption must be

---

[3] See Tseng, *Tseng Wen-cheng-kung ch'üan-chi, Wen-chi,* 3:1a-3a.

that he disregarded this program, and this assumption is strengthened by his proposals for new economic development in trade and business. What he did propagate was the development of private property and its promotion by the state, a far cry indeed from the original Taiping system. He was concerned with what he called "rule by law," which to him was to be combined with a stress on education.

Hung Jen-kan was concerned with the creation of public opinion, dependent in part on a public press. But it was the educated, the scholars, who understood the trends of the time and who were responsible for the laws. In his discussion of foreign countries he indicated his preference for the United States, and he described the election of the President by secret ballot. Under this concept, leadership is thus based on representation rather than on divine right. But for Hung Jen-kan the voting right is exercised only by "officials and people of virtue and wisdom." If his political ideas did therefore lead him to envision a future in which the educated would provide a rule by law in which these laws would represent a concept of the world held by many of his missionary friends, in which there would be state promotion of free economic activity in business and trade, in which welfare would be handled by charitable enterprises, he was, without perhaps realizing it himself, propagating a system diametrically opposed to that of the original Taiping kingdom. How little the Heavenly King himself was capable of visualizing any political system can be seen from the absence of any realization by him of the contradictions and conflicts inherent in this ideological confusion. Hung Jen-kan's state would have been very limited in its function—a state that protected private activity and encouraged rather than controlled all spheres of human life; a state that certainly did not possess the totalitarian character originally inherent in the Taiping movement. The rule by the educated seemingly connected his system to that of the Chinese past but was Western rather than Chinese. Not only was Christianity to take the place of Confucianism, the gentry's role of social leadership would end. The state was to take over through laws the public functions of regulating the life of the society and of education which in the traditional order were the very heart of the gentry's position. And the newly educated were to play a leadership role through voting and election for office in the state and not as an autonomous function in society. The dualism of the public order was therefore to disappear, while the public order itself was to provide a larger realm of freedom for individual enterprise than had ever been possible in Confucian China.

Whether Hung Jen-kan ever realized how far his ideas deviated from the original Taiping concepts appears highly doubtful. The naïve and direct way in which he revealed at Nanking his program, which differed so greatly from the Taiping system of the time, seems to indicate how little he realized this conflict in spite of his practical grasp of the political and military situation. He seems not to have been aware of the problem of getting from the Taiping leaders and forces support for a program so different in origin from the fanatical élan that had motivated them. His propositions on law, education, business, and Protestant virtues could not have much impact on the population of the rural districts and towns whose support was so vital in the battle between the Taipings and their gentry opposition. No more than Yang Hsiu-ch'ing did Hung Jen-kan succeed in gaining that popular support necessary to broaden the Taiping Rebellion from the rising of the fanatical military organization into a popular revolution. Success would only have been possible if the Taipings could have imposed their rule by force, but not against a determined opposition that could counter the Taiping claims with an appeal of its own in terms that linked an attack against Taiping atrocities with the defense of the beliefs and ideas of Chinese tradition.

If the Confucian gentry were still willing and able to defend the traditional order, the Taipings could not succeed unless they had the popular support for their program necessary for a social revolution. There is no indication that they had. And so they became just another force imposed on the countryside, filling up their ranks from desperate uprooted groups of the population, at first by voluntary enlistment but more and more through compulsory enlistment and terror.[4] In the last stage of the campaigns the recruitment of people for the army, labor service, and the administrative staff became a major task for many of the Taiping leaders.[5]

[4] See Li Kuei, *Ssu-t'ung-chi,* in Hsiang, *Tzu-liao,* IV, 463 ff.; Li Kuang-chi, *Chieh-yü tsa-shih,* in Hsiang, *Tzu-liao,* V, 309 ff.; Chang Erh-chia, *Nan-chung-chi,* in Hsiang, *Tzu-liao,* VI, 631 ff. Li Kuei describes his experience in the Taiping army between 1860 and 1862 after he had been captured near Nanking and forced, together with many others, to participate in the campaign in Chekiang, where he escaped from Hangchow to Shanghai. Li Kuang-chi describes the Taiping campaign of Hu-chou in Chekiang in 1860 and 1861; after his capture he had to serve as a copyist with a Taiping chancellor until his escape by means of a forged pass. Chang Erh-chia was captured near Hangchow at about the same time and served first as a laborer and later as a copyist with the duty of compiling soldiers' rosters.

[5] See a.o. documents 206 and 391.

The Taiping Rebellion and its extraordinary attempt to destroy the whole social and political fabric of China and replace it with a fantastic totalitarian order of its own ended thus in complete defeat, leaving no trace of its early victories nor of its faith once imposed upon its million followers. The traditional order reasserted itself for a time, and yet the prolonged and deadly battle fought between the Taipings and the defenders of the existing order contributed to the eventual collapse of this order itself. It was not the dynasty that had proved capable of defeating by its own strength the mortal challenge to its rule; it had been the gentry that defeated the attack against the Confucian social order and in so doing saved the dynasty. To permit the gentry leadership to defend the order and thus save the throne, the dynasty had to abandon its measures of political control on which the safety of the imperial government rested. The necessity of permitting the growth of military-political organizations formed against the Taipings and other rebellions in the areas of combat meant a loss of authority from which the Ch'ing government never recovered. The supremacy of the political over the social leadership had depended on the control of all military forces and on a system of checks and control within the administrative structure that guaranteed not only complete authority within this system itself but its dominance over the autonomous gentry management of the social order. The emergence of regional political organizations from this social leadership gravely undermined the government's central authority and eventually contributed to its collapse.

But if the social order was successfully defended at the time, the disintegration of the political power of the dynasty provided a weakening of the whole system that proved crucial in the decades to come. Had Chinese history run its course within the setting of the past, a new dynasty might well have eventually emerged from the regional military-political organizations within or might have been established by traditional conquests from without—or a combination of both. But this was the time when China was faced with the threatening impact of the West that had already made its inroads in the treaty ports and had shaped the character of the Taiping Rebellion itself. It was fateful for China that this confrontation with the new world of modern states came at the time of political disintegration.

The Ch'ing dynasty truly never recovered. There was no real T'ung-chih restoration. Regionalism carried over into the revolution of 1911 and even beyond. And if the last great effort to transform the Chinese

Confucian tradition into a system that could continue to play its part on commonly accepted universal precepts within the modern world failed, the political decline may well have been partly responsible. K'ang Yu-wei's great attempt at the end of the century to initiate a program of reforms based on a universalized Confucian tradition[6] was blocked as much by the lack of central authority as by the power struggle at the court itself. The court at least was too weak to deal with the immense problem of a true reform that might have staved off the revolution and the complete break with the past. And no regional leadership would have been strong enough to face this problem.

In the final outcome the Taiping Rebellion signaled thus the beginning of the end of Confucian China. Fantastic and irrational as it was, it was revolutionary in character. Its basic ideas came from the West, as much as they distorted their Western prototype. Their acceptance by the rebels showed that such ideas could find a favorable ground in China and be shaped there into a totalitarianism that in some ways preceded its Western counterpart. The very fact that large numbers of Chinese people could—in desperation—abandon their basic traditional beliefs and follow the extraordinary preachings of a fanatical doctrine should have given pause to those who regarded the Confucian ethics so ingrained in China as to exclude such revolutionary change.

There is no direct link between the Taiping Rebellion and the events of the twentieth century in China. In its chronological appearance in Chinese history, the rebellion remained an extraordinary episode. Neither the Nationalist nor the Communist tradition was connected with it, though Taiping lore has been referred to occasionally in political propaganda. As a disrupting factor and a most startling early attempt at totalitarianism the Taiping Rebellion marked a turning point in Chinese history and in primitive form brought up issues that go far beyond the Chinese historical experience and have still to be answered in the conflicts of our world today.

[6] K'ang Yu-wei's great concept will be described in Kung-chuan Hsiao's forthcoming book, "K'ang Yu-wei: Precursor of Modern China."

APPENDIX I

Maps

MAP 1
HUNG HSIU-CH'ÜAN'S NATIVE PLACE

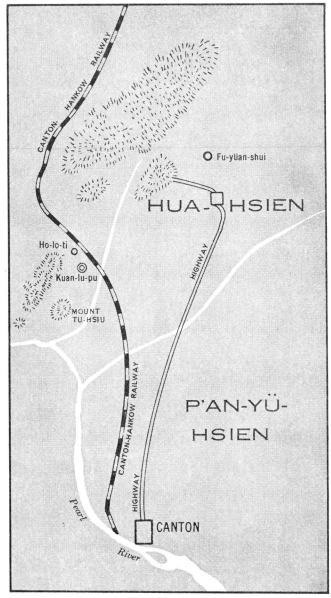

LEGEND

O Birth place of Hung (Jan. 1, 1814)

◎ Village of Hung's boyhood and youth

O Native village of the Nan Wang, Feng Yün-shan

(Modern railroad and highway added to show approximate location of places)

Source: Chien Yu-wen, T'ai-p'ing-chün Kwangsi shou-i shih, pp. 57-58.

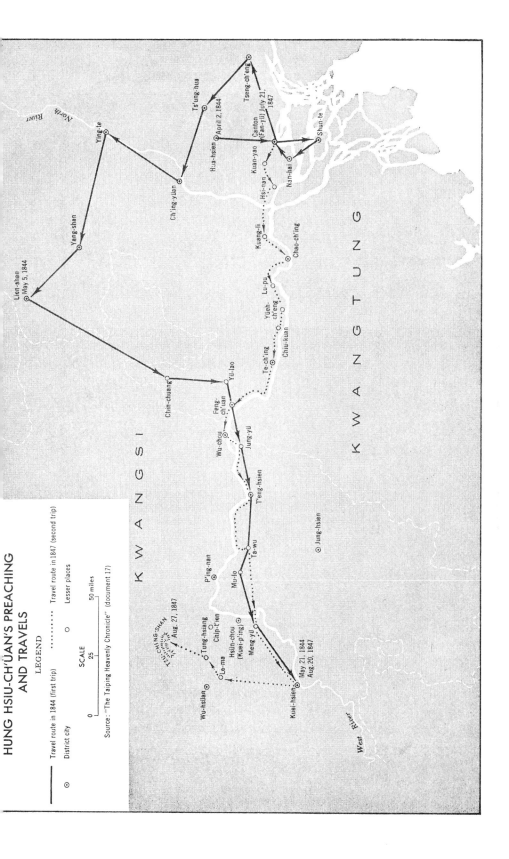

HUNG HSIU-CH'ÜAN'S PREACHING AND TRAVELS

LEGEND

——— Travel route in 1844 (first trip)   ·········· Travel route in 1847 (second trip)

⊙ District city   ○ Lesser places

SCALE

0   25   50 miles

Source: "The Taiping Heavenly Chronicle" (document 17)

K W A N G S I

K W A N G T U N G

North River

West River

Lien-shan
May 5, 1844

Yang-shan

Ying-te

Ch'ing-yüan

Ts'ung-hua

Hua-hsien April 2, 1844

Tseng-ch'eng July 21, 1847

Canton (Fan-yü)

Shun-te

Kuan-yao

Hsi-nan

Nan-hai

Kuang-li

Chao-ch'ing

Lu-pu

Yüeh-ch'eng

Te-ch'ing

Chiu-kuan

Chin-chuang

Yü-lao

Feng-ch'üan

Wu-chou

Jung-yü

Teng-hsien

Ta-wu

Mu-lo

P'ing-nan

Jung-hsien

CH'ING SHAN

Aug. 27, 1847

Tung-hsiang

Chin-t'ien

Wu-hsüan

Lo-ma

Hsün-chou (Kuei-p'ing)

Meng-yü

Kuei-hsien
May 21, 1844
Aug. 20, 1847

MAP 3
LOCATION OF THE ORIGIN OF THE TAIPINGS AND
LOCATION OF KEY LEADERS

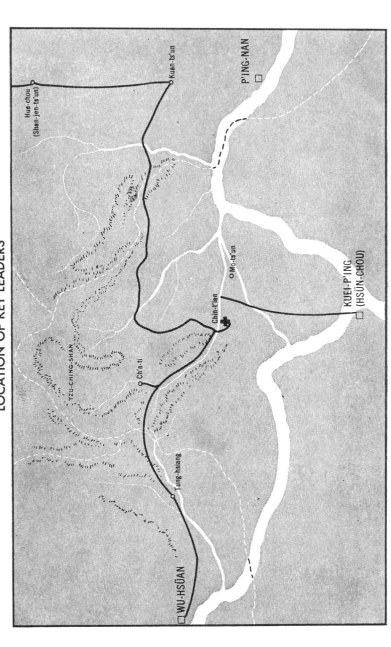

Kuan-ts'un

Hua-chou
(Shan-jen-ts'un)

P'ING-NAN

Mo-ts'un

TZU-CHING-SHAN

Ch'a-ti

Chin-t'ien

KUEI-P'ING
(HSÜN-CHOU)

Tung-hsiang

WU-HSÜAN

LEGEND

Tung-hsiang: Yang (April 15, 1851)
Hsiao (April 19, 1851)

Ch'a-ti: Yang (Aug. 9, 1851)
Hung (Aug. 29, 1851)

Hua-chou: Hung (July–Dec. 1850)

Mo-ts'un: Hsiao (Aug. 9, 1851)
Yang (Aug. 22, 1851)
Hung (Aug. 29, 1851)

Chin-t'ien: Hung (Jan. 1851) Home of Wei; center of main
forces of the Taipings in the initial period; place
of rise of the Taipings

□   District City

✚

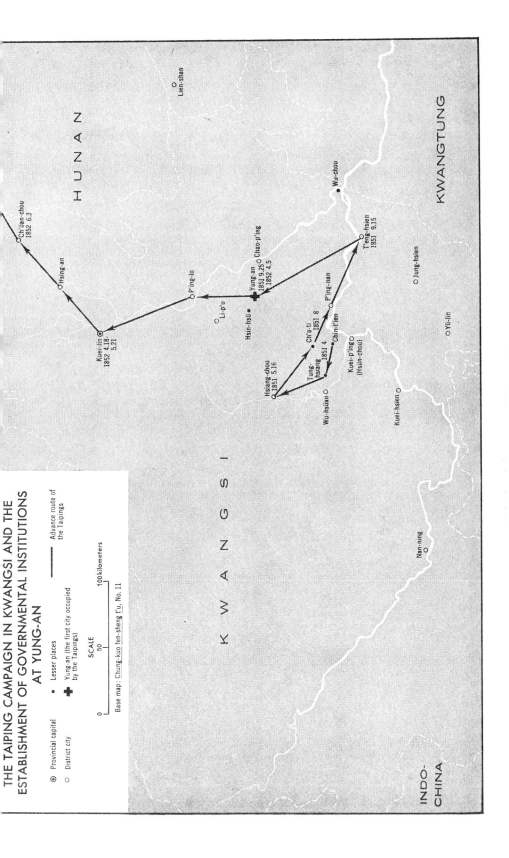

THE TAIPING CAMPAIGN IN KWANGSI AND THE
ESTABLISHMENT OF GOVERNMENTAL INSTITUTIONS
AT YUNG-AN

◉ Provincial capital

● Lesser places

——— Advance route of
the Taipings

○ District city

✚ Yung-an (the first city occupied
by the Taipings)

SCALE

0   50   100 kilometers

Base map: Chung-kuo fen-sheng t'u, No. 11

HUNAN

Lien-shan ○

Chüan-chou ◉
1852 6.3

○ Hsing-an

P'ing-lo ○

Kuei-lin ◉
1852 4.18
5.21

○ Li-p'u

Yung-an ◉ Chao-p'ing
1851 9.25○
1852 4.5

Hsin-hsü ● ✚

Wu-chou ●

T'eng-hsien ○
1851 9.15

○ Jung-hsien

P'ing-nan ○

Ch'a-ti ●
1851 8

Tung- ●
hsiang
1851 4

Chin-t'ien ●

Kuei-p'ing ○
(Hsün-chou)

Hsiang-chou ◉
1851 5.16

Wu-hsüan ○

○ Yü-lin

K W A N G S I

Kuei-hsien ○

Nan-ning ○

INDO-
CHINA

KWANGTUNG

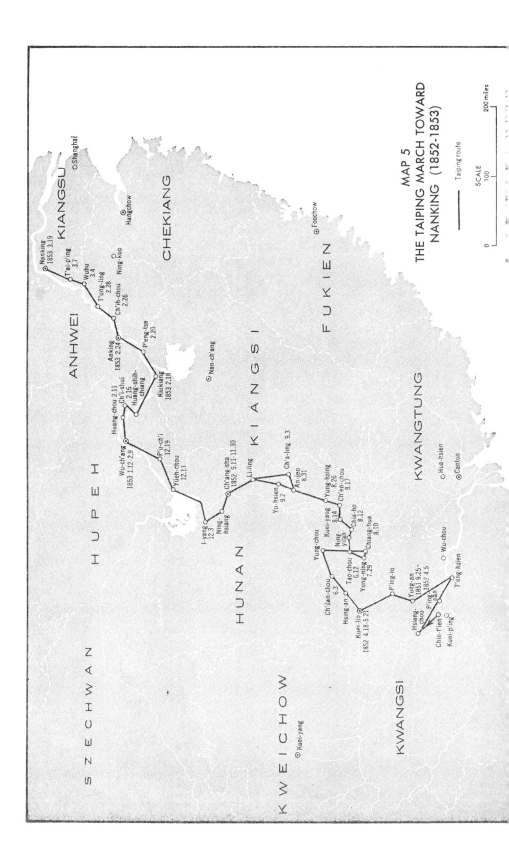

MAP 5
THE TAIPING MARCH TOWARD
NANKING (1852-1853)

SCALE

0   100   200 miles

Taiping route

SZECHWAN

HUPEH

ANHWEI

KIANGSU

Nanking 1853 3.19
T'ai-ping 3.7
Wuhu 3.4
Tung-ling 2.28
Ch'ih-chou
Ning-kuo 2.26
Anking 1853 2.24
P'eng-tse 2.20
Ch'i-shui 2.16
Huang-chou 2.11
Huang-shih-chiang
Kiukiang 1853 2.18

CHEKIANG

Shanghai
Hangchow

Wu-ch'ang 1853 1.12-2.9
P'u-ch'i 12.19
Yüeh-chou 12.13
I-yang 12.3
Ning-hsiang
Ch'ang-sha 1852 9.11-11.30
Li-ling

KIANGSI

Nan-ch'ang

FUKIEN

Foochow

HUNAN

Cha-ling 9.3
An-jen 8.31
Yu-hsien 9.2
Yung-hsing 8.26
Ch'en-chou 8.17
Kuei-yang 8.14
Chia-ho 8.12
Ning-yüan
Chiang-hua 8.10
Yung-chou
Tao-chou 6.12
Ch'i-an-chou 6.3
Yung-ning 7.29
P'ing-lo
Hsing-an
Kuei-lin 1852 4.18-5.21
Hsiang-chou
Yung-an 1851 9.25-1852 4.5
P'ing-nan
T'eng-hsien
Chin-t'ien
Kuei-p'ing

KWEICHOW

Kuei-yang

KWANGTUNG

Hua-hsien
Canton
Wu-chou

KWANGSI

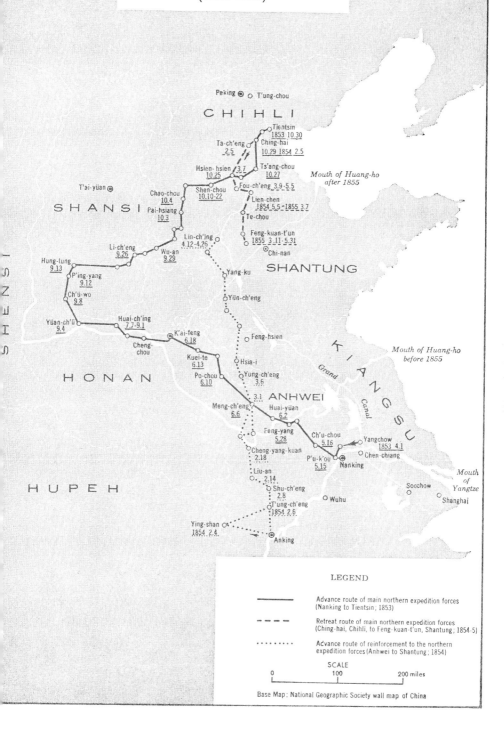

MAP 6
TAIPING NORTHERN EXPEDITIONS
(1853-1855)

Peking ◉ ○ T'ung-chou

C H I H L I

Tientsin
1853 10.30
Ta-ch'eng ○ Ching-hai
2.5   10.29 1854 2.5
Hsien-hsien ○ 3.7   Ts'ang-chou
10.25   10.27
T'ai-yüan ◉   Shen-chou ○   Fou-ch'eng 3.9-5.5
Chao-chou   10.10-22   Lien-chen
10.4   1854 5.5-1855 3.7
S H A N S I   Pai-hsiang ○   ○ Te-chou
10.3
Li-ch'eng ○   Lin-ch'ing ○   Feng-kuan-t'un
9.26   4.12-4.26   1855 3.11-5.31
Hung-tung ○   Wu-an ○   ◉ Chi-nan
9.13   9.29
P'ing-yang ○   S H A N T U N G
9.12   ○ Yang-ku
Ch'ü-wo ○
9.8   ○ Yün-ch'eng
Yüan-ch'ü ○   Huai-ch'ing ○
9.4   7.7-9.1
○ K'ai-feng   ○ Feng-hsien
Cheng-   6.18
chou ○
Kuei-te ○   ○ Hsia-i
6.13
H O N A N   Po-chou ○   ○ Yung-ch'eng
6.10   3.6
3.1 A N H W E I
Meng-ch'eng ○   Huai-yüan ○
6.6   6.2
○ Feng-yang   Ch'u-chou   Yangchow
5.28   5.16   1853 4.1
Cheng-yang-kuan ○   P'u-k'ou ○   ○ Chen-chiang
2.18   5.15   Nanking
Liu-an ○
○ 2.14
Shu-ch'eng
2.8   ○ Wuhu
H U P E H   T'ung-ch'eng
1854 2.6
Ying-shan ○
1854 2.4   ◉ Anking

Mouth of Huang-ho
after 1855

Mouth of Huang-ho
before 1855

K I A N G S U

Grand Canal

Mouth
of
Yangtze
Soochow ○
○ Shanghai

LEGEND

―――――― Advance route of main northern expedition forces
(Nanking to Tientsin; 1853)

― ― ― ― Retreat route of main northern expedition forces
(Ching-hai, Chihli, to Feng-kuan-t'un, Shantung; 1854-5)

· · · · · · · · · · Advance route of reinforcement to the northern
expedition forces (Anhwei to Shantung; 1854)

SCALE
0   100   200 miles

Base Map: National Geographic Society wall map of China

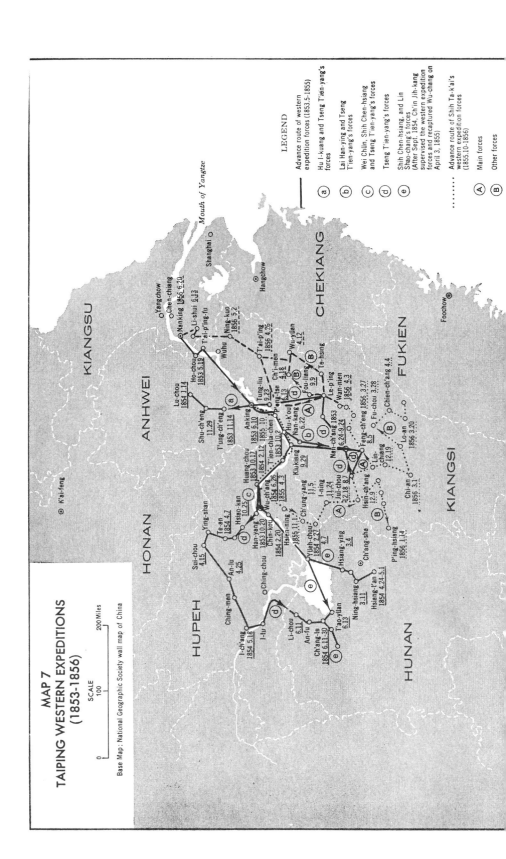

MAP 7
TAIPING WESTERN EXPEDITIONS
(1853-1856)

SCALE
0   100   200 Miles

Base Map: National Geographic Society wall map of China

LEGEND

Advance route of western
expedition forces (1853.5-1855)

(a) Hu I-kuang and Tseng T'ien-yang's
forces

(b) Lai Han-ying and Tseng
T'ien-yang's forces

(c) Wei Chün, Shih Chen-hsiang
and Tseng T'ien-yang's forces

(d) Tseng T'ien-yang's forces

(e) Shih Chen-hsiang, and Lin
Shao-chang's forces
(After Sept. 1854, Ch'in Jih-kang
supervised the western expedition
forces and recaptured Wu-chang on
April 3, 1855)

Advance route of Shih Ta-k'ai's
western expedition forces
(1855.10-1856)

(A) Main forces

(B) Other forces

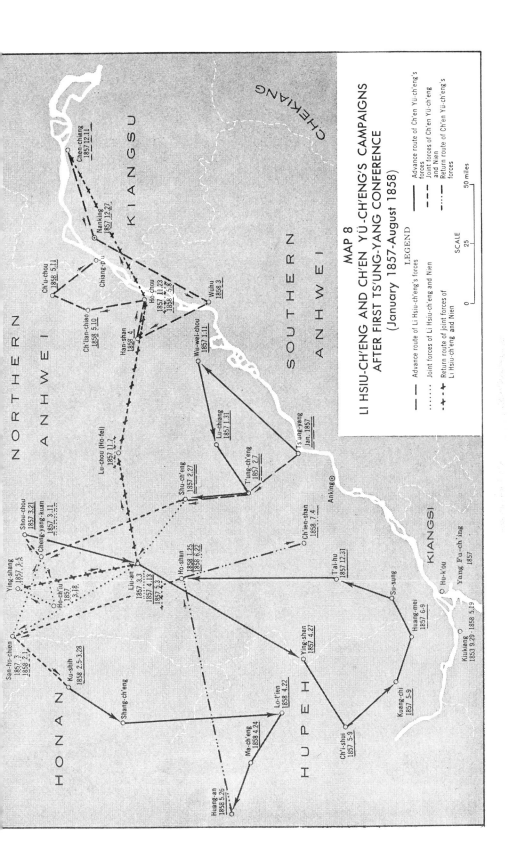

MAP 8

LI HSIU-CH'ENG AND CH'EN YÜ-CH'ENG'S CAMPAIGNS
AFTER FIRST TS'UNG-YANG CONFERENCE

(January 1857-August 1858)

LEGEND

—— Advance route of Li Hsiu-ch'eng's forces

········· Joint forces of Li Hsiu-ch'eng and Nien

—+─+ Return route of joint forces of Li Hsiu-ch'eng and Nien

— — Advance route of Ch'en Yü-ch'eng's forces

─ ─ ─ Joint forces of Ch'en Yü-ch'eng and Nien

·····>· Return route of Ch'en Yü-ch'eng's forces

SCALE

0   25   50 miles

NORTHERN ANHWEI

SOUTHERN ANHWEI

KIANGSU

CHEKIANG

KIANGSI

HONAN

HUPEH

Chen-chiang 1857 12.11

Nanking 1857 12.27

Ch'u-chou 1858 5.11

Chiang-p'u

Ho-chou 1857 11.23 1858 5.8

Wuhu 1858 3

Ch'üan-chiao 1858 5.10

Han-shan 1858 4

Wu-wei-chou 1857 1.11

Lu-chou (Ho-fei) 1857 11.2

Lu-chiang 1857 1.31

Tung-ch'eng 1857 2.7

Ts'ung-yang Jan. 1857

Shou-ch'eng 1857 2.27

Anking

Chien-shan 1858 7.4

Shou-chou 1857 3.21

Cheng-yang-kuan 1857 3.11

Ying-shang 1857 3.5

Ho-ch'iu 1857 3.18

Liu-an 1857 3.3 1857 4.13 1857 5.3

Ho-shan 1858 1.25 1858 6.22

T'ai-hu 1857 12.31

Su-sung

Hu-k'ou

Yang Fu-ch'ing 1857

San-ho-chien 1857 3 1858 2.1

Ku-shih 1858 2.5-3.28

Shang-ch'eng

Ma-ch'eng 1858 4.24

Lo-t'ien 1858 4.22

Ying-shan 1857 4.27

Huang-mei 1857 6.9

Kuang-chi 1857 5.9

Kiukiang 1853 9.29-1858 5.19

Huang-an 1858 5.26

Ch'i-shui 1857 5.9

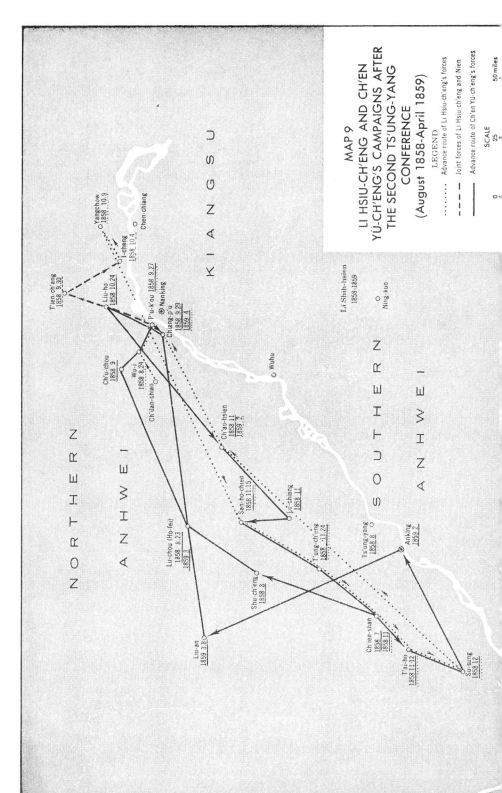

MAP 9

LI HSIU-CH'ENG AND CH'EN
YÜ-CH'ENG'S CAMPAIGNS AFTER
THE SECOND TS'UNG-YANG
CONFERENCE
(August 1858–April 1859)

LEGEND

.... Advance route of Li Hsiu-ch'eng's forces

– – – Joint forces of Li Hsiu-ch'eng and Nien

———— Advance route of Ch'en Yü-ch'eng's forces

SCALE

0   25   50 miles

KIANGSU

NORTHERN

ANHWEI

SOUTHERN

ANHWEI

Yangchow
1858 10.9

I-cheng
1858 10.4

Chen-chiang

Tien-ch'ang
1858 9.30

Lu-ho
1858 10.24

P'u-k'ou 1858 9.27

⦿ Nanking

Chiang-p'u
1858 9.29
1859 4

Ch'u-chou
1858 9

Wu-i
1858 8.24

Ch'üan-chiao

Ch'ao-hsien
1858 11
1859 2

San-ho-chen
1858 11.15

Li-chiang
1858 11

Wuhu

Li Shih-hsien
1858–1859

Ning-kuo

Lu-chou (Ho-fei)
1858 8.23
1859 3

T'ung-ch'eng
1858 11.24

Ts'ung-yang
1858 8

Anking
1859 2

Shu-ch'eng
1858 8

Chien-shan
1858 7
1858 11

Lu-an
1859 3.8

T'ai-hu
1858 11.12

Su-sung
1858 12

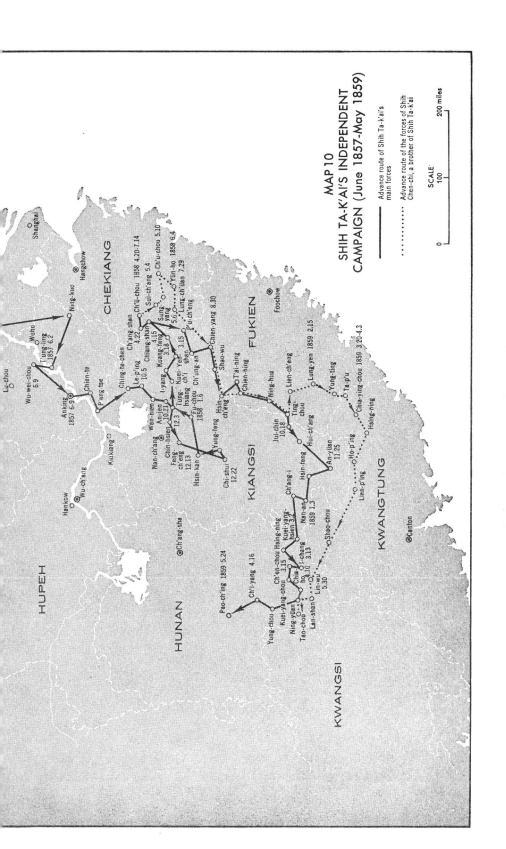

MAP 10
SHIH TA-K'AI'S INDEPENDENT
CAMPAIGN (June 1857-May 1859)

——— Advance route of Shih Ta-k'ai's
main forces

··········· Advance route of the forces of Shih
Chen-chi, a brother of Shih Ta-k'ai

SCALE
0   100   200 miles

HUPEH

CHEKIANG

FUKIEN

KIANGSI

HUNAN

KWANGTUNG

KWANGSI

Shanghai

Hangchow

Ning-kuo

Wuhu

Tung-ting
1857 6.2

Lu-chou

Wu-wei-chou
6.9

Anking
1857 6.9

P'eng-tse

Chien-te

Ching-te-chen

Ch'ang-shan

Ch'ü-chou 1858 4.20-7.14

Sui-ch'ang 5.4

Ch'u-chou 5.10

Le-p'ing
10.5

Chiang-shan
4.22

Kuang-feng
4.15

Sung-yang 5.6

Yün-ho 1858 6.4

Lung-ch'üan 7.29

i-yang
3.18

Kuei-yen
3.15

Tung-
hsiang
12.3

Yen-
shan

Chien-yang 8.30

Wen-niem

An-jen
10.21

Feng-
ch'eng
12.13

Fu-chou
1858 1.6

Ch'ung-an

Hsin-
ch'eng

Shao-wu

Ta'i-ning

Chien-ning

Nan-ch'ang

Kiukiang

Chin-hsien

Hankow

Wu-ch'ang

Hsin-kan

Yung-feng

 Chi-shui
12.22

Jui-chin
10.18

Ning-hua

Ting-
chou

Lien-ch'eng

Lung-yen 1859 2.15

Yung-ting

Ta-p'u

Foochow

Ch'i-yang 4.16

Ch'ang-i

Hsin-feng

Hui-ch'ang

Ch'en-chou Hsing-ning
3.15

Kuei-yang-
hsien 3.7

Ch'a-
ling
3.10

I-chang
3.13

Nan-an
1859 1.3

An-yüan
11.25

Ho-p'ing

Cha-ying-chou 1859 3.20-4.3

Hsing-ning

Pao-ch'ing 1859 5.24

Ch'ang-sha

Yung-chou

Kuei-yang-chou

Ning-yüan

Tao-chou

Lan-shan

Lin-wu
5.30

Shao-chou

Lien-p'ing

Lien-p'ing

Canton

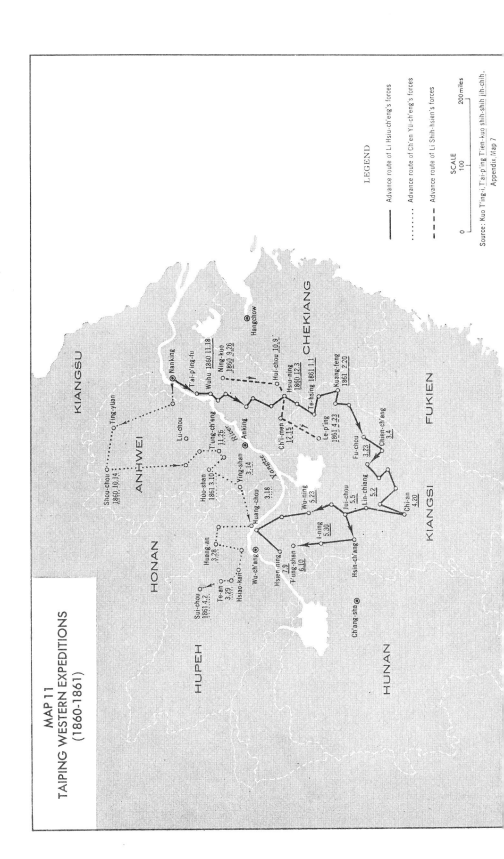

MAP 11
TAIPING WESTERN EXPEDITIONS
(1860-1861)

KIANGSU

HUPEH

HONAN

ANHWEI

KIANGSI

CHEKIANG

FUKIEN

HUNAN

Ch'ang-sha

Nanking

Tai-p'ing-fu

Wuhu 1860 11.18

Ning-kuo 1860 9.26

Hui-chou 10.9

Hsiu-ning 1860 12.3

Hangchow

Te-hsing 1861 11.1

Kuang-teng 1861 2.20

Ch'i-men 12.15

Le-p'ing 1861 4.23

Fu-chou 3.23

Chien-ch'ang 3.4

Ting-yüan

Lu-chou

Tung-ch'eng

11.26

Anking

Yangtze River

Ying-shan 3.14

Huo-shan 1861 3.10

Shou-chou 1860 10.14

Huang-chou 3.18

Wu-ning 5.5

Ju-chou 5.5

Lin-chiang 5.2

Chi-an 4.20

Huang-an 3.28

Wu-ch'ang

Hsien-ning 7.9

T'ung-shan 6.10

I-ning 5.30

Hsin-ch'ang

Sui-chou 1861 4.2

Te-an 3.29

Hsiao-kan

LEGEND

Advance route of Li Hsiu-ch'eng's forces

Advance route of Ch'en Yü-ch'eng's forces

Advance route of Li Shih-hsien's forces

SCALE
0   100   200 miles

Source: Kuo T'ing-i, T'ai-p'ing T'ien-kuo shih-shih jih-chih, Appendix Map 7

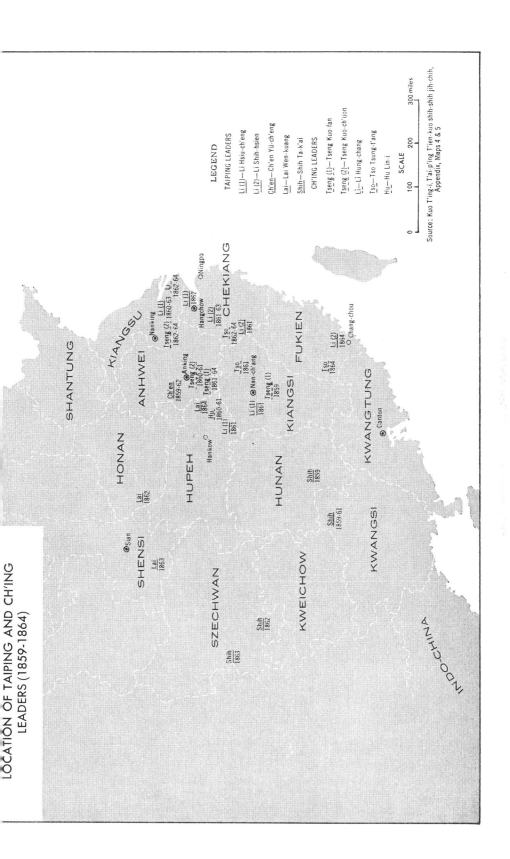

LOCATION OF TAIPING AND CH'ING
LEADERS (1859-1864)

LEGEND

TAIPING LEADERS

Li (1)—Li Hsiu-ch'eng

Li (2)—Li Shih-hsien

Ch'en—Ch'en Yü-ch'eng

Lai—Lai Wen-kuang

Shih—Shih Ta-k'ai

CH'ING LEADERS

Tseng (1)—Tseng Kuo-fan

Tseng (2)—Tseng Kuo-ch'üan

Li—Li Hung-chang

Tso—Tso Tsung-t'ang

Hu—Hu Lin-i

SCALE

0   100   200   300 miles

Source: Kuo T'ing-i, T'ai-p'ing T'ien-kuo shih-shih jih-chih,
Appendix, Maps 4 & 5

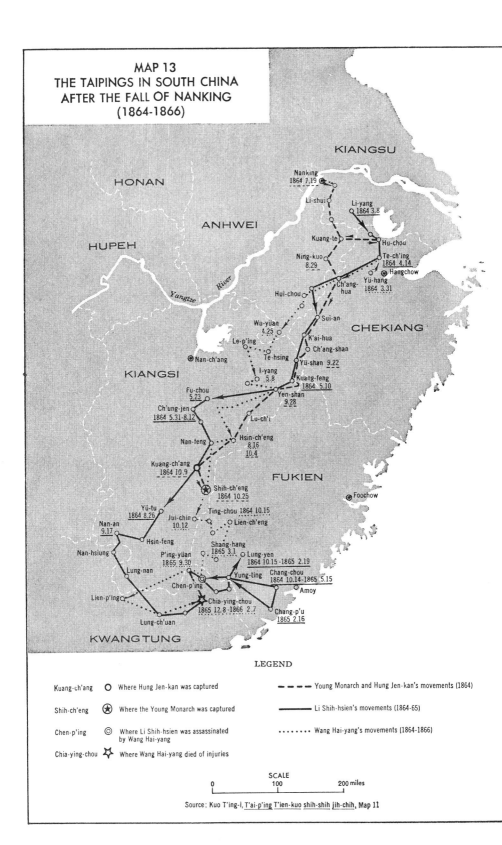

MAP 13
THE TAIPINGS IN SOUTH CHINA
AFTER THE FALL OF NANKING
(1864-1866)

KIANGSU

HONAN

ANHWEI

HUPEH

Nanking
1864 7.19

Li-shui

Li-yang
1864 3.8

Kuang-te

Hu-chou

Ning-kuo
8.29

Te-ch'ing
1864 4.14

Hui-chou

Ch'ang-
hua

Yü-hang
1864 3.31

Hangchow

Sui-an

CHEKIANG

Wu-yüan
4.25

Le-p'ing

K'ai-hua

Ch'ang-shan

Nan-ch'ang

Te-hsing

Yü-shan 9.22

KIANGSI

I-yang
5.8

Kuang-feng
1864 5.10

Fu-chou
5.23

Yen-shan
9.28

Ch'ung-jen
1864 5.31-8.12

Lu-ch'i

Nan-feng

Hsin-ch'eng
8.16
10.4

Kuang-ch'ang
1864 10.9

FUKIEN

Shih-ch'eng
1864 10.25

Foochow

Yü-tu
1864 8.26

Jui-chin
10.12

Ting-chou 1864 10.15

Lien-ch'eng

Nan-an
9.17

Hsin-feng

Shang-hang
1865 3.1

Nan-hsiung

P'ing-yüan
1865 9.30

Lung-yen
1864 10.15 -1865 2.19

Lung-nan

Yung-ting

Chang-chou
1864 10.14-1865 5.15

Chen-p'ing

Amoy

Lien-p'ing

Chia-ying-chou
1865 12.8 -1866 2.7

Chang-p'u
1865 2.16

Lung-ch'uan

KWANGTUNG

Yangtze River

LEGEND

Kuang-ch'ang O Where Hung Jen-kan was captured

Shih-ch'eng ⊛ Where the Young Monarch was captured

Chen-p'ing ◎ Where Li Shih-hsien was assassinated
by Wang Hai-yang

Chia-ying-chou � Where Wang Hai-yang died of injuries

– – – – Young Monarch and Hung Jen-kan's movements (1864)

——— Li Shih-hsien's movements (1864-65)

· · · · · · · Wang Hai-yang's movements (1864-1866)

SCALE

0   100   200 miles

Source: Kuo T'ing-i, T'ai-p'ing T'ien-kuo shih-shih jih-chih, Map 11

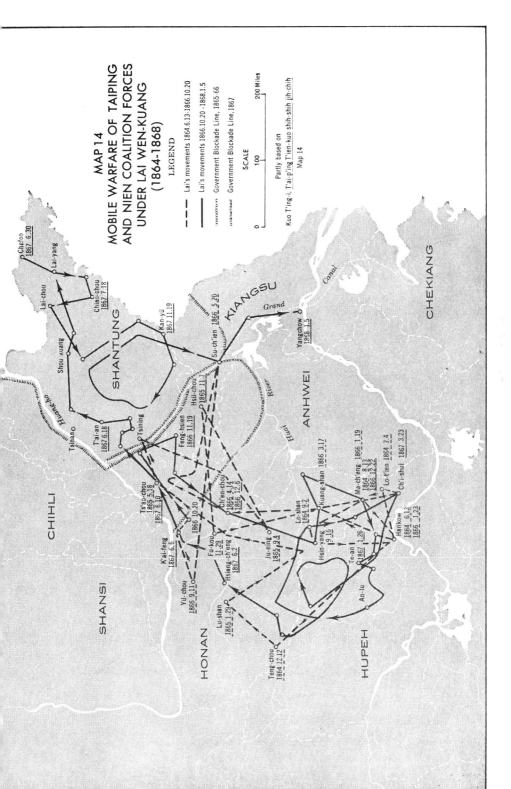

MAP 14
MOBILE WARFARE OF TAIPING
AND NIEN COALITION FORCES
UNDER LAI WEN-KUANG
(1864-1868)

LEGEND

- - - - Lai's movements 1864.6.13-1866.10.20
———— Lai's movements 1866.10.20 -1868.1.5
:::::::::: Government Blockade Line, 1865-66
⊞⊞⊞⊞ Government Blockade Line, 1867

SCALE

0   100   200 Miles

Partly based on
Kuo T'ing-i, T'ai-p'ing T'ien-kuo shih-shih jih-chih
Map 14

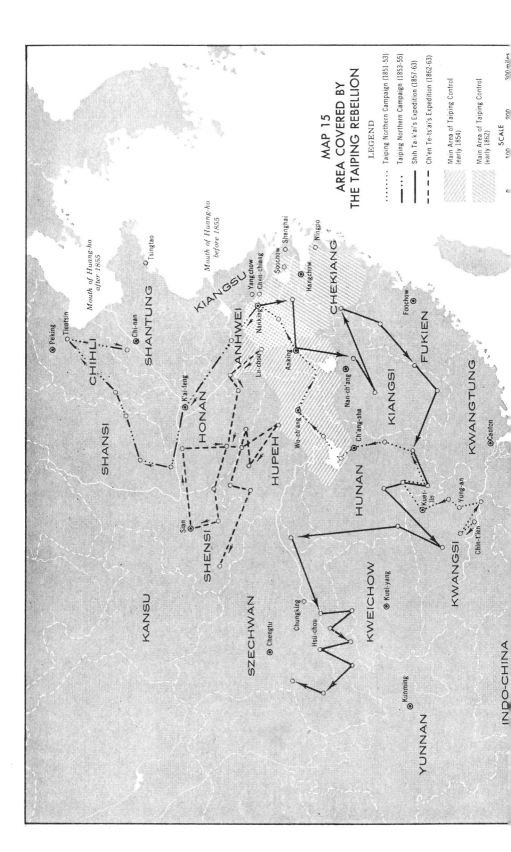

MAP 15
AREA COVERED BY
THE TAIPING REBELLION

LEGEND

.... Taiping Northern Campaign (1851-53)

—·—·— Taiping Northern Campaign (1853-55)

——— Shih Ta-k'ai's Expedition (1857-63)

– – – Ch'en Te-ts'ai's Expedition (1862-63)

▨ Main Area of Taiping Control (early 1854)

▨ Main Area of Taiping Control (early 1862)

SCALE

0   100   200   300 miles

APPENDIX II
List of Documents and Comments

Documents and Comments

(The text of these documents and comments will appear as Volumes II and III of *The Taiping Rebellion*.)

PART I

1. Hung Hsiu-ch'üan's Background
2. Gospel Jointly Witnessed and Heard by the Imperial Eldest and Second Eldest Brothers (*Wang-chang-tz'u-hsiung ch'in-mu ch'in-erh kung-cheng fu-yin-shu*)
3. Poem by Hung Hsiu-ch'üan on the Wall of Shui-k'ou Temple in Hua-hsien
4. Ode on Hearing the Birds Sing
5. Ode on the Sword
6. Ode on Repentance
7. Ode to Awaken the Minds of Men
8. Poem Refuting the Elders on the Praise of Idols
9. Ode of Praise
10. The Taiping Imperial Declaration (*T'ai-p'ing chao-shu*)
11. Ode on the Sun
12. Favorite Sayings of Hung
13. Ode Praising the Lord
14. Poem Rebuking the *Kan-wang-yeh*
15. Poem on Opium
16. Ode on Hope
17. The Taiping Heavenly Chronicle (*T'ai-p'ing t'ien-jih*)
18. A Couplet on the Stone Pillar before the Tomb of the Great-Grand-mother
19. An Ode Alluding to the State of the Country
20. Manifesto on the Right to the Throne

PART II

(a) *Official Publications*

21. Proclamation of Entitlement by the Heavenly Father, God (*T'ien-fu shang-ti yen-t'i huang-chao*)
22. The Book of Declarations of the Divine Will Made during the Heavenly Father's Descent to Earth [I] (*T'ien-fu hsia-fan chao-shu*)
23. The Book of Heavenly Decrees and Proclamations (*T'ien-ming chao-chih shu*)

218

24. The Book of Heavenly Commandments (*T'ien-t'iao-shu*)
25. The Taiping Ceremonial Regulations [I] (*T'ai-p'ing li-chih*)
26. The Taiping Military Organization (*T'ai-p'ing chün-mu*)
27. Taiping Rules and Regulations (*T'ai-p'ing t'iao-kuei*)
28. Proclamations by Imperial Sanction (*Pan-hsing chao-shu*)
29. The Trimetrical Classic (*San-tzu-ching*)
30. Ode for Youth (*Yu-hsüeh-shih*)

(b) *Proclamations, Edicts, and Memorials*

31. Proclamation on the Cause for the Campaign
32. Proclamation Denouncing Corrupt Officials
33. A Proposal to the T'ien Wang
34. Notification Announcing the Taiping Campaign
35. Proclamation to the Scholars and People of Chiang-nan
36. Proclamation to the People upon Entering Nanking

(c) *Confessions*

37. The Confession of Hung Ta-ch'üan

(d) *Poetry*

38. Hymn in Praise of the Lord

PART III

(a) *Official Publications*

39. Book of Declarations of the Divine Will Made during the Heavenly Father's Descent to Earth [II] (*T'ien-fu hsia-fan chao-shu*) Introductory Note to Documents 40 and 41
40. Hung Hsiu-ch'üan's Annotations to the Old Testament (*Chiu-i-chao sheng-shu*)
41. Hung Hsiu-ch'üan's Annotations to the New Testament (*Hsin-i-chao sheng-shu*)
42. Taiping Songs on World Salvation (*T'ai-p'ing chiu-shih-ko*)
43. Treatises on the Establishment of the Heavenly Capital in Chin-ling (*Chien T'ien-ching yü Chin-ling lun*)
44. Treatises on the Denouncement of the Demons' Den as the Criminals' Region (*Pien yao-hsüeh wei Tsui-li lun*)
45. Treatises on Affixing the Imperial Seal on Proclamations and Books for Publication (*Chao-shu kai-hsi pan-hsing lun*)
46. The Land System of the Heavenly Dynasty (*T'ien-ch'ao t'ien-mou chih-tu*)
47. Calendar by Imperial Sanction, the Third Year (*Pan-hsing li-shu*)
48. Calendar by Imperial Sanction, the Fourth Year (*Pan-hsing li-shu*)
49. Important Observations Regarding Heavenly Principles (*T'ien-li yao-lun*)
50. The Book on the Principles of the Heavenly Nature (*T'ien-ch'ing tao-li shu*)

193. A Letter by Hou Yü-t'ien Inquiring about the Nature of the British Trip up the Yangtze
194. The T'ien Wang's Manifesto to the Foreign Brothers
195. Chu Hsiung-pang's Official Note on the Delivery of the T'ien Wang's Manifesto
196. A List of Gifts Presented by the Subordinates of Chu Hsiung-pang
197. A Taiping Apology for the Exchange of Shots
198. Hou Yü-t'ien's Note to Barker on Artillery
199. Hou Yü-t'ien's Reply to Barker on Artillery

(e) *Poetry*

200. A Poem on "Our Court Suffers from Internal Misfortune"

PART V

(a) *Official Publications*

201. Theme for the Chi-wei Ninth-Year Metropolitan Examination (*Chi-wei chiu-nien hui-shih-t'i*)
202. Writings of the Imperially Ordained Chief Examiner of the Literary Examinations, the Loyal Chief of Staff, the Kan Wang (*Ch'in-ming wen-heng cheng-tsung-ts'ai ching-chung chün-shih Kan Wang pao-chih*)
203. A New Treatise on Aids to Administration (*Tzu-cheng hsin-p'ien*)
204. Calendar by Imperial Sanction, the Eleventh Year (*Pan-hsing li-shu*)
205. A Hero's Return to the Truth (*Ch'in-ting ying-chieh kuei-chen*)
206. Imperially Approved Veritable Records While Conducting Army Campaigns (*Ch'in-ting chün-tz'u shih-lu*)
207. Proclamations on the Extermination of Demons (*Chu-yao chi-wen*)
208. Imperial Regulations Governing Scholarly Ranks (*Ch'in-ting shih-chieh t'iao-li*)
209. The Young Monarch's Proclamation (*Yu-chu chao-shu*)

(b) *Proclamations, Edicts, and Memorials*

210. A Proclamation on the Enforcement of the Law
211. A Proclamation to Pacify the People
212. Shih Ta-k'ai's Reply to the T'ien Wang
213. Li Hsiu-ch'eng's Proclamation on the Election of Officials and the Registry of Households
214. A Poetical Proclamation Urging the People to Return to Their Occupations
215. A Proclamation Ordering the People to Be at Peace in Their Occupations
216. A Proclamation Urging the People to Remain in Their Occupations
217. An Edict to Li Hsiu-ch'eng on the Dispatch of Funds for the Capital
218. A Proclamation Ordering the People of Shanghai to Surrender
219. A Proclamation Urging the People to Return to Their Homes
220. A Proclamation Ordering the Protection of Foreign Property

Abbreviations

A complete annotated bibliography of works concerning the Taiping Rebellion (with the Chinese characters) and a list of the abbreviations used throughout the three volumes appear in Volume III. For the convenience of the reader who has only Volume I at hand, there are listed below the abbreviations used in Volume I, together with complete citations. For the publications for which no abbreviations are used, complete citations are given in the notes.

Boardman	Eugene P. Boardman. *Christian Influence upon the Ideology of the Taiping Rebellion, 1851-1864.* Madison, Wis., 1952.
Brine	Lindesay Brine. *The Taeping Rebellion in China.* London, 1862.
Chang, *Tse-ch'ing*	Chang Te-chien. *Tse-ch'ing hui-tsuan.* Preface 1855; published in facsimile in 1932; also reprinted in Hsiang, *Tzu-liao,* III, 25-348.
Chien, *Chin-t'ien*	Chien Yu-wen. *T'ai-p'ing t'ien-kuo tsa-chi erh-chi: Chin-t'ien chih-yu chi ch'i-t'a.* Commercial Press, Chungking, 1944; Shanghai, 1946.
Chien, *Ch'üan-shih*	Chien Yu-wen. *T'ai-p'ing t'ien-kuo ch'üan-shih.* Hong Kong, 1962.
Chien, *Shou-i-shih*	Chien Yu-wen. *T'ai-p'ing-chün Kwangsi shou-i shih.* Chungking, 1944; Shanghai, 1946.
Fishbourne	E. G. Fishbourne. *Impressions of China and the Present Revolution.* London, 1855.

Forrest

Robert James Forrest. "The Christianity of Hung Tsiu Tsuen, A Review of Taeping Books," *Journal of the North China Branch of the Royal Asiatic Society*," n.s., IV (Dec., 1867), 187-208.

Hail

William James Hail, *Tseng Kuo-fan and the Taiping Rebellion*. New Haven and London, 1927.

Hamberg

Theodore Hamberg. *The Visions of Hung-Siu-tshuen and Origin of the Kwang-si Insurrection*. Hong Kong, 1854.

Hsiang, *Tzu-liao*

T'ai-p'ing t'ien-kuo. Hsiang Ta *et al.* (compilers). Vol. II of *Chung-kuo chin-tai-shih tzu-liao ts'ung-k'an.*

Hsieh, *Lun-ts'ung*

Hsieh Hsing-yao. *T'ai-p'ing t'ien-kuo shih-shih lun-ts'ung*. Shanghai, 1935.

Kuo, *Jih-chih*

Kuo T'ing-i. *T'ai-p'ing t'ien-kuo shih-shih jih-chih*. Chungking and Shanghai, 1946.

Kuo, *Li-fa-k'ao*

Kuo T'ing-i. *T'ai-p'ing t'ien-kuo li-fa k'ao-ting*. Shanghai, 1937.

Lindley

Augustus F. Lindley (Lin-le). *Ti-Ping Tien-Kwoh; the History of the Ti-Ping Revolution*. London, 1866.

Lo, "Ching-chi-k'ao"

Lo Erh-kang, "T'ai-p'ing t'ien-kuo ching-chi-k'ao," *Hsüeh-yüan*, Vol. II, No. 1 (Nanking, May, 1948).

Lo, *K'ao-cheng-chi*

Lo Erh-kang. *T'ai-p'ing t'ien-kuo-shih k'ao-cheng-chi*. Shanghai, 1948.

Lo, *Li-hsiang-kuo*

Lo Erh-kang. *T'ai-p'ing t'ien-kuo ti li-hsiang-kuo*. Shanghai, 1950.

Lo, *Nien-p'u*

Lo Erh-kang. *Chin-t'ien ch'i-i-ch'ien Hung Hsiu-ch'üan nien-p'u*. Chungking, 1941.

Lo, *Shih-kang*

Lo Erh-kang. *T'ai-p'ing t'ien-kuo shih-kang*. Shanghai, 1937.

Lo, *Shih-kao*	Lo Erh-kang. *T'ai-p'ing t'ien-kuo shih-kao.* Peking, 1951.
Lo, *Ts'ung-k'ao*	Lo Erh-kang. *T'ai-p'ing t'ien-kuo shih ts'ung-k'ao.* Shanghai, 1947.
Lo and Shen, *Shih-wen-ch'ao*	*T'ai-p'ing t'ien-kuo shih-wen-ch'ao.* Lo Yung and Shen Tsu-chi (compilers). Rev. ed. Shanghai, 1934.
Mackie	John M. Mackie. *Life of Tai-Ping-Wang, Chief of the Chinese Insurrection.* New York, 1857.
Meadows	Thomas T. Meadows. *The Chinese and Their Rebellions.* London, 1856.
NCH	*North China Herald.* Shanghai.
Oliphant	Laurence Oliphant. *Narrative of the Earl of Elgin's Mission to China and Japan.* Edinburgh, 1860.
Parliamentary Papers, 1853	Great Britain: *Parliamentary Papers. Papers Respecting the Civil War in China,* presented to the House of Commons, 1853.
Parliamentary Papers, 1861	Great Britain: *Parliamentary Papers. Correspondence Respecting the Opening of the Yang-tze-kiang River to Foreign Trade, 1861.*
Parliamentary Papers, April 8, 1862	Great Britain: *Parliamentary Papers. Papers Relating to the Rebellion in China and Trade in the Yang-tze-kiang River,* April 8, 1862.
Teng	Teng Ssu-yü. *New Light on the History of the Taiping Rebellion.* Cambridge, Mass., 1950.
Tseng, *Tsou-kao*	Tseng Kuo-fan. *Tseng Wen-cheng-kung ch'üan-chi. Tsou-kao.*
Yüeh-fei chi-lüeh	Tu Wen-lan. *P'ing-ting Yüeh-fei chi-lüeh.* 1869, 1871, 1888.

Index

235